2nd Edition

EARTH
Matters

Studies for our Global Future

Edited by Pamela Wasserman

ZPG

Zero Population Growth, Inc.
Washington, DC

Printed on recycled paper with soy ink

Published by
Zero Population Growth
1400 16th Street, N.W., Suite 320
Washington, DC 20036
(202) 332-2200

Designed by
Lindsay Raue
Raue & Associates
Alexandria, VA

Printed in the United States of America by
DeLancey Printing
Alexandria, VA

Library of Congress Cataloging-in-Publication Data
Earth matters: studies for our global future / edited by Pamela Wasserman
      p.   cm.
      Rev. ed of: Earth matters / by Pamela Wasserman, Andrea Doyle,
      c 1991
      ISBN 0-9445219-15-6
      Includes bibliographical references.
      1. Environmental sciences — Study and teaching (Secondary)
I. Wasserman, Pamela, 1965-   . II. Wasserman, Pamela, 1965-
Earth matters
GE70. E16 1998
363.7   —dc21   98-38881
                                                      CIP

Introduction to the Second Edition

Welcome to the second edition of *Earth Matters: Studies for our Global Future*. Whether this is your first introduction to the curriculum or you have been a loyal devotee of the original edition, you will find much in this updated edition to recommend to your students and colleagues.

Since the original *Earth Matters* was released in early 1992, it has been lauded by educators nationwide and internationally. The American Association for the Advancement of Science recommended that "a course that used this text would be valuable in all high school curricula, as students would be stimulated to learn more about global reality and what must be done to achieve sustainable socioeconomic systems" (Science Books and Films). The California Department of Education and the California Energy Commission awarded *Earth Matters* an "A" in their *Compendium for Human Communities* (1994) and featured it at state educational conferences. In 1996, the book transcended North American boundaries and was translated into Japanese by ERIC, the Educational Resource and Innovation Center in Tokyo for distribution throughout Japan.

But even well-respected resources can be improved and made accessible to new audiences. Since the original edition was released nearly seven years ago, the world has witnessed a number of geopolitical changes and changes in environmental trends. New reports have been issued and international conferences convened on a number of *Earth Matters* topics from climate change and food scarcity to the status of women and human habitat. Rewriting the "Student Readings" and updating the activities gave us the opportunity to incorporate the suggestions of educators, scientists and policy experts, and to reflect current realities.

In this new edition, all of the information in readings is footnoted for easy reference and further research. Most of the activities have been revised and updated and many have been expanded. Two new activities on community sustainability are included in the "Finding Solutions" chapter. The Teacher's Guide has been expanded to include a reference of how each of the interdisciplinary activities meet the latest standards for seven subject areas. A completely revised and updated section on "Suggested Resources for Further Research," including Internet sources, appears at the end. And, in response to Canadian educators, we have attempted to make this new edition more relevant to our northern neighbors.

As secondary and post-secondary educators have been doing for seven years, you are free to use this new edition of *Earth Matters* in creative ways to supplement your textbooks or to develop an entire course on issues of local and global importance. We welcome your feedback and wish you and your students rewarding learning experiences.

Pamela Wasserman

Pamela Wasserman
Director of Education
Zero Population Growth, Inc.

Acknowledgments

Project Manager and Editor: Pamela Wasserman

Lead Researcher: Joy Fishel

Writers: Pamela Wasserman, Andrea Axel, Joy Fishel, Nick Boutis, Maureen Hickey, Melissa Young, Lisa Colson and Gretchen Roberts

Research Assistants: Lisa Engel, Jodi Schwartz

ZPG Population Education Staff: Pamela Wasserman, *Director, Population Education Program*
Nick Boutis, *Population Education Associate*
Maureen Hickey, *Teacher Training Coordinator*
Melissa Young, *Population Education Assistant*

Special thanks to Andrea Axel for co-authoring the original edition of *Earth Matters* in 1991. Her creative activities have stood the test of time.

Our thanks to the following expert reviewers for their suggestions and fact checking on the Student Readings:

Peter Belden
Fellow, Population Reference Bureau

Joel Darmstadter
Senior Fellow, Resources for the Future

Richard Denison
Senior Scientist,
Environmental Defense Fund

Richard Heede
Research Scholar,
Rocky Mountain Institute

Frances Houck
Training Specialist,
The Futures Group International

Michael Leahy
Forest Campaign Coordinator,
National Audubon Society

Nicole Levesque
Project Coordinator, Center for
Development and Population Activities

Julie Middleton
Program Director, Save Our Streams (SOS),
Izaak Walton League

Mary Minette
Director, Endangered Species Campaign,
National Audubon Society

Jennifer Morgan
Coordinator, U.S. Climate Action Network

Ed Pembleton
Independent Consultant

David Pimentel
Department of Agriculture and Life
Sciences, Cornell University

Michael Rubinstein
Local Media Associate, Bread for the World

Dr. Gerald Shively
Department of Environmental and Natural
Resource Economics, Purdue University

Heather Weiner
Policy Analyst, Earthjustice Legal Defense Fund

Leah Yasenchak, Prudence Goforth,
Christine Sansevero
Office of Air and Radiation,
U.S. Environmental Protection Agency

Our gratitude to the following educators for reviewing the activities which have appeared in both the old and new editions of Earth Matters *and for offering advice on further improvements:*

Peter Chappell
Killarney Secondary School, Vancouver, BC

Eugene Kutscher
Science Chair, Roslyn Schools, NY

Martha Monroe
School of Forest Resources and Conservation
University of Florida

Wayne Moyer
Coordinator, Secondary Science,
Montgomery County Public Schools, MD

William C. Ritz
Director of Science Education, California State University,
Long Beach, CA

Ruth Stas
Social Studies Program Coordinator, Manheim Township School
District, PA

Gina Zappariello
Ocean City High School, Ocean City, NJ

Earth Matters: Studies for our Global Future (2nd Edition) was made possible by the generous support of the Fred H. Bixby Foundation, Carolyn Foundation, Geraldine R. Dodge Foundation, Fred Gellert Foundation, William and Flora Hewlett Foundation, The Huber Foundation, Harris and Eliza Kempner Fund and the David and Lucile Packard Foundation.

Table of Contents

Table of Contents

Teacher's Guide

Teacher's Guide

Why *Earth Matters*?

"Before you eat breakfast this morning, you've depended on more than half the world. This is the way our universe is structured. . . We aren't going to have peace on earth until we recognize this basic fact of the interrelated structure of all reality."

~Dr. Martin Luther King, Jr.

Today's students inhabit a rapidly changing world of increasing global interdependence. Our global economy is evident in everything from the sources of clothes we wear and the foods we eat to the cars we drive and the computers that link us to each other in seconds. Our global environment is shaped by everyone's actions and depends on everyone's vigilance. Air and water pollution and climate change know no national boundaries. Loss of biodiversity due to urban development in one area can affect the future of medical discovery. And a child from any part of the globe, who is nurtured with a sense of self-worth and a decent education, could grow up to be a great scientist, artist or statesman with the potential to enhance quality of life for all humanity.

Central to any discussion of global interdependence are people — our numbers and our activities. Most of the threats to our global ecosystems and social structures are human-made, and are worsened when increasing numbers place stress on finite resources and fragile economies. *Earth Matters* helps students explore these connections by linking human population growth and lifestyles to the health and well-being of the planet and all its inhabitants.

Through 12 readings and 34 innovative activities, *Earth Matters* introduces high school students to issues of the global environment and society, while challenging them to evaluate these issues critically and motivating them to develop solutions.

How to Use *Earth Matters*

Because the issues covered in *Earth Matters* are interdisciplinary, this book is designed for use in several curriculum areas. The readings and activities develop knowledge and skills applicable to high school social studies, science, math, language arts and family life education, and can be easily integrated into existing curriculum plans. The charts on the following pages briefly describe the activities and indicate which skills and subject areas are emphasized in each. Many of these activities also lend themselves to a team-teaching approach, where educators from different disciplines facilitate the lessons.

In this second edition of *Earth Matters*, we have also added a section to the "Teacher's Guide" indicating how each activity meets the objectives for the latest content standards for seven different subject areas. These standards clearly indicate a role for population education in the sciences and social sciences, and even in mathematics and the humanities.

There are a variety of ways to use *Earth Matters*. Although the book forms a complete unit on global environmental and social issues, each chapter or activity can stand alone to emphasize one particular topic or idea. We recommend that students complete the reading section in each chapter before participating in the corresponding activities. Words in **bold** in the readings are new terms which you may want to review with students. For more in-depth information on each issue, students and teachers should refer to the list of suggested resources at the end of the book.

All of the activities in *Earth Matters* are designed to engage students. A variety of teaching strategies, including role-playing simulations, laboratory experiments, problem-solving challenges, mathematical exercises, cooperative learning projects, research and discussion are employed to meet the needs of different educators and their individual teaching styles. The range of activities has been designed to develop a number of student skills, including critical thinking, research, public speaking, writing, data collection and analysis, cooperation, decision making, creative problem solving, reading comprehension, conflict resolution and values clarification.

Twelve of the 13 chapters in *Earth Matters* address specific issues of the global society and environment, such as climate change, biodiversity loss and gender equality. The final chapter, "Finding Solutions," includes several activities which encompass all of the preceding topics. These activities encourage personal decision making and individual actions on critical issues that shape our lives. In this way, *Earth Matters* aims not only to enlighten students but also to build skills, concern and commitment to effective global and local citizenship.

Teacher's Guide

Environmental Studies

The Acid Tests
Are People the Problem?
Bye, Bye Birdie
Clearing the Air
Demographic Facts of Life
Eco-Ethics
An Energizing Policy
Getting Around
Go for the Green
Good News, Bad News
In Search of Sustainable Life
An International Greenhouse
It's In the Bag
Lots of Lemna
Methane Matters
No Water Off A Duck's Back
A Nonbearing Account
Population Growth — It All Adds Up
Population Scavenger Hunt
Power of the Pyramids
Roll on Mighty River
Talkin' Trash in Tropico
Think Globally, Act Locally
To Log or Not to Log
Toss of the Dice
Waste A-Weigh
Water, Water Everywhere

Biology/Life Sciences

The Acid Tests
Bye, Bye Birdie
Clearing the Air
Demographic Facts of Life
Go for the Green
An International Greenhouse
Lots of Lemna
Methane Matters

No Water Off A Duck's Back
Power of the Pyramids
Toss of the Dice
Waste A-Weigh
Water, Water Everywhere

Math

Demographic Facts of Life
The Lion's Share
Lots of Lemna
Power of the Pyramids
Toss of the Dice
Water, Water Everywhere

Social Studies

Are People the Problem?
Changing Values
Clearing the Air
Demographic Facts of Life
Eco-Ethics
Gender Quest
An Energizing Policy
Generations Apart
Getting Around
Go For the Green
Good News, Bad News
The Hunger Banquet
In Search of Sustainable Life
An International Greenhouse
The Lion's Share
Living on $500 a Year
A Nonbearing Account
Population Growth — It All Adds Up
Population Scavenger Hunt
Power of the Pyramids
Roll on Mighty River
Think Globally, Act Locally
To Log or Not to Log
A Woman's Place

Economics

Changing Values
An Energizing Policy
Go For the Green
The Hunger Banquet
The Lion's Share
Living on $500 a Year
Population Growth — It All Adds Up
Talkin' Trash on Tropico
To Log or Not to Log

Language Arts

Bye, Bye Birdie
An Energizing Policy
Gender Quest
Generations Apart
An International Greenhouse
It's In the Bag
Living on $500 a Year
A Nonbearing Account
To Log or Not to Log
A Woman's Place

Family Life Education

Changing Values
Eco-Ethics
Gender Quest
Getting Around
The Hunger Banquet
It's In the Bag
The Lion's Share
Living on $500 a Year
Population Growth — It All Adds Up
Think Globally, Act Locally
Water, Water Everywhere
A Woman's Place

Teacher's Guide

Chapter	Activity	Description	Skills
I. Population Dynamics	1. Lots of Lemma	Students collect data on the exponential growth of *Lemma* (duckweed) plants.	Collecting and recording data, analyzing and interpreting data, estimation, graphing math calculations
	2. A Toss of the Dice	Students use dice to model exponential growth, as well as two other kinds of population growth.	Math calculations, interpreting data
	3. Power of the Pyramids	Students construct and interpret population pyramids which illustrate age and sex distribution of populations in different countries. They use this information to discuss population projections for those countries.	Calculating, graphing, analyzing and interpreting data
	4. Demographic Facts of Life	Students calculate the rate of natural increase and corresponding doubling times for several countries and discuss differences. Students also examine the impact of world disasters on population growth.	Collecting, analyzing and interpreting data, math calculations
	5. Population Scavenger Hunt	Students attempt to accomplish up to 35 tasks related to improving their population literacy, earning points for each completed task.	Varies according to each of 35 tasks
II. Climate Change	6. An International Greenhouse	Students act as delegates to the United Nations Environmental Programme in this model United Nations simulation focusing on climate change issues.	Public speaking, research parliamentary procedure, conflict resolution, negotiation
	7. Methane Matters	Students study possible relationships between several human activities and production of methane, a greenhouse gas.	Analyzing data, diagramming, graphing
III. Air Pollution	8. The Acid Tests	Students measure the effects of various pH solutions on beans to determine the effect of acid rain on plant growth.	Laboratory preparation, collecting, recording and analyzing data graphing, measuring, observation, drawing
	9. Clearing the Air	Students collect articles on air pollution problems throughout the world and create charts, depicting causes, effects and possible solutions.	Research, collecting and recording data, analyzing and interpreting data, reading comprehension

Teacher's Guide

Chapter	Activity	Description	Skills
IV. Water Resources	10. Water, Water Everywhere	Students observe a brief demonstration on the distribution of the world's water and then calculate their daily water use from direct and indirect sources.	Estimation, math calculations, graphing observation, research, writing
	11. Roll on Mighty River	Students participate in a simulation to determine problems associated with water quality and distribution.	Public speaking, debate, library research, decision making
V. Deforestation	12. To Log or Not to Log	Students participate in a mock trial pitting loggers against environmentalists in a land use conflict over old-growth forests in the United States.	Research, public speaking, persuasion, evaluation, critical thinking
	13. Go for the Green	Students play a board game in which they make economic and environmental decisions regarding tropical rainforests.	Decision making, strategizing
VI. Food and Hunger	14. The Hunger Banquet	Students attend a luncheon where they are randomly assigned to a global economic area and get a first-hand look at the inequitable distribution of food and wealth worldwide.	Communication, negotiation, conflict resolution, strategic planning, writing
	15. Good News, Bad News	Students analyze statements about population and food issues and determine whether to categorize them as "good news" or "bad news." They then evaluate the statements as a whole to gain a total picture of the food and hunger situation.	Evaluating and ranking data, critical thinking, research, writing
VII. Waste Disposal	16. Talkin' Trash in Tropico	Students design a solid waste disposal program for a mythical island after researching all of their options.	Research, writing, evaluation, cooperation, decision making
	17. It's In the Bag	Students debate which grocery bag (paper or plastic) is better for the environment.	Critical thinking, debate, writing, research, public speaking
	18. Waste A-Weigh	Students weigh their food wastes each day in the cafeteria and compete with other classes to reduce waste.	Brainstorming, collecting and recording data, applying knowledge

Teacher's Guide

Chapter	Activity	Description	Skills
VIII. Wildlife Endangerment	19. Bye, Bye Birdie	Students research various endangered species and develop criteria for determining which species should be "saved," given limited resources.	Critical thinking, cooperation, research, writing, public speaking, evaluation
	20. No Water Off a Duck's Back	Students conduct experiments on bird eggs and feathers to identify adverse effects of oil spills on wildlife.	Laboratory preparation, mathematic calculations, observation, graphing, drawing, analyzing data, discussion
IX. Energy Issues	21. Are People the Problem?	Students compare U.S. energy consumption habits with those of other countries and discuss the relationship between population and energy use.	Mathematic calculations, collecting and recording data, analyzing and interpreting data, estimation, graphing
	22. Getting Around	Students devise a survey on transportation habits, administer it in the community and evaluate findings.	Developing and administrating a survey, tabulating and interpreting data, evaluation
	23. An Energizing Policy	Students act as presidential advisors to formulate their own energy policies for the nation.	Critical thinking, research, writing, decision making, persuasion
X. Rich and Poor	24. The Lion's Share	Students study the relationship between income and family size as an aid to seeing how a country's per capita income varies with its population and gross domestic product (GDP).	Analyzing data, mathematic calculations, research and preparing a budget
	25. Living on $500 a Year	Students read and discuss how the average person lives in less developed countries and brainstorm possible ways to alleviate global inequities.	Brainstorming, problem solving, cooperation, evaluation, critical thinking
XI. Population and Economics	26. Population Growth—It All Adds Up	Students collect advertisements which promote growth and discuss whether an increased quality of life can be achieved without growth.	Collecting and analyzing data, critical thinking, research, discussion
	27. Changing Values	Students examine principles of growth that have been traditionally held in North America and determine whether they have changed in recent years.	Critical thinking, values-clarification

Teacher's Guide

Chapter	Activity	Description	Skills
XII. The World's Women	28. A Woman's Place	Students examine the status of women in different countries.	Cooperation, observation, research, public speaking/discussion, calculating averages and probability, analyzing data
	29. Gender Quest	Students act as anthropologists from a mythical planet to analyze women's place in contemporary American culture.	Observation, cooperation, research, interpretation, public speaking, analyzing data
XIII. Finding Solutions	30. Eco-Ethics	Students determine their personal code of environmental ethics by choosing responses to specific environmental dilemmas.	Decision making, writing, discussion, critical thinking
	31. Think Globally, Act Locally	Students list possible individual actions they can take to alleviate each of the problems addressed in this book, and determine the feasibility of each action.	Brainstorming, evaluation, critical thinking
	32. A Nonbearing Account	Students analyze a proposal for combating overpopulation and then devise their own plans.	Critical thinking, discussion, creative thinking, writing
	33. In Search of Sustainable Life	Students develop a Quality of Life Index for their communities.	Brainstorming, problem solving, decision making, writing, researching
	34. Generations Apart	Students interview older community residents to learn about changes in population and technology and how they affect their quality of life.	Research, writing, public speaking, interviewing

Teacher's Guide

Meeting the Standards with Earth Matters

Match the codes on the matrix to the *Guide to Selected National Standards* on page xviii.

Activity	English Language Arts	Geography	Health	History	Math	Science	Social Studies
1. Lots of Lemna				WH Era 9: 2A WHAE: 1	1, 3, 4	C-part 1 F	
2. Toss of the Dice				WH Era 9: 2C WHAE: 1	1, 3, 4	F-part 1	
3. Power of the Pyramids				U.S. History ERA 10: 2B	1, 3, 4	F, C	
4. Demographic Facts of Life		4-d; 9-a; 12-d		WH Era 9: 2A	1, 3, 4	F-part 1; C	IX-d
5. Population Scavenger Hunt	1, 7	4-d; 12-d; 14-a,b,c	IV.3	US Era 10: 2B WH Era 9: 2A	1, 3, 4	C, F	1-a,d; III-h,k VIII-a,f; IX-c,d X-d,i,j
6. An International Greenhouse	1, 7	4-d; 6-b; 8-c; 10-b; 13-b; 14-a,b,c; 15-a; 16-c	IV.3, VII.5	WH Era 9: 2A WHAE: 1		C, F	1-a; II-e; III-e,k V-b; VI-f; VIII-b,f; IX-d,e; X-d,i,j
7. Methane Matters		4-d; 8-c; 14-b,c; 16-c	VII.5 I.5, III.4	WH Era 9: 2A WHAE: 1	3, 4	C, F	IX-d; VIII-b; III-e
8. The Acid Tests		8-c; 14-a		WHAE: 1		C, F	III-e; IX-d
9. Clearing the Air	1, 5, 7	4-d; 8-c; 12-d; 14-a,b,c 15-a; 16-c	IV.3; I.5; III.4	WHAE: 1 WH Era 9: 2A		C, F	III-e, h, k; IX-d; X-d
10. Water, Water Everywhere	1, 7	8-c; 14-a, b, c		WHAE: 1 WH Era 9: 2A	3, 4	C, F	VI-c; VII-h; IX-h
11. Roll On Mighty River	1, 7	4-d; 8-c; 9-a; 13-a; 14-a,c; 15-a; 16-c		WHAE: 1		F	I-a; III-k; VI-c,f; IX-b,e,f; X-i,j
12. To Log or Not to Log	1, 5, 7	4-d; 6-a; 8-c; 9-a; 13-a; 14-b,c; 16-c,e		WHAE: 1 WH Era 9: 2A, 2B		C, F	III-k; V-b; VI-c,h,f VII-c,h; IX-b,d,e,h; X-f,i,j

Meeting the Standards with Earth Matters

Match the codes on the matrix to the *Guide to Selected National Standards* on page xviii.

Activity	English Language Arts	Geography	Health	History	Math	Science	Social Studies
13. Go for the Green	1, 7	8-b,c; 13-a; 14-a,b; 16-e		WHAE: 1 WH Era 9: 2A		C-, F	II-e; III-e; VI-c; VII-h; IX-b,c,d,h
14. The Hunger Banquet	5	4-d; 6-b; 8-b,c; 14-a,b; 16-c	III.4	WHAE: 1 WH Era 9: 2A, 2B, 3			III-e; VI-a,f IX-b,d,g; X-d
15. Good News, Bad News — Where Do We Stand?	1, 5, 7	14-a	IV.3	WHAE: 1 WH 2A			II-e; III-e,h; VI-g VIII-a,b; IX-c,d
16. Talkin' Trash on Tropico	7	4-d; 8-c, 9-a; 12-d 14-a, 15-a; 16-d,e	I.5, III.4 IV.3, VII.5	WHAE: 1 WH Era 9: 2A		C, F	III-k, VII-h; VIII-a, IX-d; X-d,j
17. It's in the Bag	5, 7	14-a; 15-a; 16-e		WHAE: 1 WH Era 9: 2A			III-k, VI-f; VII-h; IX-h; X-i
18. Waste A-Weigh		8-c; 16-c,d	III.4, VII.5	WHAE: 1 WH Era 9: 2A		F	II-e; III-k X-d,i,j
19. Bye-Bye Birdie	1, 5, 7	8-b,c; 14-a,b,c		WHAE: 1 WH Era 9: 2A		F, C	VII-h; IX-d
20. No Water Off a Duck's Back	1, 5, 7	8-b,c; 14-a,b,c; 15-a	I.5	WHAE: 1 WH Era 9: 2A		F, C	IX-d
21. Are People the Problem?		4-d; 9-d; 12-d; 14-a 15-a; 16-c		WHAE: 1 WH Era 9: 2A, 2B	1, 3	F, C	IX-d,h
22. Getting Around	5	4-d; 8-c; 9-d 14-a,b,c; 16-c	IV.3, III.4	WHAE: 1 WH Era 9: 2A		F, C	III-e,h; VIII-a,f IX-c,d,h
23. An Energizing Policy	1, 5, 7	8-c; 14-c; 16-c		WHAE: 1 WH Era 9: 2A, 2B		F, C	III-k; VI-j; VII-f,h IX-c,d,h
24. The Lion's Share	1, 7	6-b; 9-d; 10-b; 16-c		WH Era 9: 2A, 2B, 3	1, 3, 4	F-part 1	II-e; VII-h; IX-d,e

Meeting the Standards with Earth Matters

Match the codes on the matrix to the *Guide to Selected National Standards* on page xviii.

Activity	English Language Arts	Geography	Health	History	Math	Science	Social Studies
25. Living on $500 a Year	7	4-c; 6-a,b; 10-b; 16-c	III.4, VII.5 VI.3	WH Era 9: 2A, 2B, 3		F, part 1	II-e; III-e,k; IX-d,h; X-j
26. Population Growth—It All Adds Up	5, 7	4-c,d; 6-c; 8-b,c; 9-a; 12-d,e; 13-c; 14-b; 15-a	I.5, III.4			F, C	II-e; III-h; VII-h VIII-b; IX-d; X-d,j
27. Changing Values		6-a,b; 14-b		U.S. ERA 10: 2B			II-b,e; III-h, VII-h VIII-b, X-d
28. A Woman's Place	5	4-c; 6-a,b; 10-b		WHAE: 1 WH Era 9: 2A, 2C, 3		F, C	II-e; VI-a; IX-d X-j
29. Gender Quest	5	4-c; 6-a; 10-b		WH Era 9: 2C, 3 US Era 10:2A, 2E			II-e; VI-a; IX-d X-j
30. Eco-Ethics	7	6-a; 8-c; 14-a,b	V.7				
31. Think Globally, Act Locally	7	4-d; 8-b,c; 10-b; 12-d,e; 14-a,b,c; 15-a; 16-c	III.4 VII.5	WHAE: 1 WH Era 9: 2A, 2C, 3		F, C	II-e; VI-a; VIII-f; IX-d; X-d,i,j
32. A Nonbearing Account	7			WH Era 9: 2A, 2C		F, C IX-d; X-i,j	II-e; VII-h;
33. In Search of Sustainable Life	5	4-c; 8-c; 12-c; 14-a,b	I.5, III.4, IV3, VII.5	WH Era 9: 2A WHAE: 1		F, C	II-e; VI-c; IX-d,h; X-d,j
34. Generations Apart	5	4-a,c,d; 6-a,c; 9-d; 12-a,b,e; 14-a,b; 15-a		WHAE: 1 WH Era 9: 2A US Era 10: 2A			II-b,c,e; III-h,i X-j

Teacher's Guide

A Guide to Selected National Standards

English Language Arts

(International Reading Association and National Council of Teachers of English, 1996)
IRA, P.O. Box 8139, Newark, DE 18714-8139
NCTE, 1111 W. Kenyon Rd. Urbana, IL 61801-1096

Standard 1:
Students read a wide range of print and non-print texts to build an understanding of texts, of themselves, and of the cultures of the United States and the world; to acquire new information; to respond to the needs and demands of society and the workplace; and for personal fulfillment. Among these texts are fiction and non-fiction, classic and contemporary works.

Standard 5:
Students employ a wide range of strategies as they write and use different writing process elements appropriate to communicate with different audiences for a variety of purposes.

Standard 7:
Students conduct research on issues and interests by generating ideas and questions, and by posing problems. They gather, evaluate, and synthesize data from a variety of sources (e.g. print and non-print texts, artifacts, people) to communicate discoveries in ways that suit their purpose and audience.

Geography

National Council for Geographic Education, 1994
Geography Standards Project, 1600 M Street, NW, Washington, DC 20036

II. **Places and Regions**
4. Knows and understands the physical and human characteristics of place.
6. Knows and understands how culture and experience influence people's perceptions of places and regions.

III. **Physical Systems**
8. Knows and understands the characteristics and spatial distribution of ecosystems and Earth's surface.

IV. **Human Systems**
9. Knows and understands the characteristics, distribution, and migration of human populations on the Earth's surface.
10. Knows and understands the characteristics, distribution and complexity of Earth's cultural mosaics.
12. Knows and understands the processes, patterns, and functions of human settlements.
13. Knows and understands how the forces of cooperation and conflict among people influence the division and control of Earth's surface.

V. **Environment and Society**
14. Knows and understands how human actions modify the physical environment.
15. Knows and understands how physical systems affect human systems.
16. Knows and understands the changes that occur in the meaning, use, distribution, and importance of resources.

Health Education

Joint Committee on National Health Education Standards, 1995

I. Students will comprehend concepts related to health promotion and disease prevention.
5. Analyze effectively how the environment influences the health of the community.

III. Students will demonstrate the ability to access valid health-enhancing behaviors and reduce health risks.
4. Develop strategies to improve or maintain personal, family and community health.

IV. Students will analyze the influence of culture, media, technology and other factors on health.
3. Evaluate the impact of technology on personal, family and community health.

V. Students will demonstrate the ability to use interpersonal communication skills to enhance health.
7. Analyze the possible causes of conflict in schools, families and communities.

VI. Students will demonstrate the ability to use goal-setting and decision-making skills to enhance health.
3. Predict immediate and long-term impact of health decisions on the individual, family and community.

VII. Students will demonstrate the ability to advocate for personal, family and community health.
5. Demonstrate the ability to work cooperatively when advocating for healthy communities.

History

National Center for History in the Schools at UCLA, 1996
231 Moore Hall 405 Hilgard Avenue, Los Angeles, CA 90024

U.S. History
Era 10: Contemporary U.S. (1968 - present)
II. Economic, social and cultural developments in contemporary United States
A. Understands economic patterns since 1968.
B. Understands the new immigration and demographic shifts.

World History
Era 9: The 20th Century Since 1945
II. The search for community, stability, and peace in an interdependent world
A. Understands how population explosion and environmental changes have altered conditions of life around the world.
B. Understands how increasing economic interdependence has transformed human society.
C. Understands how liberal democracy, market economies, and human rights have reshaped political and social life.
D. Understands major sources of tension and conflict in the contemporary world and efforts that have been made to address them.
III. Major global trends since World War II
Understands major global trends since World War II.

World History Across the Eras
I. Long-term changes and recurring patterns in world history.
Understands long-term changes and recurring patterns in world history.

Mathematics

National Council of Teachers of Mathematics, 1989
1906 Association Dr., Reston, VA 22091

I. **Mathematics as Problem Solving**
- apply integrated mathematical problem-solving strategies to solve problems from within and outside mathematics.
- recognize and formulate problems from situations within and outside mathematics.
- apply the process of mathematical modeling to real-world problem situations.

III. **Mathematics as Reasoning**
- make and test conjectures
- formulate counterexamples
- follow logical arguments
- judge the validity of arguments

IV. **Mathematical Connections**
- use and value the connections between mathematics and other disciplines

E. Understands how a democratic polity debates social issues and mediates between individual or group rights and the common good.

Teacher's Guide

Science

National Science Education Standards of the National Research Council, 1996
2101 Constitution Ave., NW, Washington, DC 20418

CONTENT STANDARD C: Life Science
Students in grades 9-12 should develop understanding of
- Interdependence of organisms
- Matter, energy, and organization in living systems
- Behavior of organisms

CONTENT STANDARD F:
Science in Personal and Social Perspective
Students in grades 9-12 should develop understanding of
- Personal and community health
- Population growth
- Natural resources
- Environmental quality
- Natural and human-induced hazards
- Science and technology in local, national, and global challenges

Social Studies

National Council for the Social Studies, 1995
3501 Newark St. N.W., Washington, DC 20016
Performance Expectations

I. Culture
A. Analyze and explain the ways groups, societies, and cultures address human needs and concerns.
D. Compare and analyze societal patterns for preserving and transmitting culture while adapting to environmental or social change.
H. Explain and apply ideas, theories, and modes of inquiry drawn from anthropology and sociology in the examination of persistent issues and social problems.

II. Time, Continuity, and Change
B. Apply key concepts such as chronology, causality, change, conflict, and complexity to explain, analyze, and show connections among patterns of historical change and continuity.
C. Identify and describe significant historical periods and patterns of change within and across cultures.
D. Investigate, interpret, and analyze multiple historical and contemporary viewpoints within and across cultures related to important events, recurring dilemmas, and persistent issues, while employing empathy, skepticism, and critical judgment.

III. People, Places, and Environment
C. Describe, differentiate, and explain the relationships among various regional and global patterns of geographic phenomena such as landforms, climate, vegetation, natural resources, and population.

H. Examine, interpret, and analyze physical and cultural patterns and their interactions, such as land use, settlement patterns, cultural transmission of customs and ideas, and ecosystem changes.
I. Describe and assess ways that historical events have been influenced by, and have influenced, physical and human geographic factors, in local, regional, national, and global settings.
K. Propose, compare, and evaluate alternative policies for the use of land and other resources in communities, regions, nations and the world.

V. Individuals, Groups, and Institutions
B. Analyze group and institutional influences on people, events, and elements of culture in both historical and contemporary settings.

VI. Power, Authority, and Governance
A. Examine persistent issues involving the rights, roles and status of the individual in relation to the general welfare.
C. Analyze and explain ideas and mechanisms to meet needs and wants of citizens, regulate territory, manage conflict, and establish order and security, and balance competing conceptions of a just society.
F. Analyze and evaluate conditions, actions and motivations that contribute to conflict and cooperation within and among nations.
G. Evaluate the role of technology in communications, transportation, information-processing, weapons development, or other areas as it contributes to or helps resolve conflicts.
H. Explain and apply ideas, theories, and modes of inquiry drawn from political science to the examination of persistent issues and social problems.
J. Prepare a public policy paper and present and defend it before an appropriate forum in school or community.

VII. Production, Distribution, and Consumption
A. Explain how the scarcity of productive resources (human, capital, technological and natural) requires the development of economic systems to make decisions about how goods and services are to be produced and distributed.
C. Consider the costs and benefits to society of allocating goods and services through private and public sectors (potential activity on this).
F. Compare how values and beliefs influence economic decisions in different societies.
H. Apply economic concepts and reasoning when evaluating historical and contemporary social developments and issues.
I. Apply knowledge of production, distribution and consumption in the analysis of a public issue such as the allocation of health care or the consumption of energy, and devise and economic plan for accomplishing a socially desirable outcome related to that issue.

VIII. Science, Technology, and Society
A. Identify and describe both current and historical examples of the interaction and interdependence of science, technology, and society in a variety of cultural settings.
B. Make judgments about how science and technology have transformed the physical world and human society and our understanding of time, space, place and human-environment interaction.
F. Formulate strategies and develop policies for influencing public discussions associated with technology-society issues, such as the greenhouse effect.

IX. Global Connections
B. Explain conditions and motivations that contribute to conflict, cooperation and interdependence among groups, societies and nations.
C. Analyze and evaluate the effects of changing technologies on the global community.
D. Analyze the causes, consequences and possible solutions to persistent, contemporary, and emerging global issues, such as health, security, resource allocation, economic development, and environmental quality.
E. Analyze the relationships and tensions between national sovereignty and global interests in such matters as territory, economic development, nuclear and other weapons, use of natural resources, and human rights concerns.
F. Analyze or formulate policy statements demonstrating an understanding of concerns, standards, issues, and conflicts related to universal human rights.
G. Describe and evaluate the role of international and multinational organizations in the global arena.
H. Illustrate how individual behaviors and decisions connect with global systems.

X. Civics Ideals and Practices
D. Practice forms of civic discussion and participation consistent with the ideals of citizens in a democratic republic.
F. Analyze a variety of public policies and issues from the perspective of formal and informal political actors.
I. Construct a policy statement and an action plan to achieve one or more goals related to an issue of public concern.
J. Participate in activities to strengthen the "common good" based upon careful evaluation of possible options for citizen action.

Population Dynamics

The People Connection

"Population growth may be the most pressing issue we face as we enter the new millenium."
~National Geographic Magazine, January 1998

Central to so many of the environmental, social and economic issues facing the planet today are people — our numbers and our behaviors. Although barely noticeable on a day-to-day basis, human population pressures threaten the health of our ecosystems and the quality of life for Earth's inhabitants.

Consider that in the six seconds it takes to read this sentence, 16 more people will inhabit the globe. In fact, the world's population grows at nearly a record pace, adding a New York City every month, a Germany each year and almost an India every decade.[1] At the turn of the century there are six billion of us and counting. This growth in human numbers has been described as a "population explosion," doubling ever faster over the past 300 years.

What Ignited the Explosion?

Rapid population increases have been a very recent development in the scope of human history. People lived on Earth for about three million years before the world population reached 500 million around 1600. Until then, **birth rates** and **death rates** were in balance, keeping the population stable. Although birth rates were high, death rates — particularly among children — also remained high.

By the 17th century, this balance of birth and death rates began to change as advances in medical care, sanitation, food production and nutrition increased **life expectancy** for children and adults. Death rates dropped, but birth rates remained high and the population grew steadily. By 1800, at the height of the Industrial Revolution in North America and Europe, global population reached one billion.

As industrialization grew throughout the Western world, people exchanged their agrarian lifestyles for homes and jobs in burgeoning cities. Without land to farm, large families became neither necessary nor practical. Slowly, birth rates dropped in rapidly industrializing nations. This three-part population pattern — from high birth and death rates, to high birth and low death rates, and finally to low birth and death rates — is now referred to as the **demographic transition**.

In the non-industrialized nations of Africa, Latin America and Asia, however, birth rates remained high at the same time that death rates dropped, as new agricultural and medical technologies were imported from more developed countries. Economic conditions in these nations did not always improve as life spans increased. The result has been a population explosion and stagnation in the middle of the demographic transition pattern throughout much of the globe. By 1960, the world population reached three billion. Just 15 years later, in 1975, the population soared to four billion and topped five billion in 1987. In 1999, the population reached six billion, completely doubling in less than 40 years. It now appears that global population growth is finally turning a corner as birth rates begin to fall worldwide. Even so,

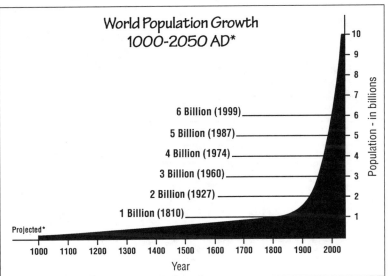

World Population Growth 1000-2050 AD*

6 Billion (1999)
5 Billion (1987)
4 Billion (1974)
3 Billion (1960)
2 Billion (1927)
1 Billion (1810)

Projected*

Year: 1000 1100 1200 1300 1400 1500 1600 1700 1800 1900 2000

Population - in billions: 1 2 3 4 5 6 7 8 9 10

demographers now project that the global population will continue to grow, albeit more slowly than in the past century, adding an additional two to five billion more people by the middle of the 21st century.[2]

How does the quality of life on Earth vary now from what it was when there were half as many people? How might it be in the future when there are many more of us? How many people can the Earth support sustainably?

The People Connection

Crowding the Earth

No one knows for sure how many people the Earth can support. Every environment has a carrying capacity — the point at which there are not enough natural resources to support any more members of a given species. In *How Many People Can the Earth Support*, author Joel Cohen attempted to answer that very question by collecting dozens of expert estimates made in recent decades. Finding the Earth's carrying capacity is difficult because the number of people the Earth can support depends greatly on how people use the Earth's resources. Although estimates varied, Cohen was able to conclude from scholars that,

The possibility must be considered seriously that the number of people on Earth has reached, or will reach within the next century, the maximum number the Earth can support in modes of life that we and our children and their children will choose to want.[3]

The population issue, then, is not one of numbers but of carrying capacity. The entire world population could fit into Texas, and each person could have an area equal to the floor space of a typical North American home. But this ignores the amount of land required to provide each of us with the raw materials for survival (food, water, shelter, clothing and energy) and all that has become essential to our modern lifestyles (transportation, electronic communication, consumer goods and services). Scientists in Vancouver, Canada tried to calculate local residents' "ecological footprint," the land and water area that would be required to support the area's population and material standard indefinitely. They found that the Vancouver area's population requires an area 19 times larger than its home territory to support its present consumer lifestyles — wheat fields in Alberta, oil fields in Saudi Arabia, tomato fields in California. [4]

While the continents are vast, only a small fraction (1/10) of all the land in the world is arable.[5] The rest has been built up into cities and towns or is inhospitable to growing crops. While the number of people continues to grow, the small portion of land which must support these people remains the same, or shrinks as cities expand. The size of the human population affects virtually every environmental condition facing our planet. As our population grows, demands for resources increase, adding to pollution and waste. More energy is used, escalating the problems of climate change, acid rain, oil spills and nuclear waste. More land is required for agriculture, leading to deforestation and soil erosion. More homes, factories and roads must be built, occupying habitat lost to other species which share the planet, leading increasingly to their extinction. Simply put, the more people inhabiting our finite planet, the greater stress on its resources.

The People Connection

Population Growth: North American-style

With over 90 percent of the population increase today occurring in developing countries, many North Americans feel that they neither contribute to nor are affected by the problem. In fact, the United States is the fastest growing industrialized country, growing by 2.6 million people each year. This is of particular concern to the global environment, as affluent lifestyles in North America place disproportionate demands on the world's resources and leave a much larger "ecological footprint." At current consumption levels, the next 20 million Americans, for example, will consume more barrels of oil than the over 600 million people living in Sub-Saharan Africa.[6] The 47 million people expected to be added to the U.S. population over the next 20 years will produce more carbon dioxide emissions than the 470 million people expected be added to China and India for the same time period.[7]

Evidence of population growth surrounds us — intensifying traffic congestion, urban and suburban sprawl, and landfill space too full to handle the mounting garbage and hazardous waste which North Americans create daily. In the last 200 years, the United States has lost 71 percent of its topsoil, 50 percent of its wetlands, 90 percent of its old-growth forests, 99 percent of its tallgrass prairie, and up to 490 species of native plants and animals with another 9,000 now at risk.[8] We are currently developing rural land at the rate of nine square miles per day[9], and paving 1.3 million acres each year — an area roughly the size of Delaware.[10] Many attribute these problems solely to wasteful habits. However, as we in North America increase our population, we compound our ecological impact. Efforts to relieve environmental stress by cutting consumption would be undermined, if not negated, by continued population growth or by stabilization at a size larger than our resources can sustain.

In making its policy recommendations to the President of the United States in 1996, the President's Council for Sustainable Development (PCSD) stated clearly that "human impact on the environment is a function of both population and consumption patterns" and recommends policies to move toward voluntary population stabilization at the national level.[11]

What Can Be Done?

There is much that can and has been done toward stabilizing the world population and preserving the environment. Two recent United Nations conferences have brought attention to the importance of slowing population growth. At the 1992 U.N. Conference on Environment and Development (Earth Summit) in Rio de Janeiro, Brazil, 179 governments adopted a plan of action which recognizes that "the growth of world population and production combined with unsustainable consumption patterns places increasingly severe stress on the life supporting capacities of our planet."[12]

World Population Clock, 1998

1998 Population (est.)		World 5.9 billion	United States 270 million
Births per:	Year	136,967,149	4,053,000
	Month	11,413,929	377,750
	Week	2,633,984	77,942
	Day	375,252	11,135
	Hour	15,636	463
	Minute	261	7.7
	Second	4.3	—
Deaths per:	Year	53,282,252	2,431,800
	Month	4,440,188	202,650
	Week	1,024,659	46,765
	Day	145,979	6,680
	Hour	6,082	278
	Minute	101	4.6
	Second	1.7	—
Natural Increase per:	Year	83,684,897	1,621,200*
	Month	16,973,741	175,100*
	Week	1,609,325	31,177*
	Day	229,274	4,455*
	Hour	9,553	185*
	Minute	159	3.1*
	Second	2.7	—*

*These figures do not include net immigration, which is also a significant factor in U.S. population increase.

The U.N. International Conference on Population and Development (ICPD) in Cairo, Egypt, which followed two years later, expanded on many of the principles laid out in Rio. The

The People Connection

plan of action developed at the Cairo conference states that early stabilization of world population would make a "crucial contribution" toward improving the lives of people around the planet.[13]

It only takes very small changes in **fertility rates** (the average number of children born to each woman) to make a big difference in when the population will stabilize, and how many people there will be when that happens. According to the United Nations, a drop in the average number of children a woman has in her lifetime by one child per woman could mean a difference of four billion people in the projected population for 2050![14]

Recent trends show that the population growth rate has begun to decrease, due at least in part to policies enacted or strengthened in response to the recommendations of the U.N. conferences. Programs that expand access to health care, education and family planning services, which enable women to choose the timing and number of their children, as well as those that have improved the status of women and employment opportunities, all work to lower fertility levels. In 1960, the average woman gave birth to more than five children. Today, the average woman gives birth to just over three children.

However, these positive indicators do not mean that rapid population growth no longer poses a threat to the world's people and resources. High growth rates in recent decades mean that almost one-third of the world's people are under age 15 and have not yet entered their child-bearing years.[15] This age structure means there is still potential for steady population increases and the need for international cooperation to continue successful programs. In order to achieve **zero population growth** (stable population) while maintaining low death rates, average births will need to total only about two children per woman worldwide in the years to come.

Endnotes

[1] 1997 *World Population Data Sheet*, Population Reference Bureau .

[2] *World Population Prospects, The 1996 Revision*. New York: United Nations, 1996.

[3] Joel E. Cohen. *How Many People Can the Earth Support?* New York: W.W. Norton and Co., 1995.

[4] Mathis Wackernagel and William Rees. *Our Ecological Footprint: Reducing Human Impact on the Earth*. Canada: New Society Publishers, 1996.

[5] *1996 Human Development Report*, United Nations. Table 22: Natural Resources Balance Sheet. Figure is for 1993.

[6] Statistics on oil consumption for 1994 from *1996 World Development Report*, The World Bank. Table 8: Commercial Energy Use.

[7] Population estimates from the U.S. Census Bureau homepage, "International Database" www.census.gov/ipc/www/idbprint.html. Carbon Dioxide emission data is for 1992 found in op. cit. note 6.

[8] The World Resources Institute. *The 1993 Information Please Environmental Almanac*. Boston and New York: Houghton Mifflin, 1993.

[9] Alan T. Durning. *How Much is Enough? The Consumer Society and the Future of the Earth*. New York: W.W. Norton and Company, 1992.

[10] David Pimentel (panelist). "United States Carrying Capacity Overview," Carrying Capacity Network Conference. Washington, DC: 1993.

[11] The President's Council on Sustainable Development. *Sustainable America: A New Consensus for Prosperity, Opportunity, and a Healthy Environment for the Future*. Washington, DC: U.S. Government Printing Office, 1996.

[12] Agenda 21: United Nations Programme of Action from Rio, para. 5.3.

[13] Programme of Action adopted at the International Conference on Population and Development, Cairo, Egypt, 1994, paragraph 1.11.

[14] Population Division of the Department of Economic and Social Affairs of the United Nations Secretariat. *World Population Projections to 2150*. New York: United Nations, 1998.

[15] Op. cit. note 1.

Lots of *Lemna*

Introduction:

When modeling exponential growth in the science classroom, it is useful to use living organisms whose growth can be easily measured. This activity uses a small, floating aquatic flowering plant of the genus *Lemna* (duckweed) to investigate geometric population growth. *Lemna* is small enough to have a sufficiently rapid reproduction rate yet large enough to be easily seen and counted. As individual *Lemna* leaves grow and enlarge, they break apart from the parent plant and form new plants. *Lemna* can reproduce and double its number in less than five days if the growing conditions are adequate. As *Lemna* grows and reproduces, it forms a population of floating plants on the surface of the water. Within three months, a definite J-curve can be obtained, and within five to six months, *Lemna* will entirely cover the surface of a 10-gallon aquarium with an estimated 10,000 individual plants.

Procedure:

Because of the time involved with this activity, it is necessary to start the lab five months prior to when the lesson on population is introduced.

1. Several days prior to the class period when the lesson is introduced to the students, set up the aquarium as follows: Prepare a 10-gallon aquarium with aged water aerated with a single pump. On the day you begin the activity with students, place 10 *Lemna* plants in the tank. *Lemna* can be field collected or purchased at a supply house. They often grow in aquaria at tropical fish shops. Leave the aquarium light on at all time. When water begins to evaporate from the tank, replace with aged tap water.

2. Let students know that they will be collecting data on the population growth of *Lemna*. You might like to have the class predict the reproduction rate and doubling time of *Lemna*.

3. You may wish to have the students study the *Lemna* plant under a microscope. Students can do background reading on the genus, investigating such information as the geographic range of *Lemna* and the best ecological conditions for growth.

4. Have students construct a data collection sheet in their notebooks with a column for the day recorded and one for population size. Explain how to collect and record the population size. Counting the number of plants should take only a few minutes every couple of days. The students will discover that for several days, no population increase will occur, and then within one day, the population will increase significantly. These "spurts" in reproduction are to be expected and represent important lessons in growth and development. After several months, the number of plants becomes too large to easily count. Try to get the students to devise a method of measurement that is appropriate for large numbers. One method is to:

    a) Calculate the surface area of the aquarium, (in sq. cm.).
    b) Average, from 10 samples, the number of *Lemna* plants per square cm.
    c) Estimate the percentage of the surface covered by the plants.
    d) Calculate the population size by multiplying a x b x c.

At this point students should note on their data sheets the percentage of surface covered by the *Lemna*. Students who count on the same day may not have the same number of population sizes on their data sheets. Although students should be taught the importance of accurate data collection, the time that students count the number of plants will vary and small errors will be more common as the population size increases and as students estimate the population size with indirect measures.

5. After students have finished collecting data, (when the tank is full of *Lemna*) ask them to graph the results. The graph will be a typical geometric curve. Discuss with them the nature of the curve and how geometric growth is different from arithmetic growth. Perhaps you will want the students to predict future populations if the growth rate continues. What are the implications when population growth is "out of control?" If organisms follow a geometric growth curve, why isn't the world hopelessly overpopulated with

Concept:
Populations grow exponentially in environments without limiting factors.

Objectives:
Students will be able to:
• Utilize direct and indirect methods for measuring population size.
• Conduct population measurements and plot results.
• Interpret a graph of population growth.
• Apply concepts of exponential growth to a theoretical example.

Subjects:
Biology, math, environmental science

Skills:
Collecting and recording data, analyzing and interpretating data, estimation, mathematical calculations, graphing

Method:
Students collect data on the geometric growth of a *Lemna* (duckweed) population and graph results. They then draw parallels between observed *Lemna* growth and human population growth.

Materials:
10 *Lemna* plants (duckweed)
10-gallon aquarium with water and aerator

Lots of Lemna

plants and animals? Why haven't most populations of organisms followed the J-curve? Why don't populations of natural organisms go out of control? Have the students identify natural factors which help control population sizes. What might limit *Lemna* growth in the wild, as in a pond?

Follow-up Activities:

Activity 1: A Human J-Curve

Students can now extend the concept of exponential growth into the area of human population growth. Copy the table below onto the chalkboard. Have the students graph human population growth. How does the human population graph compare to the *Lemna* population graph? What is the future for human populations? What decisions must be made? What are the implications of human population growth for future resource use, for disease control or for environmental quality?

Activity 2: Bacteria Bottles

This puzzle illustrates the concept of exponential growth using bacteria. Invite students to try it on friends and family.

Bacteria multiply by division. One bacterium becomes two. Then two divide into four; the four divide into eight, and so on. For a certain strain of bacteria, the time for this division process is one minute. If you put one bacterium in a bottle at 11:00 p.m., by midnight the entire bottle will be full.

World Population History	
Year	**Population (in millions)**
1 A.D.	170
200	190
400	190
600	200
800	220
1000	265
1100	320
1200	360
1300	360
1400	350
1500	425
1600	545
1700	610
1750	760
1800	900
1850	1,211
1900	1,625
1950	2,515
2000*	6,080
2050*	9,400

*Projected

Data: For 1 A.D. through 1975: The Atlas of World Population History by C. McEvedy and R. Jones, New York: Penguin Books, 1978. For 1975 to 1959: Population Reference Bureau, 1875 Connecticut Avenue, N.W., Suite 520, Washington, D.C. 20009. For 2000 projection: World Population Prospects, The United Nations, 1994 revision, Middle Series. For 2050 Projection: World Population Prospects, The United Nations, 1996 Revision, Middle Series.

1. When would the bottle be half-full? How do you know?
   The bottle was half full at 11:59 p.m. because the doubling time is one minute and the bottle was full at midnight.

2. Suppose you could be a bacterium in this bottle. At what time would you first realize that you were running out of space?
   Answers will vary. To clarify, ask students: "At 11:55 p.m., when the bottle was only 3% full and 97% empty, would it be easy to perceive that there was a space problem?"

3. Suppose that at 11:58 some bacteria realize that they are running out of space in the bottle. So they launch a search for new bottles. They look far and wide. Finally, offshore in the Arctic Ocean, they find three new empty bottles. Great sighs of relief come from all the bacteria. This is three times the number of bottles they've known. Surely, they think, their space problems are over. Is that so? Explain why the bacteria are still in trouble. Since their space resources have quadrupled, how long can their growth continue?
   With space resources quadrupled, the bacteria have two more doubling times, or two minutes before they will run out of space.
   11:58 p.m.: Bottle 1 is one-quarter full.
   11:59 p.m.: Bottle 1 is half-full.
   12:00 a.m.: Bottle 1 is full.
   12:01 a.m.: Bottles 1 and 2 are full.
   12:02 a.m.: Bottles 1, 2, 3 and 4 are all full.

4. Does what you have learned about bacteria suggest something about human population growth?

Adapted by permission from the National Association of Biology Teachers. The original activity, "Using Lemna to Study Geometric Population Growth" by Larry DeBuhr, appears in The American Biology Teacher, Vol. 53, No. 4, April 1991, pp. 229-232.

Toss of the Dice

Introduction:

Population, non-renewable resource consumption, food production, industrial output and pollution generation have all been increasing exponentially. To understand the resource and environmental crises, one must understand exponential growth. This lab is designed to give that understanding, while illustrating three models of population growth.

Procedure:

In this experiment, students will use dice to model population growth. Each die represents a person. Each throw represents a year. A *3* or a *6* represents the birth of a child, so each time one of them comes up, add a die to the population. If a *1* comes up, a death has occurred, so remove that die from the population. Hence, you are modeling a situation where the birth rate is twice the death rate. You also have a population growth rate of 1/6 or about 17 percent.

Have students follow these instructions:

Part A: Unrestricted Exponential Growth

Put ten ordinary dice into a container (Adam, Eve, Cain, Abel, Sally, Alice, Dick, Jane, Bob and Sue). Shake the container and dump the contents out onto a smooth, hard floor. Remove and count all the *1*'s that appear. A *1* is analogous to a death. Record the number of deaths on the chart for Part A. Count up all the *3*'s and *6*'s that appear. Since they correspond to births, add a die to the container for each of them. Then fill in the required information in the chart. Repeat the above procedure until the total population exceeds 500 people. When the population grows beyond the number of dice or cubes that you have available, either roll twice or double your results.

Part B: The Effect of Instituting a Limited Family Planning Program

Return to the year where your population was almost 100 people. Put that many dice into the container. But now introduce a limited birth control program. This will be modeled by saying that a *3* represents a birth, as before, and so does every other *6*. However, the remaining half of the *6*'s represent women who use contraceptives (or whose male partner uses contraceptives) and so a birth has been prevented. If an odd number of *6*'s comes up, round off in favor of a birth half of the time, and in favor of a prevented birth in the half of the cases. Model this situation, from where you start, for 12 throws of the dice. You have essentially cut the population growth rate from 17 percent to 8 percent.

Part C: The Zero Population Growth Plan

Again return to the year where your population was almost 100 people. Put that many dice into the container. But now introduce a large scale family planning program. This will be modeled by saying that all *6*'s represent women using effective contraceptives or women whose male partners use effective contraceptives. Hence, a *1* represents a death, a *3* represents a birth, and a *6* represents a prevented birth. Model this situation from where you start for twelve throws of the dice.

Part D: World Population Trends

See page 8 for a listing of estimates of world population from 1 A.D. to 2050. Figures such as these are compiled by the United Nations and are published in most almanacs.

Adapted by permission from Kendall/Hunt Publishing Company. The original activity, "Modelling Exponential Growth," appears in Global Science: Energy, Resources, Environment Laboratory Manual. Copyright 1981, 1984, 1991, 1996 by Kendall/Hunt Publishing Company.

Concept:
Within the last two centuries, human population growth has increased exponentially. The absence of widespread family planning contributes to the geometric growth of human populations.

Objectives:
Students will be able to:
• Model population growth using dice.
• Understand exponential growth.
• Compare and contrast three different population growth models.

Subjects:
Math, biology, environmental science

Skills:
Mathematical calculations, interpreting data

Method:
Students roll dice to model exponential growth, as well as two other population growth models.

Materials:
200-300 dice (or wood or sugar cubes with different colored sides)

2 large, open-ended container (e.g., coffee can, milk carton, etc.)

Copies of Student Worksheet

Graph paper

Note: Dice can be purchased at game stores. *The Growth Model*, including 250 dice, can be purchased for $42.00 from Scott Resources, P.O. Box 2121, Fort Collins, CO 80522; (800) 289-9299.

Toss of the Dice

Part A: Unrestricted Exponential Growth

Throw No. (Year)	Number of Births	Number of Deaths (Population)	Number of Dice	Population Growth Rate
0	—	—	10	—
1				
2				
3				
4				
5				
6				
7				
8				
9				
10				
11				
12				
13				
14				
15				
16				
17				
18				
19				
20				
21				
22				
23				
24				
25				
26				
27				
28				
29				
30				

Toss of the Dice

Part B: The Effect of Instituting a Limited Family Planning Program

Throw No. (Year)	Number of Births	Number of Deaths (Population)	Number of Dice	Population Growth Rate

Part C: The Zero Population Growth Program

Throw No. (Year)	Number of Births	Number of Deaths (Population)	Number of Dice	Population Growth Rate

Power of the Pyramids

Concept:
The age and gender distribution of a regional or national population affects its growth rate.

Objectives:
Students will be able to:
• Calculate percentages using raw numbers for each age/gender group in a given population.
• Construct a population age/gender distribution graph for one of six different countries.
• Make correlations between the shapes of the graphs and the coutries' different growth patterns.

Subjects:
Math, biology, social studies, environmental science

Skills:
Calculating, graphing, analyzing and interpreting data

Method:
Students construct and interpret population pyramids and discuss differences in population growth rates among several different countries.

Materials:
Student Worksheets
  (one per student)
Graph paper
Colored pencils
Ruler
Calculator

Introduction:

To help them make population projections for different countries, demographers look at the profile of the countries' residents. What are the ages of the people? How many are men? How many are women? Taking this information, they construct **population pyramids** like the ones students will create in this activity. These graphs depict the configuration of a country's population as impacted by 70 to 80 years of economic, political and natural events. These graphs can also help predict future population trends.

Procedure:

1. Display the sample world population pyramid and explain that this is a kind of graph used by demographers to study the distribution of people across age categories.

2. Assign each student or group of students one of the six countries and distribute graph paper and a copy of the student worksheet for that country.

3. The figures on the worksheet represent the population (in thousands) of each age group within each gender for each particular country. In order to construct the country's pyramid, students must first calculate the percentage of the population in each gender in each age group.
   Example: According to the worksheet, the United States' total population in 1995 was 263,119,000. The population of males ages 0-4 was 10,515,000.

   $$\frac{10,515,000}{263,119,000} = .04 \text{ or } 4\%$$

   Students should complete these calculations for each **cohort** (age group).

4. Using graph paper, students can construct a population pyramid as in the example. A line drawn down the middle of the graph separates the male and female populations. The percentages of the population will be plotted along the X-axis — females to the right, males to the left of the center line. The age groups will be running up the Y-axis with the youngest at the bottom, oldest at the top. (See "World Population Pyramid" sample.) Note: Make sure the scale on the X-axis goes up to 9% in each direction to encompass everyone's data.

5. Have students graph the percentage data for their assigned country.

6. Have students hold up their finished graphs for all to see while going through the follow-up questions in class.

Discussion Questions:

1. Where are you represented on the tables and on the graphs?
   If you live in the United States and were between 10 and 15 years old in 1995 you are represented on line 3 in the U.S. data under either male or female. On the graph you and your cohorts made up the percentage presented by the third bar from the bottom, males on the left, females on the right.

2. Can you tell from the data if there are more male or female babies in each country?
   Yes, there are more male babies. There is a slightly greater probability of giving birth to male children. For every 100 girls born, there are about 105 boys born.

3. Are there more elderly women or men? Why might that be the case?
   There are more elderly women. Throughout the world, life expectancy for women is higher than for men. This is due to a number of genetic and social factors. In general, men are more predisposed to certain health risks than women. Also, men make up the vast majority of the military, and are more likely to die during wars.

4. Can you tell from the graphs which country has the most people?
   No. The graphs represent 100 percent of the population of each country broken down by age groups. Demographers use the percentage data instead of the raw data so that each graph fits on the same size paper and can be compared to the graphs of other countries.

5. Which country has the most people? How can you tell?
   From the TOTAL line on the data sheet you can tell that China has more people than any other country.

6. Of the six graphs, which two look most like pyramids? What does that indicate about their population growth rates? What factors would change the shape of the pyramids in the future?

The graphs for Kenya and Brazil look most like pyramids. This indicates a high growth rate. Population growth occurs when the segment of the population currently in its childbearing years (ages 15-44; bars 4-9 on the graphs) has produced a generation larger than itself (bars 1-3). If the birth rate goes down, this would change the shape of the graph over time from a pyramid to more of a rectangle, indicating a more stable population.

7. Looking at the pyramids, which countries appear to have the slowest rates of population growth? How can you tell?

Austria and Japan. The graphs are closer to rectangles than pyramids, showing more uniform population size across the age groups.

8. Which are the largest age groups in the U.S.?

People aged 30-50 (in 1995) made up the biggest portion of the United States, with babies a close second. The people who were born between 1946 to 1964 are called "Babyboomers," and were born shortly after World War II, when many husbands and wives were reunited, and the country experienced greater economic prosperity than it did during the years of the Great Depression and the war. Couples felt confident of their ability to support families, and the birth rate soared as a result.

9. In which country do children make up the largest percentage of the population?

You can see on the graph that the bottom of the Kenyan and the Brazilian pyramids go out the farthest, representing the largest percentage. The percentages that you calculated show that Kenyan babies (males and females com-

bined) make up about 16% (8 + 8) of the population and the older children also make up a big percentage.

10. If you had a business and wanted to capitalize on your information about the population age distribution for the U.S. what would you sell?

Answers might include any products for people of the Baby Boom generation or their children.

11. If you had a business in Kenya and wanted to capitalize on your information about the Kenyan population, what would you sell?

Answers might include any products for children and infants.

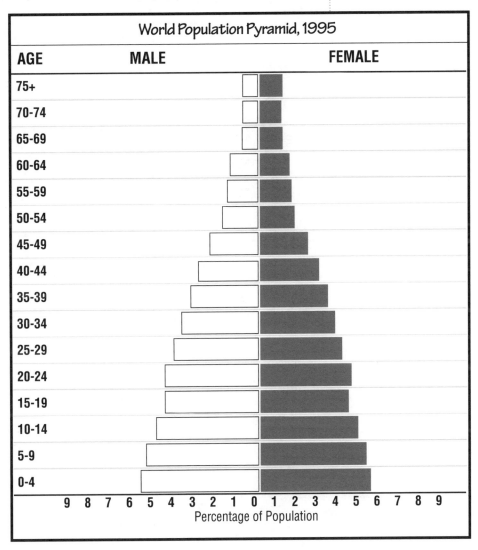

World Population Pyramid, 1995

AGE	MALE	FEMALE
75+		
70-74		
65-69		
60-64		
55-59		
50-54		
45-49		
40-44		
35-39		
30-34		
25-29		
20-24		
15-19		
10-14		
5-9		
0-4		

9 8 7 6 5 4 3 2 1 0 1 2 3 4 5 6 7 8 9

Percentage of Population

Sample Pyramids

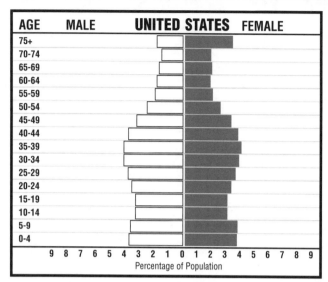

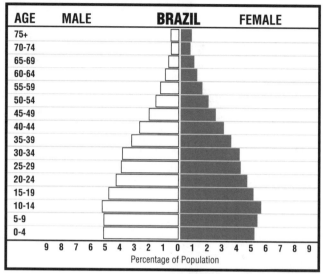

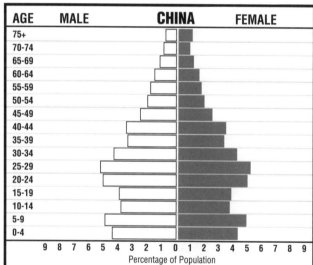

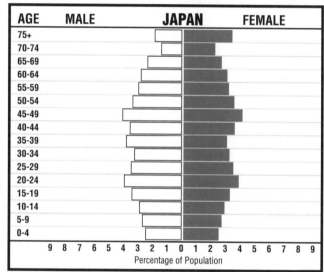

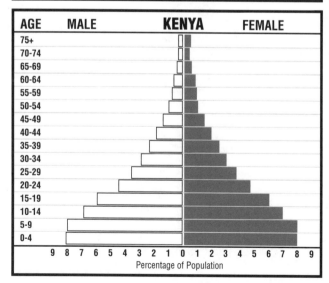

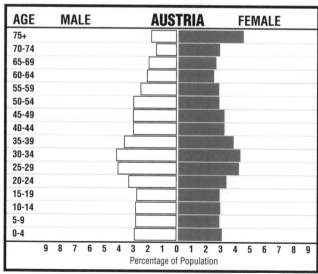

Power of the Pyramids

Population in Thousands (1995)

Age Group	United States M	United States %	United States F	United States %	Brazil M	Brazil %	Brazil F	Brazil %	China M	China %	China F	China %
0-4	10,015		10,009		8,643		8,256		55,642		51,073	
5-9	9,610		9,147		8,787		8,625		59,714		57,549	
10-14	9,445		8,982		8,874		8,800		47,233		43,974	
15-19	8,939		8,500		8,114		8,095		49,232		46,016	
20-24	9,366		8,906		7,354		7,387		62,779		58,952	
25-29	10,006		9,639		6,839		6,857		65,023		60,822	
30-34	10,990		10,848		6,652		6,690		54,417		50,205	
35-39	11,096		11,140		5,638		5,716		43,295		39,874	
40-44	10,031		10,137		4,723		4,826		44,159		41,285	
45-49	8,717		8,934		3,754		3,847		32,604		29,614	
50-54	6,739		7,026		2,911		3,005		25,235		22,416	
55-59	5,361		5,761		2,437		2,560		22,969		20,490	
60-64	4,771		5,369		1,923		2,070		20,212		18,662	
65-69	4,509		5,439		1,529		1,694		15,533		14,943	
70-74	3,876		5,173		1,060		1,224		10,807		11,324	
75+	5,043		9,097		1,083		1,373		10,272		13,007	
Total	129,012		134,107		80,319		81,055		619,126		580,206	
Total	263,119				161,374				1,199,332			

Source: The World Bank, World Population Projections 1994-95 Edition. (Baltimore: The Johns Hopkins University Press, 1994).

Power of the Pyramids

Population in Thousands (1995)

Age Group	Japan M	Japan F	Japan %	Kenya M	Kenya F	Kenya %	Austria M	Austria F	Austria %
0-4	3,224	3,074		2,249	2,214		249	236	
5-9	3,491	3,330		2,232	2,219		237	224	
10-14	3,809	3,622		1,928	1,919		242	232	
15-19	4,359	4,141		1,655	1,656		233	221	
20-24	5,116	4,868		1,290	1,296		279	267	
25-29	4,558	4,351		1,016	1,024		346	332	
30-34	4,123	4,006		820	828		354	346	
35-39	4,904	3,843		654	665		306	305	
40-44	4,494	4,450		517	531		259	258	
45-49	5,286	5,264		380	396		254	252	
50-54	4,401	4,490		265	282		253	227	
55-59	3,877	4,024		233	255		215	222	
60-64	3,608	3,839		205	225		178	195	
65-69	2,985	3,365		152	169		166	209	
70-74	1,920	2,722		105	117		127	226	
75+	2,433	4,236		112	146		151	352	
Total	61,587	62,626		13,811	13,940		3,849	4,133	
Total	125,213			27,751			7,981		

Source: The World Bank, World Population Projections 1994-95 Edition. (Baltimore: The Johns Hopkins University Press, 1994).

16 Earth Matters

Power of the Pyramids

Population in Thousands (1995)

Age Group	United States M	%	F	%	Brazil M	%	F	%	China M	%	F	%
0-4	10,015	3.8	10,009	3.8	8,643	5.4	8,256	5.1	55,642	4.6	51,073	4.3
5-9	9,610	3.7	9,147	3.5	8,787	5.4	8,625	5.3	59,714	5.0	57,549	4.8
10-14	9,445	3.6	8,982	3.4	8,874	5.5	8,800	5.5	47,233	4.0	43,974	3.7
15-19	8,939	3.4	8,500	3.2	8,114	5.0	8,095	5.0	49,232	4.1	46,016	3.8
20-24	9,366	3.6	8,906	3.4	7,354	4.6	7,387	4.6	62,779	5.2	58,952	4.9
25-29	10,006	3.8	9,639	3.7	6,839	4.2	6,857	4.2	65,023	5.4	60,822	5.1
30-34	10,990	4.2	10,848	4.1	6,652	4.1	6,690	4.1	54,417	4.5	50,205	4.2
35-39	11,096	4.2	11,140	4.2	5,638	3.5	5,716	3.5	43,295	3.6	39,874	3.3
40-44	10,031	3.8	10,137	3.9	4,723	2.9	4,826	3.0	44,159	3.7	41,285	3.4
45-49	8,717	3.3	8,934	3.4	3,754	2.3	3,847	2.4	32,604	2.7	29,614	2.5
50-54	6,739	2.6	7,026	2.7	2,911	1.8	3,005	1.9	25,235	2.1	22,416	1.9
55-59	5,361	2.0	5,761	2.2	2,437	1.5	2,560	1.6	22,969	1.9	20,490	1.7
60-64	4,771	1.8	5,369	2.0	1,923	1.2	2,070	1.3	20,212	1.7	18,662	1.6
65-69	4,509	1.7	5,439	2.1	1,529	0.9	1,694	1.1	15,533	1.3	14,943	1.2
70-74	3,876	1.5	5,173	2.0	1,060	0.7	1,224	0.8	10,807	1.0	11,324	0.9
75+	5,043	1.9	9,097	3.5	1,083	0.7	1,373	0.9	10,272	0.9	13,007	1.1
Total	129,012	49	134,107	51	80,319	50	81,055	50	619,126	52	580,206	48
Total	263,119				161,374				1,199,332			

Source: The World Bank, World Population Projections 1994-95 Edition. (Baltimore: The Johns Hopkins University Press, 1994).

Power of the Pyramids

Population in Thousands (1995)

Age Group	Japan M	%	F	%	Kenya M	%	F	%	Austria M	%	F	%
0-4	3,224	2.6	3,074	2.5	2,249	8.1	2,214	8.0	249	3.1	236	3.0
5-9	3,491	2.8	3,330	2.7	2,232	8.0	2,219	8.0	237	3.0	224	2.8
10-14	3,809	3.0	3,622	2.9	1,928	6.9	1,919	6.9	242	3.0	232	2.9
15-19	4,359	3.5	4,141	3.3	1,655	6.0	1,656	6.0	233	2.9	221	2.8
20-24	5,116	4.1	4,868	3.9	1,290	4.6	1,296	4.7	279	3.5	267	3.3
25-29	4,558	3.6	4,351	3.5	1,016	3.7	1,024	3.7	346	4.3	332	4.2
30-34	4,123	3.3	4,006	3.2	820	3.0	828	3.0	354	4.4	346	4.3
35-39	4,904	3.9	3,843	3.1	654	2.4	665	2.4	306	3.8	305	3.8
40-44	4,494	3.6	4,450	3.6	517	1.9	531	1.9	259	3.2	258	3.2
45-49	5,286	4.2	5,264	4.2	380	1.4	396	1.4	254	3.2	252	3.2
50-54	4,401	3.5	4,490	3.6	265	1.0	282	1.0	253	3.2	227	2.8
55-59	3,877	3.1	4,024	3.2	233	0.8	255	0.9	215	2.7	222	2.8
60-64	3,608	2.9	3,839	3.1	205	0.7	225	0.8	178	2.2	195	2.4
65-69	2,985	2.4	3,365	2.7	152	0.5	169	0.6	166	2.1	209	2.6
70-74	1,920	1.5	2,722	2.2	105	0.4	117	0.4	127	1.6	226	2.8
75+	2,433	1.9	4,236	3.4	112	0.4	146	0.5	151	1.9	352	4.4
Total	61,587	49*	62,626	50*	13,811	50	13,940	50	3,849	48	4,133	52
Total	125,213				27,751				7,981			

Source: The World Bank, World Population Projections 1994-95 Edition. (Baltimore: The Johns Hopkins University Press, 1994). *Due to rounding, Japan's male and female percentages do not add up to 100%.

Demographic Facts of Life

Introduction:

Birth and death rates determine the rate of population growth. If the birth and death rates are similar, a population experiences little or no growth. When the birth rate far exceeds the death rate, the population soars. These rates are expressed as the number of births or deaths for every 1,000 people in a given year. For instance, in 1998 the world's birth rate was 23 per 1,000 and the death rate was 9 per 1,000. Using the formulas below, we can determine the world's annual growth rate and the number of years it will take the population to double if the growth rate remains constant.

$$\% \text{ annual natural increase} = \frac{\text{birth rate - death rate}}{10}$$

$$\frac{23 - 9}{10} = 1.4 \%$$

$$\text{doubling time (in years)} = \frac{70}{\text{rate of increase}}$$

$$\frac{70}{1.5} = 49 \text{ years}$$

(Note: 70 is the approximate equivalent of 100 times the natural log of 2.)

Procedure:

Part 1: On the Double

Distribute copies of the *Student Worksheet 1* and have students complete the table.

Answers to table on Student Worksheet 1		
Country	**Percent annual natural increase**	**Doubling time (years)**
Brazil	1.4	50
Canada	0.5	140
China	1.0	70
India	1.8	39
Italy	0.0	No doubling
Japan	0.3	233
Mexico	2.2	32
Nigeria	3.0	23
Russia	-0.5	No doubling
U.S.	0.6	116
U.K.	0.2	350

Discussion:

1. Why do you think some countries are doubling much more rapidly than others? Why do you think some countries, such as Italy, have reached **zero population growth** (z.p.g.)?

   The doubling time is shorter in countries where the rate of growth is higher. The greater the difference between the birth rate and the death rate, the faster the population growth. Many European counties, such as Italy, have reached zero population growth because their birth and death rates are about the same.

2. Which figures differ most greatly between countries, the birth rates or the death rates? How would you explain the wide disparity in birth rates among different countries? Why are the death rates relatively low in many of the countries with high birth rates?

   The birth rates differ greatly due to differences in average family size. Death rates are relatively low in many of the countries with high birth rates because the majority of the population is young. In Kenya, for instance, 46 percent of the population is under age 15, and only three percent is age 65 or older.

3. If you were a national leader in Kenya or Iraq, would you be concerned about the rapid population growth? Why or why not? Similarly, if you were a national leader in Italy, would you be concerned that your country has reached z.p.g.? Why or why not?

   Yes. As a national leader of Kenya, you would be responsible for seeing that there are sufficient services for the expanding population such as homes, roads, jobs, health care, etc. You would find it difficult for your country to prosper in the world market, if it cannot meet the needs of its own people. As a national leader of Italy, you would not be faced with these problems and could plan for your nation's future progress.

4. The population of the United States is actually growing at the rate of about one percent each year, more than its rate of natural increase. Where is the additional population growth coming from?

Concept:

The discrepancy between a population's birth and death rates determines rate of growth. Our rapid growth rate means that even the deaths from large-scale disasters have little effect on our population size.

Objectives:

Students will be able to:
- Describe how birth and death rates affect population growth.
- Calculate rates of population growth given birth and death rates.
- Calculate doubling time at the given rate of increase.
- Draw connections between population growth and social/political and economic conditions.
- Calculate population increase per unit of time, given rate of increase.

Subjects:

Math, biology, environmental science, social studies

Skills:

Collecting, analyzing and interpreting data, math calculations

Method:

Students calculate the rate of natural increase and corresponding doubling times for several countries and discuss differences. Students also calculate the time it has taken for the world to replace the number of people lost in historic disasters.

Materials:

Copies of Student Worksheet
Calculator

Demographic Facts of Life

Immigration accounts for roughly 30 percent of population growth in the United States. In recent years, the greatest number of new Americans have come from the following countries: Mexico, Philippines, Vietnam, India, Dominican Republic, and China (mainland).

Part 2: Grim Reaper's Revenge

We are currently adding 84 million people (net growth) to the world each year, or 229,000 people each day. Conveying the importance of such figures to students can be difficult since the numbers are so large they lose their meaning. The table in *Student Worksheet 2* makes these numbers more concrete by illustrating that the numbers of people lost in history's major disasters are currently being replaced in a matter of days or weeks.

Have students complete the table in *Student Worksheet 2*.

Answers to table on Student Worksheet 2

Disaster	Replacement time
All U.S. accident deaths, 1995	9.8 hours
Bangladeshi Cyclone, 1991	14.7 hours
Total American deaths in all wars	2.6 days
Great flood, Hwang Ho River, 1887	3.9 days
Total U.S. automobile deaths through 1995	1.8 weeks
Indian famine, 1769-70	1.9 weeks
Total AIDS dead through 1996	4.0 weeks
Chinese famine, 1877-78	5.9 weeks
Influenza epidemic, 1918	3 months
Global deaths in all wars, past 500 years	5 months
Bubonic plague, 1347-51	10.8 months

Demographic Facts of Life

On the Double

Using the table below, determine the percentage of annual increase and the population doubling times for the following countries.

$$\% \text{ annual natural increase} = \frac{\text{birth rate - death rate}}{10}$$

$$\text{doubling time (in years)} = \frac{70}{\text{rate of increase}}$$

Country	Birth Rate in 1998 (per 1,000 people)	Death Rate in 1998 (per 1,000 people)	% Annual Natural Increase	Doubling Time (Years)
China	17	7		
India	29	10		
Iraq	38	10		
Italy	9	9		
Japan	10	7		
Kenya	38	12		
Mexico	27	5		
Russia	9	14		
South Africa	27	12		
United Kingdom	13	11		
United States	15	9		

Birth and death rates obtained from the 1998 World Population Data Sheet: Demographic Data and Estimates for the Countries and Regions of the World (1998, Population Reference Bureau, Washington, DC).

Demographic Facts of Life

Grim Reaper's Revenge

We are currently adding 84 million people (net growth) to the world's population each year. This means we are adding 229,000 people each day. Even the deaths from large-scale disasters have little effect on a population growing so rapidly. Below is a listing of some of the world's worst disasters, along with an approximate death toll. At today's present rate of growth, determine how many days, weeks or months it would take to replace those lost. Round off to one decimal place.

Some past disasters	Approximate # of deaths	Present world population growth replaces this # in approximately what time span?
All U.S. accident deaths, 1995	93,300	
Bangladeshi cyclone, 1991	140,000	
Total American deaths in all wars	600,000	
Great flood, Hwang Ho River, 1887	900,000	
Total U.S. automobile deaths through 1995	2,600,000	
India famine, 1769-70	3,000,000	
Total AIDS dead through 1996	6,400,000	
China famine, 1877-78	9,500,000	
Influenza epidemic, 1918	21,000,000	
Global deaths in all wars in the past 500 years	35,000,000	
Bubonic plague, 1347-51	75,000,000	

Casualty figures obtained from the 1998 World Almanac and Book of Facts (Mahwah, NJ: K-III Reference Corp., 1997), 1998 Information Please Almanac (New York: Houghton Mifflin Company, 1997).

Population Scavenger Hunt

Introduction:

This scavenger hunt encourages students to further investigate many of the concepts introduced in this curriculum. We recommend that you give students time to gather a variety of items from the list, anywhere from a week to a month. Ideally this would be a good activity to have running during the duration of a unit on population.

Procedure:

Students can work individually or in groups to collect as many items as possible on this list. Since some items involve more work than others, points are assigned to designate degree of difficulty.

1. Collect 3 newspaper clippings about an environmental or social problem that relates to overpopulation. Write a summary of each article, explaining the link to population growth. *8 points (1 extra point for each additional article, up to 5)*.

2. Make a poster showing the many effects (environmental, economic, social, etc.) of more people. *5 points*.

3. Watch a news show or special program discussing population, the environment, hunger, or poverty. Write a brief summary of the show, stating at least 5 new facts you learned about the issue. *5 points*.

4. Write an article about population growth and its effects and submit it to the school or community paper. (Or write a letter to your Congressional representatives, telling them how you feel about the issue). *10 points*.

5. Write a public service announcement about the environmental health risks of ozone layer depletion. *4 points. (5 extra points for performing it in front of the class or 10 extra for making a video of the announcement)*.

6. Make a map of North America depicting areas where the effects of acid rain have been chronicled. *4 points*.

7. Graph world temperatures as far back as you can. Write a paragraph explaining the phenomenon of global warming and whether the trend appears on your graph. *5 points*.

8. Contact the Environmental Protection Agency, or the equivalent state, provincial or local agency, about whether your city meets the national standards set for air pollution. Report your findings in writing. *5 points*.

9. Using pH paper, test a local lake, stream and drinking water for acidity levels. Turn in the pH paper and an explanation of its meaning. *10 points*.

10. Research the amount of arable land in the world. Using a map, designate the areas with fertile land. *5 points*.

11. Organize a canned food drive to help feed the hungry in your area. Record the number of cans collected and the group which received the food. *20 points*.

12. Chart your personal diet for a week. Put a star next to all of the items which came from the top of the food chain. Circle all of those you could have substituted with something lower on the food chain and write the substitution. *10 points*.

13. Make a collage or mobile using pictures or photographs of the rainforests. *6 points*.

14. Make snack food using mostly rainforest products (include your recipe). *5 points*.

15. Plant a tree in your community. *10 points (10 extra points for organizing an event where a group goes to plant trees on a certain day)*.

16. Find out rates of deforestation and reforestation in the United States. Chart or graph these rates and superimpose a population growth chart for the United States. *10 points*.

17. Monitor your household waste generation for a week. Chart your findings, including a list of the items most frequently found in your garbage can. Put a star next to those that could be recycled or composted. *10 points*.

18. Research home composting, and then start a compost pile at home. Take photographs of the system and include a written description of the progress of the compost. *20 points*.

Concept:
Population pressures affect nearly every environmental and social concern facing humankind.

Objectives:
Varies according to each of 35 tasks

Subjects:
All

Skills:
Research, creative and persuasive writing, drawing/painting, organizing

Method:
Students complete a wide variety of activities which illustrate the many areas involved with population, the environment and social issues.

Materials:
Varies according to each of 35 tasks

Population Scavenger Hunt

19. Make a poster showing various recyclable items and then the new materials they become after recycling. *6 points*.

20. Create a list of ways to reuse the following items: a shoe box, an unmatched sock, a coffee can and/or lid, a toilet paper tube, a milk carton. *1 point for every 3 ideas*.

21. Write an investigative report about the Chinook salmon (or another threatened species), explaining how human habits have contributed to the species' decrease in numbers. *10 points*.

22. Visit the zoo nearest you and record which animals are considered endangered. If possible, record how many are estimated to be in existence in the wild and in captivity. *10 points (1 extra point for each drawing or written description of the animals)*.

23. Develop a campaign to save an endangered species of your choice. Design posters, buttons, bumper stickers, etc. *5 points*.

24. Design a house dependent only on alternative energy (no fossil fuels). *8 points*.

25. Make a graph showing the per capita energy use of six different countries (3 industrialized countries and 3 less developed countries). *5 points*.

26. Do an energy audit on your home. A local power company may be of assistance. Check the meter and bills to determine how much energy your family uses. *5 points*.

27. Get to school without depending on a motorized vehicle. *1 point for each day*.

28. Research the latest technology for non-fossil fuel powered cars. Make a chart showing the advantages and disadvantages of each. *8 points*.

29. Chart how your country spends money to help the poor in your country. *5 points (3 extra points for also charting local money spent)*.

30. Find out the number of homeless or unemployed in your community. Explain how you found this information. *5 points*.

31. Make a chart or diagram illustrating how poverty can affect the environment. *5 points*.

32. Interview a woman from a less developed country. Write a report based on her observations of the differences between the role of women in the U.S. or Canada and her home country. *10 points*.

33. Conduct a survey in your community to determine the average family size. Graph your results. *10 points*.

34. Conduct a survey among classmates to determine how many children, on average, they wish to have. Chart the results. *5 points*.

35. Make up your own activity related to population growth and its environmental and social effects. *Points will be determined by the teacher*.

Climate Change

A Warm Forecast for the Planet?

In recent years the fate of our planet's climate has been a source of heated debate. Ten of the hottest years since temperature record-keeping began in 1866 were in the late 1980s and 1990s. Over the past century, the average surface temperature of the Earth has increased 0.5 to 1.1 degrees Fahrenheit (0.3 to 0.6 degrees Centigrade), and the sea level has risen 10 to 25 cm.[1] Scientists, industry and policy makers have been arguing for years about whether human actions are responsible for these changes in the Earth's climate. In 1988, the World Meteorological Organization and the United Nations created an advisory group of 2,500 scientists from over 80 countries to conduct a non-biased analysis of all the available data. In 1995, this group, the Intergovernmental Panel on Climate Change (IPCC), released a report concluding that, in fact, the observed changes are "unlikely to be entirely natural in origin" and that there is "a discernible human influence on global climate."[2] The gases our industrial world has spewed for decades are changing our atmosphere, and scientists are warning that society must take immediate action to avert disastrous consequences.

The Greenhouse Effect

The Earth's atmosphere is a complicated system of gases and energy. It allows energy from the sun to pass through to the Earth and also allows energy from Earth to escape into space. By delicately balancing this exchange of energy, the atmosphere regulates our climate.

The burning of oil, coal and natural gas has increased the concentration of certain gases in our atmosphere.[3] These gases act like a blanket, trapping Earth's heat energy and preventing it from passing through to space. This imbalance in energy exchange, with the Earth's atmosphere taking in more energy than it releases, causes the Earth to get warmer. The process works much the way a greenhouse would, hence its name. Gases which function to keep heat energy from escaping the atmosphere are called **greenhouse gases**.

Turning Up the Heat

For tens of thousands of years, the levels of oxygen, nitrogen and other gases in the Earth's atmosphere remained essentially unchanged. By the beginning of the 19th century, the world's population had grown to one billion and the Industrial Revolution in North America and Europe was starting to clear the land and taint the air with factory smoke. A century later, the population had doubled to two billion and the age of petroleum was dawning. After the Second World War, energy use skyrocketed. Between 1946 and 1968, the use of motor fuel doubled, electricity consumption nearly tripled and the production of petroleum-based plastics increased ten-fold!

Oil, coal and natural gas power our automobiles, heat our homes, provide electricity for our appliances and allow us to enjoy a standard of living unprecedented in history. However, when burned (combusted), these carbon-based, fossil fuels combine with oxygen to form **carbon dioxide** (CO_2). CO_2 is the primary greenhouse gas, responsible for more than 60 percent of all the global warming due to greenhouse gases. As a result of increased industrialization and combustion of these fuels, more and more carbon has been emitted into the atmosphere, and the concentration of CO_2 in the atmosphere has increased by 30 percent since the mid-19th century. CO_2 levels are now at their highest point in 150,000 years.[4] The levels of carbon emissions have quadrupled since the 1950's, and in 1996, a new record of 6.25 billion tons of carbon were emitted.[5] Trees and other photosynthetic organisms can take in CO_2, but not more than about three or four billion

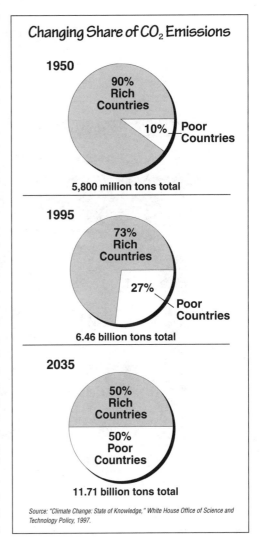

Changing Share of CO₂ Emissions

1950

90% Rich Countries

10% Poor Countries

5,800 million tons total

1995

73% Rich Countries

27% Poor Countries

6.46 billion tons total

2035

50% Rich Countries

50% Poor Countries

11.71 billion tons total

Source: "Climate Change: State of Knowledge," White House Office of Science and Technology Policy, 1997.

A Warm Forecast for the Planet?

tons worldwide. As deforestation continues, the Earth will be able to absorb less and less.

The United States emits more tons of carbon than any other country, both in raw numbers and per capita. In 1996, the United States and Canada, though just five percent of the world's population, were responsible for producing 26 percent of world's carbon emissions.[6]

However, as industrialization escalates in Asia, Africa and Latin America, carbon emissions in the developing world are increasing rapidly. China is now the world's second largest carbon emitter, at 14 percent of the global total. Even with their rapid increases, China's carbon emissions per capita are still less than one-seventh those of the United States. It is also important to point out that the vast majority of greenhouse gases already put into the atmosphere by human activities are a result of emissions from industrialized countries, and some of these gases can remain in the atmosphere for centuries.

Singer ©1993. Reprinted with permission of the artist.www.andysinger.com

Other Gases

Human activity is also directly related to the production of **methane** (CH_4), another greenhouse gas. Methane is released by natural gas leaks, coal mining, oil and gas drilling, the burning of wood and garbage and the decomposition of organic matter in rice paddies and in the intestines of cattle, sheep and termites. The atmospheric concentration of methane has increased 145 percent since pre-industrial days, and currently accounts for about 15 percent of all the global warming due to greenhouse gases.[7]

Worldwide production of methane is expected to increase as more cattle are raised and more rice is cultivated to feed increasing numbers of people. Although methane accounts for a smaller part of the greenhouse gas volume than does CO_2, it is more potent. Each methane molecule is 30 to 40 times more efficient at trapping heat than a CO_2 molecule. Further, methane remains in the atmosphere five to ten years, and levels are rising up to one percent annually.

Nitrous oxide (N_2O), also known as "laughing gas," is a byproduct of fossil fuel combustion, bacterial reactions in soil and the breakdown of widely used fertilizers. Its atmospheric concentration has increased 15 percent over pre-industrial levels, and it accounts for about five percent of the total warming due to greenhouse gases.

Chlorofluorocarbons (CFCs), unlike CO_2, methane and nitrous oxide, are completely human-made chemicals. They are used as refrigerator and air conditioner coolants, as chemical cleaners and in the manufacture of foam and in aerosol spray cans. Although CFCs cause only about ten percent of total atmospheric warming, ounce for ounce, they are the strongest insulators of the greenhouse gases. They are 10,000 to 20,000 times more effective at trapping heat than CO_2, and are likely to remain in the atmosphere 75 to 400 years.

Some of the warming effect of CFCs is slightly offset by the fact that they also deplete **ozone** in the upper atmosphere, which allows energy to leave the Earth more easily and has a net cooling effect. Depletion of the ozone layer carries its own set of severe consequences. The

A Warm Forecast for the Planet?

decrease in ozone lets in more of the sun's harmful ultraviolet light, which is known to cause skin cancer and eye disease, damage crops and destroy the phytoplankton that support the marine food chain.[8]

As a result of the Montreal Protocol in 1987, in which participating countries agreed to phase out the production of CFCs, CFC production has been falling consistently since its peak in 1988. Nonetheless, because it takes CFCs three to five years to reach the upper atmosphere, the ozone will continue to suffer their effects for years to come.

Humans are also responsible for increases in **tropospheric aerosols**, which are tiny particles suspended in the air. Aerosols cool the atmosphere but their effects tend to be short-lived and localized. While they may counteract the warming effect of greenhouse gases, aerosols can have other climate effects, such as altering rain patterns.[9]

All of the gases added to the atmosphere by energy use are responsible for over half of the increase in global temperatures. The trends point to increased energy consumption in the future, particularly in the developing world, where the population is expected to double in just 40 years. Daniel J. Evans, as Chairman of the National Academy of Sciences panel on global warming, stated in 1991 that population growth "is the biggest single driver of atmospheric pollution."

A Price for Progress

The IPCC's "best estimate" forecasts an increase in the average global temperature by the year 2100 of 3.6 degrees Fahrenheit (2 degrees Centigrade) accompanied by a rise in the average sea level of about 19.7 inches (50 cm). Does an increase of only a few degrees really make that big an impact? In the last 10,000 years, the Earth's average temperature has not changed either way by more than 1.8 degrees F (1 degree C).[10] So small differences in average temperature can make a huge difference in the Earth's climate. The following are some of the potential consequences of global warming.

• Sea levels may rise 15 to 95 cm, putting 92 million people at risk of flooding. Low-lying islands and countries such as Bangladesh would be at particularly high risk.

• Amount, frequency and intensity of rainfall may change. Floods and violent storms such as monsoons and hurricanes would become more likely.

• Droughts may occur more often and with greater severity, turning larger areas of cropland into desert.

• Tropical diseases and pests may spread, with devastating effects upon stressed crops and malnourished populations. For example, the percent of the population living in a zone of potential malaria transmission could increase from about 45 percent today to as much as 60 percent.

• Climate change will affect crop yields differently in different regions. Overall production could remain the same, with decreased productivity in the tropics, and increased productivity closer to the poles.

• A decrease in biodiversity and in the goods and services that ecosystems provide is likely as individual species respond to a changing climate.

• Deserts are expected to become hotter, but not significantly wetter, threatening more heat-sensitive species.

• Species composition of forests is likely to change. Some old forest types may disappear while others develop.

• As the climate warms, species are expected to shift upward in altitude. Species limited to mountain tops may become extinct due to disappearance of habitat.

• Geographical locations of wetlands are also expected to change in response to changes in climate and rainfall.

(All possible consequences come from the IPCC Second Assessment Report.*)*

Cool It!

A degree of uncertainty remains about the severity of global warming and the impact of human activity. However, many scientists and policymakers alike point out that if we wait until we are absolutely certain about climate change, it may be too late to take the most effective and simplest measures to combat it. The IPCC stresses: "Uncertainty does not mean

A Warm Forecast for the Planet?

that a nation or the world community cannot position itself better to cope with the broad range of possible climate changes or protect against potentially costly future outcomes."[11]

The primary precautionary measure to take against global warming is the reduction of greenhouse gas emissions. The IPCC estimates that in order to stabilize greenhouse gas concentrations at present day levels, CO_2 emissions need to be cut by 50 to 70 percent worldwide; methane emissions need to be reduced by eight percent and nitrous oxide emissions by 50 percent. At the Earth Summit in Rio de Janeiro in 1992, 166 nations signed the U.N. Framework Conference on Climate Change and agreed to reduce and stabilize emissions to 1990 levels by the year 2000; however, at the current rate, no countries, outside of a few in the European Union, are expected to meet this target.

Why are countries having a hard time cutting their greenhouse gas emissions? Because people are concerned that efforts to stabilize emissions, such as taxes placed on use of fossil fuels or changes in how factories work to make them more efficient and pollute less, can hurt economic growth. However, the IPCC Second Assessment Report and many economic studies argue that there are several ways to make emissions cuts both technically possible and economically feasible.

Altering our wasteful consumption patterns by using more energy-efficient technology in industry, recycling and using materials which produce fewer greenhouse gas emissions, driving more fuel-efficient cars, and using alternative fuels and renewable sources of energy, such as solar and wind, are essential to reducing the amount of greenhouse gas emissions. Reducing deforestation, while planting and cultivating new forests, would absorb CO_2 and preserve the biological richness of our planet. In addition, successful efforts to slow population growth would allow nations to cut CO_2 emissions more easily. Stabilizing global population is a crucial step to reducing greenhouse gas emissions, but it is not the only step. Many experts believe that a program with any chance of success must be aimed at both resource consumption and population stabilization.

In December of 1997, 160 nations met in Kyoto, Japan, to write the first-ever legally binding treaty on greenhouse gas emissions. The document produced from this conference, called the "Kyoto Protocol," requires that the industrialized nations reduce their greenhouse gas emissions by an average of 5.2 percent below 1990 levels between 2008 and 2012. The protocol, which sets legally binding limits on six greenhouse gases, is the first small step in the process of changing the fossil-fuel driven world economy to one which uses more sustainable sources of energy such as solar, wind and hydroelectric. Much work still lies ahead in to prevent potentially dangerous changes in the Earth's climate.

Endnotes

[1] *Summary for Policymakers: The Science of Climate Change*—IPCC Working Group I. The United Nations, 1995.

[2] *Climate Change 1995: The IPCC Second Assessment Report*. The United Nations, 1995.

[3] Seth Dunn. 1997. "Global Temperature Down Slightly." *Vital Signs 1997*. Washington, DC: Worldwatch Institute.

[4] Seth Dunn. 1997. "Carbon Emissions Set New Record." *Vital Signs 1997*. Washington, DC: Worldwatch Institute.

[5] Ibid.

[6] *Annual Energy Review 1996*. Washington, DC: Energy Information Agency, U.S. Department of Energy, 1997. Table 11.21. U.S.: 4.5 percent of the population, 23.5 percent of carbon emissions. Canada: 0.5 percent of the population, 2.2 percent of carbon emissions. For Canada data, see also: *Canada and Climate Change: Responding to Challenges and Opportunities*, A submission to Canada's Provincial and Federal Ministers of Energy and Environment. Joint project of the Canadian Global Change program and the Canadian Climate Program Board, November 1996.

[7] Op. cit. note 1.

[8] Anjali Acharya. "CFC Production Drop Continues." *Vital Signs 1996*. Washington, DC: Worldwatch Institute.

[9] Op. cit. note 1.

[10] Op. cit. note 2.

[11] *Summary for Policymakers: Scientific-Technical Analyses of Impacts, Adaptations and Mitigation of Climate Change*—IPCC Working Group II. United Nations, 1995.

An International Greenhouse

Introduction:

"Getting countries as diverse as industrial Ukraine and the tiny South Pacific island nation of Tuvalu to agree on any issue would be difficult. Getting them to agree to expensive, concrete solutions to a problem that is often difficult to see, hear, smell, or touch will be a mammoth undertaking... Each country (has) its own economic, environmental, and political conditions — differences that so far have made deciding what is fair for all the countries impossible."

~Washington Post, 1997

Scientists are growing ever more vocal about the risks posed by increases of carbon dioxide and other gases in our atmosphere, arguing that these gases are bringing about dangerous changes in our climate. Yet, just as there are difficulties in predicting long-range changes to our planet's climate, it can be equally challenging for diverse countries to work together to find solutions to the problem. This "mammoth undertaking" confronts the nations of the world as they seek to address climate change. In the following activity, students will learn not just about the climate change issue, but about the process that countries must go through to address complex global issues.

Procedure:

In order to focus the U.N. simulation on issues of climate change, the students will represent only those 58 nations which comprise the Governing Council of the United Nations Environment Programme (UNEP).

1. Duplicate the briefing paper, "The U.N. and Global Climate Change," for each student.

2. Assign each student a member nation to represent from the list provided at the end of this activity. Either combine two classes so that each of the 58 nations is represented or only use half the countries for one class. If you only use half the countries from the list, be sure to include a fair representation from each continent. You may wish to team-teach this activity with an instructor from a different discipline, since this activity lends itself to an interdisciplinary approach.

3. Allow students several days to research the nation they will represent. In preparing for the simulation, students should conduct background research on the history, culture, economy, demographics, geology and past international relations of their countries. Have students make full use of library resources, including the Internet, world almanacs, atlases, other books, periodicals, and newspaper clippings. Students should also be aware of specific consequences to their nations of continued climate change (see "Delegate Briefing Paper"). You should expect that some students will find more resources on their assigned countries than others.

4. If possible, you may wish to provide students with additional background reading on the issues to be addressed by the delegates. It may also be helpful to brief students on prior U.N. actions on climate change issues. This information is available from the U.N. directly, and is also chronicled in the *Model U.N. Survival Kit*.

5. Train students in the rules of procedure for the simulation. All U.N. bodies conduct business according to specific rules of procedure, even though they also function through informal channels. Model U.N. conferences usually adapt U.N. rules and procedures to fit time and other constraints. You may wish to adapt "Robert's Rules of Order" for use in the simulation. Some of the more common model U.N. rules of procedure are included in this activity. The less formal procedures of bloc politics and political interaction should also be incorporated into your simulation. A **bloc** is a group of persons or nations that form a political unit with a common interest or purpose.

6. Select or have the council select a chairperson to lead the meetings. The chairperson should be well-acquainted with the group's rules of procedure.

7. Arrange desks in a way that is most conducive for debate in your classroom or auditorium. Have each student prominently display his or her country placard.

8. The council's first meeting should open with general debate on the issue of global warming and what should or should not be done to combat climate change. This session will allow nations to articulate their broad poli-

Concept:

The Earth's atmosphere knows no national boundaries. Global cooperation is imperative if we hope to reverse present climate trends. In this activity, students conduct a model United Nations simulation in which they address the issue of global climate change.

Objectives:

Students will be able to:
• Describe the causes and effects of global climate change.
• Understand the process necessary for international cooperation to address climate change.
• Research a country and represent its interests in a model U.N. activity.

Subjects:

Social studies, language arts, environmental science, biology

Skills:

Public speaking, research, conflict resolution, negotiation, parliamentary procedure

Method:

As representatives of member nations in a model U.N. simulation, students will attempt to draft resolutions that take the next step in addressing global warming and ozone layer depletion, just as 159 countries did at the Kyoto Climate Change Convention in 1997.

Materials:

2 placards for each country on the Governing Council of the United Nations Environment Programme (UNEP)

Copies of "Delegate Briefing Paper"

An International Greenhouse

A model UN handbook is optional, but recommended.*

*The United Nations Association of the USA publishes the *Model U.N. Survival Kit*, available for $40.00. The kit includes "A Guide to Delegate Preparation," "ABCs of the U.N.," "A Global Agenda: Issues before the General Assembly," and information on how to prepare for a Model U.N. 485 Fifth Avenue, New York, NY 10017; 212-697-3232, or www.unusa.org.

The *Model United Nations Activities Sourcebook* is available through the United Nations Association in Canada. The sourcebook, which costs $10.00, includes background information on the U.N., rules of procedure, information on preparing for Model U.N. Activities, and list of resources. 130 Slater, Suite 900, Ottawa, ONT K1P 6E2, Canada, or www.unac.org.

cies and goals for the session. It provides a mechanism for the initial development of common goals between nations and interest groups.

9. After this initial meeting, delegates should break to draft proposals and resolutions. Students should seek out delegates with similar views and national interests on the issue of climate change. Caucusing and negotiation are fundamental to any model U.N. simulation. These intra- and inter-bloc meetings will ultimately produce the resolutions and proposals which will be formally considered by the council. Informal bloc meetings, which form in the hall or corner to draft a resolution, discuss potential compromises or mobilize the needed majority, are often the real work of the U.N. For help in drafting resolutions, you may wish to obtain "A Guide to Delegate Preparation" (included in the *Model U.N. Survival Kit* or available separately from the United Nations Association). You may want to restrict resolution writing to one class period.

10. In the next meeting of the council, delegates or groups of delegates will offer their proposals and a period of substantive debate on these proposals will ensue. You may wish to put a time limit on this debate. After the debate period, delegates should vote on the resolutions at hand. Resolutions or amendments can be adopted with a majority vote.

11. Share with students the outcome of the actual Kyoto Climate Change Convention (The United States, Canada, and 36 other industrialized countries agreed, by 2012, to reduce emissions 5.2% below where they were in 1990). Discuss how the actual resolutions compare to the ones the class approved? What challenges did countries encounter as they worked to reach agreements? What loose ends were left for the next meeting? What challenges does the agreement face as it moves toward being ratified by our government?

Follow-up Activity:

The international process for addressing climate change did not end with the Kyoto conference. In the words of U.N. Secretary General Kofi Annan, "Reform is not an event, but a process... Kyoto (built) on what came before, and set the stage for what comes next." There will be subsequent efforts in the years to come. As an alternative to having students simulate the Kyoto Climate Change Convention, students could model one of these future meetings.

An International Greenhouse

Member Nations of the Governing Council of the United Nations Environment Programme (As of 1997)

Africa

Algeria
Benin
Burkina Faso
Burundi
Central African Republic
Democratic Republic of Congo
Gabon
Gambia
Guinea-Bissau
Kenya
Mauritania
Morocco
Sudan
Tunisia
Zambia
Zimbabwe

Asia

China
Democratic People's Republic of Korea
India
Indonesia
Iran (Islamic Republic of)
Japan
Pakistan
Philippines
Republic of Korea
Russian Federation
Thailand
Syrian Arab Republic

Europe

Bulgaria
Czech Republic
France
Finland
Germany
Hungary
Italy
Netherlands
Poland
Slovak Republic
Spain
Sweden
Switzerland
Turkey
United Kingdom of Great Britain and N. Ireland

Latin America/Caribbean

Argentina
Brazil
Chile
Colombia
Costa Rica
Mexico
Nicaragua
Panama
Peru
Venezuela

North America

Canada
United States of America

Oceania

Australia
Marshall Islands
Samoa

Common Rules of Procedure

Procedural Motions: Actions of the body that determine how a topic is discussed and how resolutions are decided by the body. Common procedural motions include the following:

1. To adjourn the meeting/session.
2. Point of order, information and/or personal privilege.
3. To close debate on an item, resolution or amendment.
4. To reconsider an item, resolution or amendment.

Substantive motions: Actions of the body in the form of resolutions, amendments or decisions. Common substantive motions include the following:

1. To consider a resolution.
2. To consider an amendment.
3. Interventions made by delegates on 1 and 2 (e.g., speeches, statements, etc.).

Rules about voting include the following:

1. The order in which recorded votes are taken.
2. The number of votes required for adoption of resolutions or amendments [this could be a simple majority (50 percent plus 1 of the members present and voting) or two-thirds majority].
3. Division of the question (taking each section of a resolution or amendment and voting separately on each).
4. A non-recorded vote or a hand vote.

An International Greenhouse

The Executive Secretary of the United Nations wishes to notify Your Excellency's Government of the forthcoming session of the Conference of Parties to the Convention on Climate Change. The session will include a high level segment attended by Ministers and other Heads of Delegation.

The U.N. and Global Climate Change

The United Nations has committed itself to work toward international solutions to critical environmental problems, because issues of the global environment affect every nation in the world. Climate change is one such problem: No one nation is solely responsible for global warming and ozone depletion, and no one nation can stop the momentum of the changes. If the present atmospheric changes are to be reversed in order to avoid catastrophic consequences, all nations must work on cooperative solutions.

The international community has become increasingly concerned about global climate change. In 1988, the United Nations Environment Programme (UNEP) and the World Meteorological Organization established the Intergovernmental Panel on Climate Change (IPCC) to study the science and impacts of climate change, and to recommend possible policy responses. Nearly 2,000 of the world's top climate scientists participated in the assessments in the IPCC.

In its first assessment, the IPCC concluded that global warming was likely to happen: "The greenhouse gases already emitted as a result of human activities have committed the world to an unprecedentedly rapid warming. Earth is now 0.5 degrees warmer than in pre-industrial times, and by the end of the next century, we can expect it to be at least three degrees warmer. If we do not act soon to reduce emissions, the best we can expect is that within a century, the world will be warmer than at any time since the start of agricultural civilization six thousand years ago." [IPCC, 1990]

The IPCC's report cited numerous climatic and health effects of continued warming, including rising sea level resulting in flooding of delta areas, changing rainfall patterns and increased health risks. Based on these findings, the IPCC recommended immediate and drastic reductions in carbon dioxide emissions (60-80 percent), a reduction in methane emissions (15-20 percent), as well as early implementation of the phase-out of chlorofluorocarbons and more research into ways of reducing nitrous oxide.

The international community first pledged action in 1992, at the Earth Summit in Rio de Janeiro. Although mandatory cuts in greenhouse gases were rejected, countries agreed to voluntarily stabilize their production of these pollutants, so that by the year 2000, each country would only be producing as much as it did in 1990.

The IPCC issued its second assessment in 1995, this time finding evidence that global warming, no longer a theory, was already beginning to happen. By this time, it had also become clear that most countries will not meet the goals agreed to in Rio. Voluntary goals would not be sufficient to address the problem, and it appeared that mandatory cuts in the emission of greenhouse gases would be necessary.

Competing Interests

Actions to combat global warming are complex, difficult and expensive. Even if nations agree that global warming must be reversed, leaders may find it difficult to agree on a plan of action which is equally beneficial to all countries.

We live in a demographically divided world of industrialized nations and less developed nations. These differences in standards of living shape perspectives on appropriate actions to stem climate change.

Developed and developing nations often conflict over the economic ramifications of protecting the environment. One camp says that poverty causes environmental destruction because people are forced to choose between long-term stewardship or short-term survival. This camp argues that a crash program to bring Western-style development to poor nations is the best approach.

The other camp says Western-style development is the problem: Today the United States, comprising five percent of the world's population, produces 23.5% percent of all human-made atmospheric carbon dioxide (U.S. Dept of Energy, 1997), and uses more energy

An International Greenhouse

relative to its economic size than any western country except Canada. Any world policy to tackle global warming will mean a radical reduction and restructuring of North American energy consumption, and will require hard political and economic decisions.

This is not to say that the problem is just a North American one. Although people in the developing world emit only 23 percent of all greenhouse gases, their emissions are now increasing faster than those of the industrialized countries, as they pursue greater economic expansion and install the same polluting technologies that made industrialized nations rich. If present rates continue, greenhouse gas emissions of developing nations will catch up to those of industrialized nations by the year 2035 (White House Office of Science and Technology Policy, 1997), fueled by population growth rates of over 80 million people a year (Population Reference Bureau, 1998). Even if the industrialized world were to completely stop all emissions of greenhouse gases, global warming would continue to accelerate" (UNEP, 1991).

Clearly, much negotiation is required to arrive at solutions to global warming which meet the basic needs of all nations. As Benjamin Franklin said, "We will hang together or assuredly we will hang separately."

Global Warming: Who Stands to Lose the Most?

Every corner of the world will feel the effect of global warming, but less developed countries will be hardest hit by the negative consequences since they do not possess the financial and technical resources to adapt to the climate changes that could result in rising sea levels, increasing incidence of drought and floods and greater frequency of savage storms.

Scientists are already speculating as to which nations will stand to lose the most by climate change. In Southern Europe, the United States, Central America, parts of South

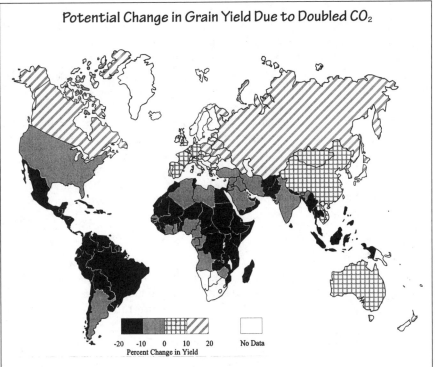

Potential Change in Grain Yield Due to Doubled CO_2

Percent Change in Yield: -20 -10 0 10 20   No Data

*Source: Based on GISS model; physiological CO_2 effects included Rosenzweig, Cynthia and Daniel Hillel, 1993. "Agriculture in a Greenhouse World: Potential Consequences of Climate Change," National Geographic Research and Exploration 9 (2); 208-221.

America, Africa and Southeast Asia, crop yields may drop dramatically. In the humid tropics, where much of the world's rice harvest is produced, it is thought that the Southeast Asian monsoon may intensify, bringing more rain in the summer and possibly less in the winter. Shortfalls in food production in these areas could be offset by production increases in higher latitudes, particularly in the Northern Hemisphere. This may produce more favorable agricultural conditions in Canada, the former Soviet Union, and Scandinavia.

Due to the expected rise in sea level, unprotected delta areas will be flooded. Millions of Bengalis will lose their homes, while nations such as Egypt, China, Indonesia, and India could lose important tracts of productive land to flooding. With the world's oceans calculated to rise anywhere from 15 to 90 cm by the end of the next century (IPCC, 1995), some 300 Pacific atolls could disappear and the existence of several island nations in the Pacific, Indian Ocean, and the Caribbean could be threatened.

Methane Matters

Concept:
Production of methane, a greenhouse gas, can be linked directly to human activity.

Objectives:
Students will be able to:
• Graph increase in atmospheric methane over time.
• Address the ways in which human activity affects atmospheric methane concentrations.
• Draw conclusions about future conditions based on current trends.

Subjects:
Biology, chemistry, environmental science, math

Skills:
Data analysis, diagramming, graphing

Method:
Students will study possible relationships between several human activities and methane production.

Materials:
Copies of Student Worksheet
Graph paper

Introduction:

The amount of methane (often called natural gas) in the air has increased 145 percent since pre-industrial times. Its high rate of increase is a concern, because methane absorbs heat, and so bears significant responsibility for global warming. There is no clear consensus about why the concentration of methane is rising so rapidly. Much of it comes from the breakdown of plant material in the absence of oxygen, as happens in swamps and inside cattle. Methane is also produced through certain human activities which have increased as our population has grown.

Procedure:

Distribute copies of the student worksheets and allow students about 30 minutes to work through the questions and graphing exercises, either individually or in groups. Go over answers in remaining class time.

Suggested answers to Student Worksheet:

1. Increased:

Wetlands — crops like rice paddies and cranberries

Cattle — due to meat eaters

Forest and grass burning — for land to grow food and graze cattle

Mining and natural gas — demand for goods mined and need for fuel (natural gas)

Landfills — increasing amount of waste

Termites — termite population increases from deforestation

Lakes — more dams for electricity

Decreased:

Wetlands— from humans draining them for other uses

2. *All the causes have not been pinpointed but the increases coincide with such important historical events as the colonization and clearing of the Americas, the Industrial Revolution, and a six-fold increase in human population.*

3. *Increased human population → need for agricultural land area → deforestation → broken wood, dead roots → increased termite population → wood digesting microorganisims → methane as a digestive waste → increased atmospheric methane.*

4. *Much work has been done recently to reduce leakage from the natural gas pipelines of Russia.*

5. *The melting of the frozen water will release the methane into the atmosphere.*

6. *The only solution is to decrease the amount of cattle raised in the U.S. Obviously, this would require individuals changing their habits and eating less meat.*

7. a) *Both are increasing.*

   b) *Human population growth causes increased methane production.*

   c) *Very large amounts of people and methane are present.*

   d) *Stabilizing population growth and reducing activities which cause methane production (see answers to #1 on the Student Worksheet for examples).*

Follow-up Activities:

In addition to methane (CH_4), other greenhouse gases include: carbon dioxide (CO_2), chlorofluorocarbons (CFCs), tropospheric ozone (O_3) and nitrous oxides (N_2O).

Explain the links, if any, between human population growth and the increase in levels of each of these greenhouse gases. *Many answers are possible.*

Adapted with permission from the Climate Protection Institute. The original, "Human Activity and Methane Production," appears in Global Warming Activities for High School Science Classes by Dorothy Rosenthal and Richard Golden, Climate Protection Institute, Oakland, CA, 1991.

Gas	Source
carbon dioxide (CO_2)	power plants, all fossil fuel burning, deforestation
chlorofluorocarbons (CFCs)	refrigerant, insulation, foams, aerosol propellant, industrial chemicals
tropospheric ozone (O_3)	natural part of atmosphere but concentration increasing due to increases in carbon monoxide
nitrous oxides (N_2O)	ammonia- and urea-based fertilizers, natural microbial soil activity, spread of agriculture, burning of timber, crop residues and fossil fuels

Methane Matters

Introduction:

Methane (CH_4), our most abundant hydrocarbon, often called natural gas, is a very efficient absorber of infrared radiation. Although its present atmospheric concentration is only 1.72 parts per million, its high rate of increase is a cause of concern. If methane emissions remain constant, the concentration of the gas in the atmosphere will increase to 1.82 parts per million over the next forty years.

Ice bubble analysis has shown that methane concentration held steady for the last 10,000 years. About 300 years ago the level began to rise and 100 years ago it began to soar. The concentration of methane gas in the atmosphere has increased 145 percent since pre-industrial times, dwarfing the 30 percent increase in the concentration of CO_2. CO_2 is the only greenhouse gas responsible for a larger share of global warming than methane.

There is no clear consensus among scientists about why the concentration of methane is rising so rapidly. Much of it comes from the breakdown of plant material in the absence of oxygen, as in swamps and inside cattle. However, much methane is also produced through certain human activities which have increased as the human population has grown.

Methane Facts and Questions:

1. Below is a list of sources of methane in order of volume produced — highest to lowest.

- wetlands, swamps
- cattle
- tropical rainforest and grass savanna burning
- natural gas and mining
- man-made dumps, landfills
- termites and other insects
- oceans
- lakes
- tundra

Which of the above have increased because of human activities and/or human population growth?
Have any decreased with human activity? Explain your selections.

2. Ice bubble analysis has shown that methane concentration has held steady for the last 10,000 years.
About 300 years ago the amount of methane in the atmosphere began to rise and 100 years ago it began to soar.
What do you think might have been the historical causes for these increases?

Methane Matters

3. Microorganisms capable of digesting wood live in the gut of termites. One of their waste products is methane. As deforestation has continued around the world, the supply of rotting wood has increased. This abundant food source has expanded the termite population. A significant part of the increase in atmospheric methane is thought to be due to this source.

   Re-order the following statements and then use a flow chart diagram to show how they are related.

   Increased atmospheric methane
   Increased termite population
   Increased human population
   Deforestation
   Need for agricultural land area
   Wood digesting microorganisms
   Broken wood, dead roots
   Methane as a digestive waste

4. Methane emissions in Russia decreased substantially in recent years, around the same time that the state petroleum industry began to be privatized.
   What do you think brought about this decrease in methane emissions?

5. The permafrosts of tundra regions and of polar ocean sediments contain vast quantities of methane trapped by frozen water molecules.
   What may happen if, partly due to the increase in atmospheric methane, the environment gets warmer and the frozen water melts?

6. Cattle, goats and sheep emit methane as they digest grass and other fibrous plants. Each head of American beef cattle belches out about a third of a pound of methane per pound of beef it yields. Add the carbon released from fuels burned in animal farming, and every pound of steak has the same greenhouse warming effect as a 25-mile drive in a typical American car.
   What, if anything, could be done individually or nationally to reduce cattle's contribution to climate change?

Methane Matters

7. On graph paper, construct a chart with the years 1500 - 2000 A.D. listed along the horizontal axis, "world population (in billions)" written along the right vertical axis and "methane concentration (ppm)" written along the left vertical axis. Using the data below, construct two line graphs on your chart: one showing world population growth through time and the other showing the increase in atmospheric methane.

Year	Methane (ppm)	World Population (in billions)
1500	0.64	0.43
1590	0.66	0.53
1670	0.65	0.58
1750	0.70	0.76
1790	0.78	0.91
1820	0.76	1.05
1850	0.80	1.21
1870	0.84	1.36
1879	0.86	1.44
1915	0.95	1.80
1950	1.15	2.52
1970	1.30	3.70
1979	1.54	4.37
1983	1.60	4.69
1984	1.63	4.77
1986	1.65	4.94
1988	1.68	5.11
1990	1.72	5.28
1993	1.73	5.51
1996	1.74	5.77

Sources: National Oceanic and Atmospheric Agency (NOAA), Climate Monitoring and Diagnostics Laboratory; Population Reference Bureau.

Questions:

a) Using the graph, how does the growth in human population compare with the increase in concentration of methane in the atmosphere?

b) How can you explain the relationship that the two graphs seem to show?

c) If present trends continue, what would you predict for the year 2050?

d) What might change present trends?

Air Pollution

Gasping for Clean Air

The sky's the limit for the billions of tons of pollutants people pump out of factories, homes and cars each year. These pollutants create problems such as urban smog, acid rain and toxic gases. Increased global industrialization and rapid population growth are combining to create more of these pollutants, threatening the very air we breathe. The health of humans and that of our ecosystem are suffering as a result of the largely preventable amounts of pollution with which we poison our air.

In many cities, it is actually hazardous to breathe. In 1996, around 47 million people in the United States and 1.5 billion people worldwide had to breathe air contaminated by dangerous levels of air pollution.[1] Breathing the air in Bombay, India, is equivalent to smoking ten cigarettes a day. And in Mexico City, the world's most polluted and populated city, infectious diseases like salmonella and hepatitis can be contracted simply by inhaling bacteria suspended in the air.

Smog Alert

The most common urban air-quality problem in the United States is **ozone**. High in the atmosphere, ozone forms a layer that filters out harmful ultraviolet radiation, thus protecting life on Earth. But ozone is also formed at the Earth's surface under certain conditions when sunlight reacts with high concentrations of nitrogen oxides and volatile organic compounds in the air. There are thousands of sources of these gases, the two most common are power plants that burn fossil fuels, and combustion of gasoline in the engines of cars, buses and trucks. Other sources include paint solvents, wood fires like those we have in our fireplaces, and coal-fired boilers; some emissions even come from trees.

Although concentrations of many air pollutants have fallen significantly in the United States in recent years (due to Clean Air Act regulations), elevated ozone levels continue to be a pervasive and damaging problem in many large and smaller cities and some rural areas as well. According to the U.S. Environmental Protection Agency (EPA), in 1996, around 47 million Americans lived in areas that exceeded EPA's ozone standard.[2] In Canada, the annual average ozone concentration increased 20 percent between 1981 and 1990.[3]

Adverse health effects of ozone pollution include shortness of breath, chest pain when inhaling deeply, wheezing and coughing. Long-term exposure may lead to permanent lung tissue damage.[4] A 1996 American Lung Association report estimated that in the 13 metropolitan areas studied, ozone was linked to 10,000 to 15,000 hospital admissions and an estimated 30,000 to 50,000 emergency room visits per year.[5]

Ozone can affect the health of trees, crops and other plants at concentrations even lower than those that harm humans. Ozone has been shown to reduce plant growth by interfering with the plant's ability to produce and store food, and it can make plants more susceptible to disease, insect attacks and harsh weather.[6] Forest declines in several parts of the country have been attributed to ozone and other pollutants. Ozone causes an estimated 1 to 2 billion dollars worth of loss to crop yields in the United States each year.[7]

The second most common vehicle-related pollutant, behind ozone, is **carbon monoxide** (CO). Motor vehicle exhaust is responsible for 60 percent of CO emissions nationwide, and in cities, vehicle exhaust can create as much as 95 percent of all CO emissions. CO concentrations in the air dropped 37 percent in the United States over the last ten years, and 45 percent in Canada between 1981 and 1990, largely due to the addition of car pollution control devices called **catalytic converters** which help remove CO from car exhaust.[8] However, in the United States in 1996, almost 13 million people lived in areas which failed to meet the EPA's health standard for CO emissions.[9]

Carbon monoxide is absorbed into the bloodstream more quickly than oxygen, creating numerous health risks. Exposure to even low levels of CO reduces the body's delivery of oxygen to its organs and tissues, producing impaired perception and thinking, slowed reflexes and drowsiness. Long-term exposure to CO is believed to aggravate arteriosclerosis and cardiovascular disease.

Gasping for Clean Air

Coal Toll

Other dangerous elements that pollute our air and threaten our well-being include **sulfur dioxide** (SO_2), **particulate matter** (suspended particles of soot, ash, dust and chemicals), **nitrogen dioxide** and **lead**. Emissions of these elements have been greatly reduced in industrialized countries with the aid of pollution control equipment and improvements in energy efficiency. In much of the world, however, these elements pose dire threats to human and environmental health. In Eastern Europe and the former Soviet Union, hasty industrialization after World War II, powered by high-sulfur, brown coal, has led to widespread environmental degradation and human illness. In India, SO_2 emissions from coal and oil have nearly tripled since the early 1960s.

The World Health Organization (WHO) estimates that around three million people die every year from exposure to particulate matter. The vast majority of deaths occur in developing countries where indoor air pollution results from burning **biomass fuel** (including firewood and cow dung) and coal for heating and cooking.[10] Particulate matter causes problems in the industrialized world as well. The National Resources Defense Council and the Harvard School of Public Health estimate that about 60,000 deaths occur every year in the United States from particulate pollution caused by fuel combustion and vehicle exhaust. That's more fatalities than are caused by car accidents and homicides combined.[11]

Acid Attack

Excessive levels of pollutants are just as damaging to the planet's health as they are to its inhabitants, especially in the form of **acid rain**. When sulfur and nitrogen oxides combine with oxygen and moisture in the atmosphere, they become sulfuric and nitric acids. These acidic pollutants fall to the ground, often hundreds of miles from their origins, as dry particles or in rain, snow, frost, fog and dew.

Acid rain damages wildlife through direct contact and by leaching or dissolving minerals in the soil. Acid rain leaches away nutrients and, at the same time, releases toxic elements such as aluminum into the soil where they can be harmful to plants and animals. In areas severely affected by acid rain, trees decline in growth and die prematurely, plants and

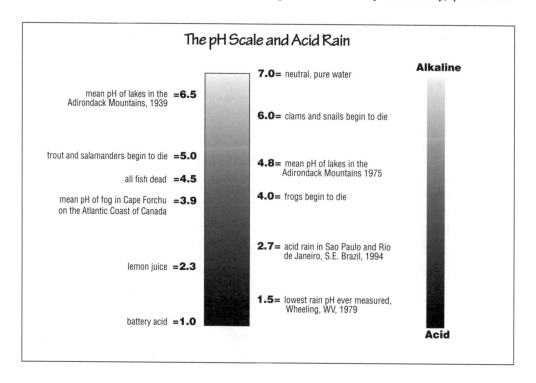

The pH Scale and Acid Rain

Alkaline

7.0= neutral, pure water

mean pH of lakes in the Adirondack Mountains, 1939 =**6.5**

6.0= clams and snails begin to die

trout and salamanders begin to die =**5.0**

4.8= mean pH of lakes in the Adirondack Mountains 1975

all fish dead =**4.5**

mean pH of fog in Cape Forchu on the Atlantic Coast of Canada =**3.9**

4.0= frogs begin to die

2.7= acid rain in Sao Paulo and Rio de Janeiro, S.E. Brazil, 1994

lemon juice =**2.3**

1.5= lowest rain pH ever measured, Wheeling, WV, 1979

battery acid =**1.0**

Acid

Gasping for Clean Air

microorganisms crucial to the wildlife food chain die, and lakes become too acidic to support fish and birds. Acid precipitation is believed to be responsible for dieback and deterioration of white birch trees in southeastern New Brunswick, Canada, and of red spruce in higher-elevation areas of the United States.[12]

In Canada, 150,000 lakes are severely affected by acid rain originating from metal smelting in eastern Canada, coal-burning utilities in Canada and the United States and vehicle emissions on both sides of the border.[13] In the Netherlands, acid rain has caused the decline of species of songbirds by depleting the soils of calcium, which is essential for the snails that the birds eat.[14]

Acid rain can also take its toll on the human body. Sulfuric and nitrogen oxide emissions have been linked to increased frequency of asthma, heart disease and lung disease, especially among children and the elderly. Even the water you drink may be tainted. Acid rain can cause a leaching of toxic substances both out of the soil and out of pipes that carry drinking water to millions of people.

Acid rain corrodes our bridges, buildings and monuments, and destroys priceless works of art. It is estimated that ancient monuments in Athens, Greece, have deteriorated more in the past 20 to 25 years from pollution than in the previous 2,400 years. Because the effects of acid rain are not necessarily felt in the same places where contributing chemicals are released, it has been difficult to enforce certain air quality policies. Clearly, individual states and countries cannot solve their problems alone.

Changing Fuel-ish Ways

The Clean Air Act of 1970 and the strengthening amendments of 1977 directed the EPA to establish air quality standards for six of the most common and widespread air pollutants. Under the Act, state governments were directed to develop and implement strategies to meet and maintain these air quality standards. Considerable progress was made in cutting urban air pollution, especially with the development of the catalytic converter and the shift to unleaded gas for motor vehicles. The EPA points out that because of the Clean Air Act, air quality in the United States is better today than it was in 1970 despite the fact that the total U.S. population has increased 29 percent, the vehicle miles traveled every year have increased 121 percent, and the size of the economy has doubled.[15] While it is frightening to think how bad the air quality could be without federal and state imposed restrictions on pollutants and emission rates, concentrations still remain quite high.

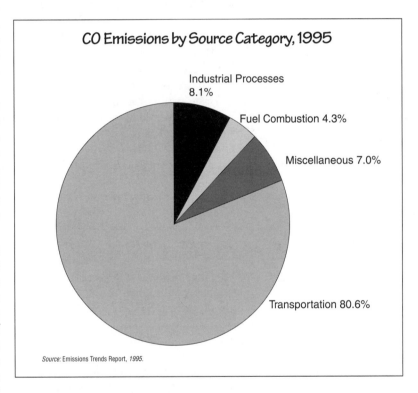

CO Emissions by Source Category, 1995

Industrial Processes 8.1%

Fuel Combustion 4.3%

Miscellaneous 7.0%

Transportation 80.6%

Source: Emissions Trends Report, *1995.*

In 1990, Congress amended the Clean Air Act. The new amendments call for enhanced car inspection and maintenance programs, tougher regulations on vehicle exhaust, and development of cleaner-burning fuels. Congress also established an "emissions trading" system which assigned allowances (one allowance = one ton of sulfur dioxide per year) to electric utilities and other industries that produce sulfur dioxide. The system lets each utility or factory decide what is the most cost-effective way to reduce its emissions; then it may sell the allowances it no longer needs after the reductions. In the year 2000, emissions will be limited to 895 million tons per year. Also that year, the EPA will begin to regulate less-polluting industries, so that a greater number of businesses will have to divide a set number of allowances. This cap on emissions plus more competition for allowances will provide an incentive for further reductions and ensure that the level of sulfur dioxide from industry sources will not increase. In addition, the amendments give the EPA greater power to enforce air quality standards and punish those who fail to comply. In 1997, the EPA re-evaluated and strengthened their national air quality standards for ozone and particulate matter.

Although these measures may allow us to breathe a little easier, the economy continues to grow, and the number of air-polluting cars on the road is expected to increase. Since 1960, the United States has added 87 million people to its population who, in turn, have almost tripled the number of vehicles on the road. Spurred by population growth, vehicle miles traveled in the United States are growing on average by more than 50 billion miles per year![16] As the population of our country continues to grow, and our urban areas sprawl out farther and farther, the number of cars on the road and the number of miles traveled will continue to grow. This growth is being accompanied by an increase in the demand for electric power from the growing population. These increases will continue to compromise the improvements in air quality made by technological advances which allow cars to burn fuel more efficiently and with less emissions and enable cleaner electric power generation.

Air pollution is undoubtedly a complex problem with no easy, inexpensive short-term solutions. Development of cleaner fuels, better emission-control technology, strengthened federal fuel economy standards for motor vehicles, and a more efficient mix of transportation alternatives, such as mass transit systems, could all play a significant role in achieving clean air in cities. If current population trends continue, however, it will become increasingly more difficult for Americans to clear the air.

Endnotes

[1] *National Air Quality and Emissions Trends Report, 1996.* U.S. Environmental Protection Agency, Office of Air Quality and Planning Standards, 1997. World Health Organization homepage: www.who.org.

[2] *National Air Quality and Emissions Trends Report, 1996.* U.S. Environmental Protection Agency, Office of Air Quality and Planning Standards, 1997.

[3] Tom Furmanczyk. *National Urban Air Quality Report, 1981-1990.* Pollution Data Branch, Response Assessment Directorate, Environmental Protection Service, Environment Canada.

[4] American Lung Association homepage: www.lungusa.org

[5] Ibid.

[6] Op. cit. note 2.

[7] *National Air Quality and Emissions Trends Report, 1995.* U.S. Environmental Protection Agency, Office of Air Quality and Planning Standards, 1996, p. 21.

[8] U.S. statistics: op. cit. note 2; Canada Statistics: Op. cit. note 3.

[9] Op. cit. note 2.

[10] World Health Organization homepage: www.who.org.

[11] Op. cit. note 4.

[12] Environment Canada hopepage: www.doe.ca.

[13] *Environmental Almanac 1993.* Boston: Houghton Mifflin.

[14] J. Graveland et al. "Poor Reproduction in Forest Passerines from Decline of Snail Abundance on Acidified Soils." *Nature*, vol. 368. March 31, 1994.

[15] Op. cit. note 2.

[16] U.S. Bureau of Transportation homepage: www.bts.gov.

The Acid Tests

Introduction:

Acid rain is something of a misnomer, because rain is naturally acidic, with a pH of about 5.6. When we speak of acid rain, therefore, we refer to rain with a pH lower than 5.6. Acid rain is produced when sulfur and nitrogen compounds are released into the atmosphere, where they combine with water to form sulfuric acid and nitric acids. Sulfur compounds may come from such natural sources as decomposing organic matter, volcanos and geysers. The environmental problem known as acid rain, however, does not arise from natural sources. It is caused primarily by fossil fuel combustion. When coal, oil and gas are burned, large amounts of sulfur and nitrogen are released as gases to make the rain more acidic than usual. Acid rain has many effects on an ecosystem. In this investigation, students will examine just one of those effects.

Procedure:

Set up:

You will need to make the water solutions before class, using 10% sulfuric acid (H_2SO_4). If you have not worked with these chemicals before, consult with the chemistry teacher about correct safety procedure. (Note: As you add drops of H_2SO_4, be sure the solution is thoroughly stirred. The number of drops recommended for each solution is approximate, so it is important that you take several pH measurements for each solution.) Use the following recipe:

a) 500 ml of spring water = pH 6

b) 500 ml of spring water + approximately 5 drops of 10% H_2SO_4 = pH 5

c) 500 ml of spring water + approximately 15 drops of 10% H_2SO_4 = pH 4

d) 500 ml of spring water + approximately 25 drops of 10% H_2SO_4 = pH 3

e) 500 ml of spring water + approximately 30 drops of 10% H_2SO_4 = pH 2

f) 500 ml of spring water + approximately 35 drops of 10% H_2SO_4 = pH 1

Facilitating the Activity:

1. Distribute copies of the student worksheets and divide the class into lab pairs. Each pair will receive a set of materials as listed above. Be sure to label each pH solution and assign a different pH (from 1 to 6) to each group.

2. On Day 1, students will set up the experiment according to directions in Part A. On Days 2-10, students will observe and record findings as indicated in Part B.

3. While students are completing their experiment, you should set up a petri dish with bean seeds and rainwater. Record these results with those of the students on the class graph. Have students answer the worksheet discussion questions and supply rainwater samples for students to check their guesses. Discuss the answers with the whole class.

Follow-up Activities:

1. More advanced students could mix their own solutions for testing. They could also experiment with different kinds of acids (sulfuric, nitric, etc.) and levels. Of course, proper safety procedures would have to be strictly observed. Also, each group could have several dishes to observe, to compare and graph the results.

2. Have students test samples of lake or pond water and soil with pH paper in their local areas to determine levels of acidity. They can then compare their findings to those of their classmates who collected samples from different sources.

3. Plants are not the only organisms affected by acid rain. Have students list ecosystems that are negatively affected by acid precipitation. What might be the long-term affects of acid rain for these areas?

Adapted with permission from Biological Sciences Curriculum Study (BSCS). The original activity, "The Effects of Acid Rain on Seed Germination," appears in Biological Science: An Ecological Approach (Kendall/Hunt Publishing Company, 1987, 1992, 1998).

Concept:
Acid rain, produced by fossil fuel combustion, is detrimental to the growth of many plant species.

Objectives:
Students will be able to:
• Determine the acidity of a substance by testing it with pH paper.
• Measure and graph the results of lab experiment with radish seeds.
• Compare the effects of different levels of acidity on plant growth.

Subjects:
Biology, chemistry, environmental science

Skills:
Lab preparation, collecting, recording and analyzing data, graphing, measuring, observation, drawing

Method:
Students test different pH solutions on bean seeds to determine optimal level for seed germination. They then test the acidity of pond water in their local areas.

Materials:
Copies of Student Worksheets
2 pairs of safety goggles
2 lab aprons
2 pairs of plastic gloves
Petri dish
4 bean seeds
Glass-marking pencil
Scissors
Transparent metric ruler
Graph paper
Absorbent paper towel
Colored chalk or markers
Rainwater
pH paper
water solution ranging in pH from 1 to 6

The Acid Tests

Part A - Day 1

1. Cut 4 paper discs the size of the petri dish from the absorbent paper towel.

2. Dampen the paper discs with the water assigned to you by your teacher. Use pH paper to test the pH of your assigned water and note the pH in your data book.

3. Place 2 of the paper discs on the bottom of the petri dish.

4. Measure the length of your 4 seeds and determine the average length.

5. Record the average length in millimeters at Day 1 in your data book.

6. Arrange the seeds in the petri dish and cover with the 2 remaining discs. Make sure the discs are still moist. If not, add more of your assigned pH solution.

7. Replace lid on petri dish and label both the lid and the dish with your team name.

8. Wash your hands thoroughly before leaving the laboratory.

9. Make a guess as to the ideal pH for bean seed growth. Record your guess in your data book.

Part B - Days 2-10

1. Remove the lid from the petri dish and remove the paper discs covering the four seeds. Test the pH of the water remaining in the dish. (If it is different from your initial recorded reading, drain the remaining water and replace with the correct level.)

2. Measure the length of the seeds in millimeters. Average the lengths and record the average in your data book.

3. Sketch the shape of the seeds and note their color.

4. Cover the seeds with the paper discs. Moisten the paper if necessary with the assigned pH solution and replace the lid. (Remember, always test the pH level of the solution before using it.)

5. On the piece of graph paper, set up a graph with age in days on the horizontal axis and length of seeds in millimeters on the vertical axis.

6. Plot the average length of your seeds for the 2 measurements (Day 1 and Day 2) you have made.

7. Repeat procedures 1-6 each day for the length of the investigation. If the seeds begin to germinate during this time, include the length of any growth in your measurement.

8. Students who are working with the same pH should average their results and have one representative for each pH record the data on the class graph. Use the color assigned to your particular pH.

9. Each day, wash your hands thoroughly before leaving the laboratory.

Discussion Questions:

1. Observe the data on the completed class graph. What appears to be the optimal pH solution for successful radish seed germination?

2. What appears to be the least ideal pH solution for successful radish seed germination?

3. What pH do you think the rainwater has, based on the data gathered? Check your guess by determining its pH with pH paper.

4. Based on the data gathered, what would be the impact of rainwater with increased acidity?

5. Do you think there is reason for concern?

Clearing the Air

Introduction:

Air pollution is becoming a serious problem in many parts of the world. For example, each year in the United States, 60,000 deaths are caused by particulates found in air pollution.[1] Breathing the air in Bombay, India is equivalent to smoking ten cigarettes a day. Every twenty-fourth disability and every seventeenth death in Hungary is caused by air pollution, according to their National Institute of Public Health. And diplomats stationed in Mexico City are awarded hardship pay for breathing the polluted air.[2] While these examples are extreme, cities worldwide are facing increased problems from industrialization's unwelcome side effect, air pollution.

Procedure:

Set-Up:

Before class, copy the air pollution diagram from the *Student Worksheet* onto the butcher paper or poster board. Make sure to leave enough space under each category so that students will be able to fill in the information from their articles. The middle circle can simply be labeled "Air Pollution," rather than trying to list all the article titles. Post this master in an easy-to-reach location so that students will be able to add to it during the class.

Facilitating the Activity:

1. A few days before the activity, have students collect at least two articles or resources about air pollution. Suggest that they make use of the local library(ies) and their home supply of newspapers and/or magazines. If they have access to the Internet, they can do a search of articles on the topic through a major newspaper's archives. They may also write a summary of a news show or documentary on television. The following list of topics can serve as a guideline for students in their search:

   - Smog in Los Angeles (or other polluted cities)
   - Effects of Eastern Europe's rapid industrialization

   - Mexico City's efforts to control airborne poisons
   - Legislation passed to curb air pollution
   - Health studies about effects of breathing dirty air
   - Damage to outdoor art due to air pollution
   - Traffic and industry's role in climate change
   - The connection between air pollution and acid rain (& effects of acid rain)

2. After allowing a couple of days for students to collect their articles and summaries, pass out the Student Worksheets and have students diagram the information from their resources. See chart on the following page for an example of how to use the diagram. You might want to chart a sample article on the master chart so that students understand the concept. Emphasize that students should include as much information as possible on their chart, but that not every category will have something listed. Allow about 15-20 minutes to complete their two charts.

3. As students finish their own charts, they may begin adding to the class version. (You might want to check students' copies for errors before they add to the main chart.) When information is duplicated, students should make tally marks next to the original entry, rather than take up extra space duplicating the information. As some areas become crowded with information, students may need to use arrows to continue the lists. Hang the completed chart in the classroom, and encourage students to add to it if they find further articles or learn more information about air pollution.

Discussion Questions:

1. Which of the causes on the chart are increased with population growth? Do any of the causes seem unrelated to a growing number of humans?

2. Make a list of important factors for a realistic plan to reduce air pollution. Using these guidelines, which ideas mentioned in the "solution" section seem most feasible? Which seem least feasible?

Concept:
Current industrial and individual practices must be modified to avoid further environmental and health problems caused by air pollution.

Objectives:
Students will be able to:
- Find and use publications on current events to understand an issue.
- Identify and categorize useful information from publications.
- Compare and discuss research findings with other students in the class.

Subjects:
Environmental science, health, social studies, biology

Skills:
Research, collecting and recording data, analyzing and interpreting data, reading comprehension

Method:
Students find articles about air pollution issues and as a class use the information to create a chart depicting the causes and effects of air pollution and possible solutions.

Materials:
Copies of Student Worksheet

Large sheet of butcher paper or poster board and writing utensils

Optional: Newspapers, news magazines and other resources

Clearing the Air

3. What differences exist between the air pollution problems in heavily industrialized countries and those in less developed countries? Are there also differences in the kinds of solutions they seek? What factors contribute to these differences?

4. Are there any direct links between specific causes of air pollution and certain effects? Which of the causes tend to create more health problems? Which tend to contribute more to environmental damage?

5. What health or environmental risks are most closely associated with acid rain?

6. Considering the air pollution problems in many big cities, why do people continue to gravitate to these heavily polluted urban areas?

Follow-up Activities:

1. Students can research one of the topics listed in the guide at the beginning of this activity and write an investigative report on the subject.

2. Have students chart the population growth rate and airborne poisons increase in cities like Mexico City and Los Angeles, if this information is available.

Endnotes

[1] American Lung Association homepage: www.lungusa.org

[2] Lester Brown, et al. *State of the World 1990*. New York: W.W. Norton and Co., 1990.

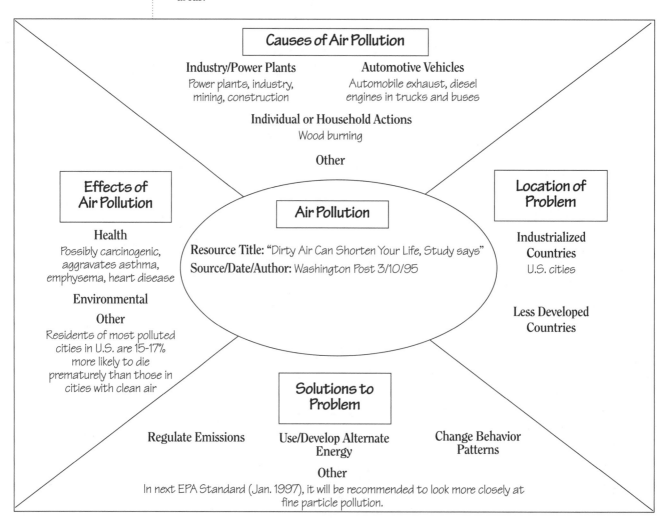

Causes of Air Pollution

Industry/Power Plants
Power plants, industry, mining, construction

Automotive Vehicles
Automobile exhaust, diesel engines in trucks and buses

Individual or Household Actions
Wood burning

Other

Effects of Air Pollution

Health
Possibly carcinogenic, aggravates asthma, emphysema, heart disease

Environmental

Other
Residents of most polluted cities in U.S. are 15-17% more likely to die prematurely than those in cities with clean air

Air Pollution

Resource Title: "Dirty Air Can Shorten Your Life, Study says"
Source/Date/Author: Washington Post 3/10/95

Location of Problem

Industrialized Countries
U.S. cities

Less Developed Countries

Solutions to Problem

Regulate Emissions

Use/Develop Alternate Energy

Change Behavior Patterns

Other
In next EPA Standard (Jan. 1997), it will be recommended to look more closely at fine particle pollution.

Clearing the Air

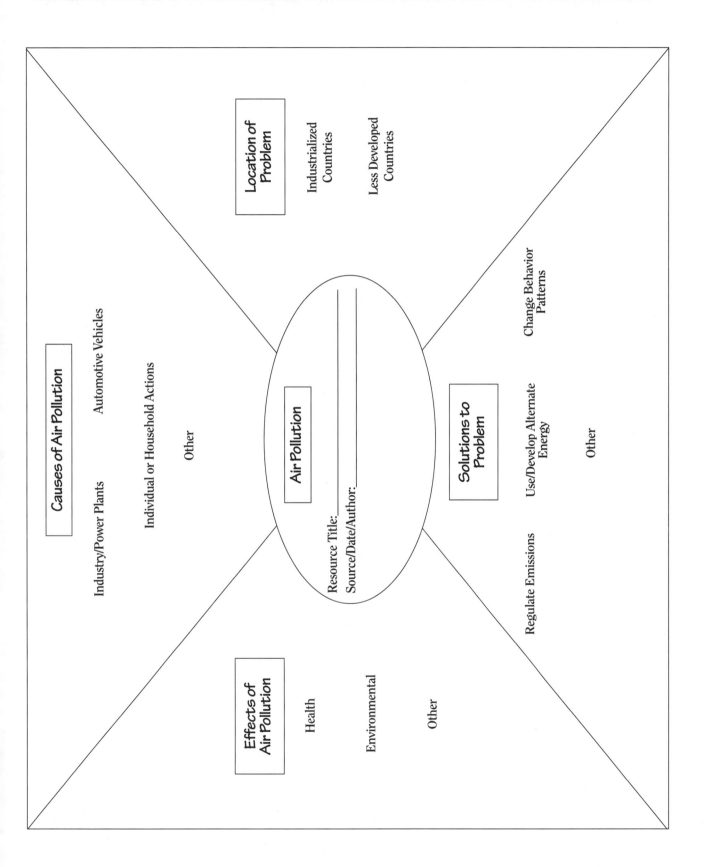

Location of Problem

Industrialized Countries

Less Developed Countries

Causes of Air Pollution

Automotive Vehicles

Industry/Power Plants

Individual or Household Actions

Other

Air Pollution

Resource Title:

Source/Date/Author:

Solutions to Problem

Change Behavior Patterns

Use/Develop Alternate Energy

Other

Regulate Emissions

Effects of Air Pollution

Health

Environmental

Other

Water Resources

Troubled Water

Many people take for granted that a clean, plentiful water supply will always be available. Unfortunately, overconsumption and pollution pose dire threats to this critical life support system. As the world's population escalates, so does the demand for water. Population growth and economic expansion have caused global withdrawals of fresh water to more than quadruple between 1940 and 1990.[1] Residents of rapidly expanding U.S. states like Florida, Arizona, and California, as well as citizens of other countries, are dealing with the dilemma of strained water resources on a daily basis.

Because many people live in arid regions, we have developed the ability to transport water and satisfy demands for water in many different ways. However, we have not developed adequate methods of ensuring the best and most efficient use of this limited resource. Twenty countries already suffer water shortages extreme enough to impede development and harm human health, and by 2050, the number of people living in water-scarce countries is projected to be between 1 and 2.5 billion people — equal to 13 to 20 percent of the world population.[2] According to the 1996 United Nations Human Development Report, nearly 1.3 billion people in the developing world still lack access to safe water, and efforts to supply it are falling behind population growth rates.

Americans get water from two main sources: the surface water of rivers, lakes, streams and reservoirs, and underground water supplies contained in aquifers. An **aquifer** is a permeable layer of sand, gravel or rock where water collects. This **groundwater** provides drinking water for half the nation. As our demand for water depletes surface water resources, groundwater sources must supply more of the water we use. One example of a strained surface water resource in the United States is the Colorado River. The amount of river water allotted to each state or city by law actually adds up to more water than flows in the river. In China, unsustainable use of groundwater for domestic, industrial and agricultural needs has lowered the water table under Beijing from 5 meters below ground level to around 50 meters.[3]

According to David Seckler, Director General of the International Irrigation Management Institute, slowing down the rate at which the amount of water available per person is decreasing may depend more on stabilizing population than anything else that policy-makers can do.[4]

An Unquenchable Thirst

Irrigation and other agricultural practices are responsible for about 69 percent of all water withdrawals on a global scale.[5] In fact, the irrigation of land solely for livestock feed accounts for a major portion of the United States water consumption.

Aside from irrigation, water is used for manufacturing and food processing. Hydroelectric power plants use water to generate electricity. Nuclear power plants and other industries use water for cooling purposes. Water is used countless times each day by individuals for bathing, drinking, washing clothes and dishes, and flushing toilets.

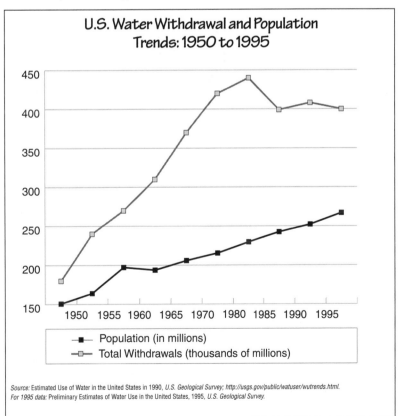

U.S. Water Withdrawal and Population Trends: 1950 to 1995

- ■ Population (in millions)
- □ Total Withdrawals (thousands of millions)

Source: Estimated Use of Water in the United States in 1990, U.S. Geological Survey; http://usgs.gov/public/watuser/wutrends.html. For 1995 data: Preliminary Estimates of Water Use in the United States, 1995, U.S. Geological Survey.

Troubled Water

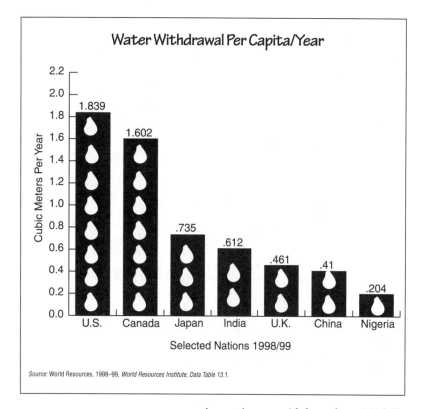

Water Withdrawal Per Capita/Year

- U.S. 1.839
- Canada 1.602
- Japan .735
- India .612
- U.K. .461
- China .41
- Nigeria .204

Cubic Meters Per Year

Selected Nations 1998/99

Source: World Resources, 1998–99, *World Resources Institute, Data Table 13.1.*

As a nation, we withdraw about 400 billion gallons of water each day for residential, industrial and agricultural purposes. This figure translates into approximately 1,500 gallons per person; only about 150 gallons of this is what we use directly in our households every day.[6] Although per capita water use has stabilized with improved technology and water conservation in recent years, Americans still use more water, both in total and in per capita terms, than any other industrialized country in the world. An average resident of Germany or France, for example, uses about one-third the water of a typical American.[7]

Muddying the Waters

Pollution further compounds water shortages. Various human activities and water uses have degraded the nature and quality of the world's water supply. The health of two-thirds of the world's population is endangered by the water they drink and use to cook and bathe. Polluted and poisoned by sewage, agricultural runoff and industrial wastes, water flows back into our streams, rivers, lakes and oceans.

In cities of the developing world, some 90 percent of sewage is released untreated into surface water.[8] Frequently these wastes pollute waters used for drinking and irrigation. As urbanization in developing countries increases, more people may be exposed to unsafe drinking water.

There are three main areas of water pollution: Ocean pollution, groundwater contamination and surface water contamination. Comprising 71 percent of the Earth's surface, the oceans receive most of the world's wastes. In recent years, unmanaged urban growth, coastal construction, intensive agriculture, off-shore oil drilling, mineral extraction, deforestation, boating, overfishing and acid rain have increasingly fouled the seas around us. The industrialized countries of the world now put more tons of trash into the ocean each year than they take out in tons of fish. More than 1,300 major industrial facilities in the United States have federal permits to dump their waste directly into coastal waterways. This waste includes hundreds of chemicals, as well as many persistent toxins.

Another source of ocean pollution is spilled oil. Great attention was brought to this phenomenon when the Exxon Valdez went aground in Alaska's Prince William Sound in 1989, spilling nearly 11 million gallons of crude oil, soiling more than 700 miles of beach, and killing thousands of birds and marine wildlife.[9] During the 1991 Persian Gulf War, Iraq's leader, Saddam Hussein, ordered oil spills as a military tactic. The destruction caused by these spills was estimated to be more than a dozen times greater than the Valdez disaster.[10] The United Nations has tried to control the pollution and overexploitation of the oceans through international conferences and global initiatives, but there is still much to be done in cleaning up global waters.

A Deadly Drink

Groundwater and surface water contamination is also a grave concern throughout the world. In developing countries, **water-borne biological hazards** (bacteria, viruses, parasites, etc.) are responsible for high infant mortality rates. Parasites, resulting from water pollution

Troubled Water

or poor sanitation practices, are found in surface waters of many semi-arid countries. Microbiological agents and parasites can be contracted from swimming in polluted waters or from eating contaminated shellfish. This problem is not only found in less developed countries. Popular tourist beaches around the world are dealing with this pollution in varying degrees of intensity.

While water-borne germs are found mostly in less developed countries, developed nations suffer chemical pollution, which has emerged as a serious threat to all countries which have introduced industrialization and chemically-supported agriculture. The most immediate stress on human health is the consumption of contaminated water. Thus far, 800 different organic and inorganic chemicals have been found in drinking water. Some organic contaminants occur naturally, but inorganic constituents of drinking water are usually the result of various industrial solvents discharged from manufacturing plants, small trade sources, and households.

In Milwaukee, Wisconsin, in April of 1993, almost 400,000 people were victims of **cryptosporidiosis**, a water-borne disease outbreak, as a result of poor water treatment methods. According to the U.S. Environmental Protection Agency (EPA), 80 large water systems throughout the United States have failed to meet regulations for basic filtration.[11]

When human wastes and pesticide and herbicide runoff wash into surface water sources or oceans, they alter the nutrient and chemical composition of the water, making it more suitable for various kinds of algae. The algae blocks light and, when it decays, uses oxygen needed by fish and other aquatic species to survive. This process, called **eutrophication**, is very hazardous to aquatic habitats. Although substantial global research has been done on this phenomenon, it is still considered one of the most serious water quality problems and continues to increase in many parts of the world.

Just over half of all Americans are dependent on groundwater, at least in part, as a source of drinking water.[12] Any pollutant that comes in contact with the ground may contaminate groundwater. Underground toxic storage tanks, pesticides, toxic waste dumps and septic

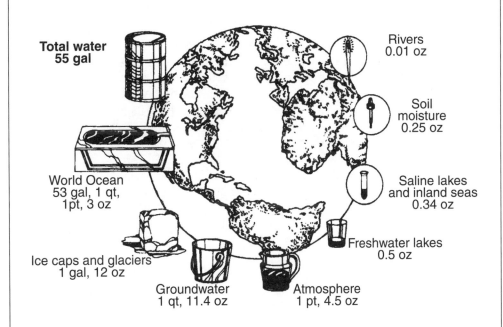

A Drop in the Barrel

Total water 55 gal

World Ocean 53 gal, 1 qt, 1pt, 3 oz

Ice caps and glaciers 1 gal, 12 oz

Groundwater 1 qt, 11.4 oz

Atmosphere 1 pt, 4.5 oz

Rivers 0.01 oz

Soil moisture 0.25 oz

Saline lakes and inland seas 0.34 oz

Freshwater lakes 0.5 oz

Though the earth contains vast water resources, only a small part of the water in the hydrosphere is available at any one time for use by people. This figure indicates the world's distribution of water, treating the whole supply as if it were 55 gallons. The primary sources of water for human use are from groundwater, freshwater lakes, and rivers.

Source: Reprinted with permission from Prentice Hall, as printed in Environmental Science, by Charles E. Kupchella and Margaret C. Hyland, 1989.

Troubled Water

tanks all pose serious threats to groundwater quality. For example, a single gallon of used motor oil which comes into contact with a source of fresh water can render one million gallons of that fresh water undrinkable. More than 65 percent of all water pollutants originate in our homes: the sinks and toilets in American households often become the conduits for caustics and household cleaning products. The oil that drips from our cars and the chemicals washed from our lawns can also enter drains and reach groundwater supplies. These practices comprise a huge source of often unmonitored hazardous wastes.

Staying Above Water

In 1972, deciding that something needed to be done on a federal level concerning contamination of waters, the U.S. Congress passed the Clean Water Act. This was the most comprehensive and expensive environmental legislation in the nation's history. The bill commenced a major change in the country's approach to water pollution control by limiting the contaminated discharges and setting water quality standards. Although great strides have been made in cleaning up the nation's waters, significant levels of water pollution still persist.

Very little has been done on the federal level to address water shortages in much of the western United States. Although water withdrawals are lower than they were in 1980, parts of the country are suffering from a decreasing fresh water supply. For example, the amount of irrigated land in four Great Plains states has decreased due to a drawing down of the Ogallala aquifer.[13] Water crises extend around the globe, especially in areas experiencing growth and increased urbanization, where supplies of clean water are rapidly diminishing.

Every effort should be made to preserve the precious two percent of Earth's waters that we depend on to sustain life. Individuals can aid this effort by using water judiciously and disposing of toxins safely. National governments can encourage cleaner, more plentiful water supplies by strictly regulating industry and agriculture's water use. Because the vast oceans belong to all the world's people, international cooperation is essential for ensuring water quality for present and future generations.

Endnotes

[1] *World Resources: A Guide to the Global Environment, 1996-1997.* New York: Oxford University Press, 1996, p. 301.

[2] Ibid., p. 302.

[3] Lester R. Brown. "Facing the Prospect of Food Scarcity." *State of the World 1997.* Washington, DC: Worldwatch Institute, 1997, p. 30.

[4] Ibid. p. 31.

[5] Op. cit. note 1.

[6] "Preliminary Estimates of Water Use in the United States, 1995" U.S. Geological Survey homepage: www.usgs.gov.

[7] Op. cit. note 1, pp. 306-307.

[8] Op. cit. note 1, pp. 71-72.

[9] Timothy Egan. "Alaska Wants $1.2 Billion to Drop Suit Over Spill." *The New York Times,* January 31, 1991.

[10] Sharon Begley. "Saddam's Ecoterror." *Newsweek,* February 4, 1990.

[11] *EPA Journal: Clean Water Agenda; Remaking the Laws that Protect our Water Resources.* Vol. 20, No. 1-2. Summer 1994.

[12] *National Water Quality Inventory: 1994 Report to Congress.* U.S. Environmental Protection Agency.

[13] Op. cit. note 3.

Water, Water Everywhere

Introduction:

Although 75% of the Earth's surface is covered with water, only a very small fraction is available for human use. Of the water that is available to us, some becomes contaminated from human actions, such as toxic run-off from agriculture, factories or pollutants that we dump in the water supply from our sinks at home. Population growth over the past 30 years has caused demand for water to double in about half the countries in the world. Residents of states with rapidly growing populations, as well as citizens of other countries, often experience water shortages. In the following activity, students will gain an appreciation for the ways we use water and the need to conserve it.

Procedure:

Part 1:

Set-up:

1. Gather all materials.

2. Fill one small container with sand.

3. Fill a one-liter container with water, add 4 drops of blue food coloring and stir.

4. Label the other 5 containers as follows: a one-liter container "oceans"; a small plastic container "polar ice"; a small container "deep groundwater"; a small container "fresh water."

5. Make a transparency of the adjacent diagram.

6. Measure and set aside 34 grams of salt.

Facilitating the Activity:

Perform the following class demonstration to help students visualize the distribution of the Earth's water resources:

1. Display the seven containers prepared for this activity.

2. Display a transparency of the figure on the right. Use a graduated cylinder to distribute the one liter of water into the five empty containers according to the percentages indicated in the figure. (For example, 97.1 percent of the water on the Earth is found in the oceans. Because one liter contains 1000 milliliters, 97.1 percent of one liter is 971 milliliters. Therefore, pour 971 milliliters into the container marked "oceans.")

3. After you have filled the empty containers with the appropriate amounts of water, continue with the demonstration as follows:

   a) Add 34 grams of salt to "ocean" container; this will match the salinity of the water sample with the salinity of the earth's oceans (3.5 percent)

   b) Place the plastic "polar ice" container in the freezer.

   c) Set the "other" container aside. We do not have access to this water.

   d) Pour the "deep ground water" into the container of sand.

   e) Ask the students which of the containers represents fresh water that is readily available for human use. (They should easily see that only the jar marked "freshwater" has the readily available supply.) Initiate a discussion on the limits of fresh water supplies, the problems of population growth and distribution, and the contamination of existing supplies. Only a small part of this fresh water (.003 percent of the Earth's total water supply) is accessible. The rest is too remote (found in Amazon or Siberian rivers) to locate, too expensive to retrieve or too polluted to use. Hold a plate in front of the class and dramatically drop the usable portion of fresh water onto it. (Represent this portion as one drop of water from an eye dropper.)

Adapted by permission from the National Science Foundation. The original activity appears in the National Science and Technology Week Activity Guide, 1988, by the National Science Foundation, Washington, DC.

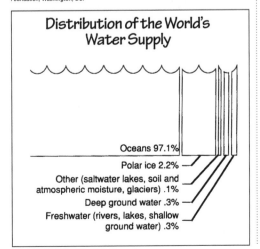

Distribution of the World's Water Supply

Oceans 97.1%
Polar ice 2.2%
Other (saltwater lakes, soil and atmospheric moisture, glaciers) .1%
Deep ground water .3%
Freshwater (rivers, lakes, shallow ground water) .3%

Concept:

Although water covers three-quarters of the Earth's surface, only a small fraction is available for human consumption. As the population grows, water efficiency and conservation become more important.

Objectives:

Students will be able to:
• Understand aspects of a shared natural resource, such as availability and distribution.
• Estimate the amount of resources they use and compare that figure to actual use.
• Design a graph to show current resource use and use after conservation measures have been taken.

Subjects:

Biology, environmental science, math, family life

Skills:

Estimation, graphing, mathematic calculation, observation, research, writing

Method:

Students observe a brief demonstration on the distribution of the world's water and then calculate how much water they use on a daily basis, both directly and indirectly.

Materials:

7 clear containers (2 one-liter containers; 5 smaller containers, one of which is plastic.)
1 plate
Overhead projector
Masking tape
Marking pen
One liter of water
Salt (34 grams)
Sand (approximately 250 ml)
Blue food coloring
1000 ml graduated cylinder
One eye dropper
Graph paper
Calculators (optional)
Copies of Student Worksheet
Freezer

Water, Water Everywhere

Part 2:

1. Have students record how many gallons of water they think they use individually in an average day. Later, they will compare this estimated daily water use with their calculated daily water use.

2. As a group, have them list all the ways members of their class use water on a day-to-day basis.

3. Using the data in the table, "Domestic Uses of Water," have them determine their individual water use per day for each activity that the class listed in step 2. They should include their share of general family uses such as dishwasher and clothes washer. Then they can determine their individual total water use per day.

4. Students should compare the individual water use calculated in step 3 with the water use estimated in step 1. Are their calculated figures higher or lower than their estimated figures? Ask students whether they consider themselves typical water users. Have them explain their answers.

5. Students should now draw a bar graph to illustrate how much water is used by their class for each activity. Which activities require the most water? Using the class average, students should also calculate the average use of their town and/or state.

Suggested Answers to Student Worksheet Questions:

1. *Water is needed to grow the food and grasses the calf would consume.*

2. *Student answers will vary.*

3. *Student answers will vary.*

4. *Possible answers: purchasing and eating foods which require less water to cultivate (eating lower on the food chain); recycling items to prevent excessive use of water in manufacturing; driving less.*

5. *Possible answers: take showers instead of baths; don't let water run while brushing teeth or shaving; fix leaky faucets; install water-saving devices for toilet and shower; water lawn less frequently; run dishwasher and washing machine only when you have full loads.*

6. *Student answers will vary. For further information on water contamination, you may wish to contact the U.S. Environmental Protection Agency, Public Information Center, 401 M Street, SW, Washington, DC 20460; 202/829-3535; www.epa.gov.*

Follow-up Activities:

1. Have students investigate new household products which conserve water (such as low-flush toilets, new shower heads, timed sprinklers, etc.) Each student or group of students could be responsible for writing up a brief synopsis of the costs and benefits of one or two of these products.

   (Note: Free catalogs listing water conservation devices are available from: Eco Source, 610 Wendell Court, Atlanta, GA 30336, 800/864-2737; and Gaiam Inc., 1 Mill St., Suite A26, Burlington, VT 05401, 800/456-1177.)

2. Have students read their home water meters daily for a week, at the same time each day, and report back to the class. They can then compare these readings to their estimates of daily water use. They can then read the meter for a second week, in which they implement many of the conservation measures suggested above.

Adapted by permission from Biological Science Curriculum Study. The original activity appears in Biological Science: An Ecological Approach (Kendall/Hunt Publishing Company, 1987, 1992, 1998).

Water, Water Everywhere

Domestic Uses of Water

Activity	Gallons Used
Brushing teeth	2-10
Washing hands	2
Shaving	20 (2/min.)
Showering	20-25 (5/min.)
Tub bathing	25-35
Flushing toilet	3.5 - 8
Getting a drink	0.25
Cooking a meal	5-7
Washing dishes	30 (8-10/meal)
Automatic dishwasher	15
House cleaning	7
Washing machine	24-50
Watering lawn	10/min. (102/1000 m^2)
Leaking faucet	25-50/day

(Faucet and toilet leaks in New York City = 757 million gallons/day)

Indirect Uses of Water

Agricultural

Item	Gallons Used
1 kg corn	374
1 loaf of bread	150
1 kg rice	1,232
1 kg grain-fed beef	1,760
1 kg cotton	4,400

Industrial

Item	Gallons Used
1 gallon gasoline	10
1 kg steel	25
1 kw electricity	80
1 kg paper	220
1 kg synthetic rubber	660
1 kg aluminum	2,200
1 car	100,000

Water, Water Everywhere

1. There are many water uses that are not obvious to most people. Consider, for example, that 1.2 million gallons of water are needed to raise one calf until it is fully grown. Why do you think so much water is needed to raise a calf?

2. Make a list of the ways you use water indirectly, for example, in the production of food you eat or materials you use.

3. Compare your list with the table above, "Indirect Uses of Water." How many of these uses did you list?

4. How could you reduce your indirect use of water?

5. What could you do to reduce your direct use of water?

6. Is there any evidence that the water supply you use daily is decreasing in size or is being contaminated by pollutants? How could you go about obtaining this information?

Roll on Mighty River

Introduction:

The Colorado River runs like a lifeline through some of the most arid regions in the United States and Mexico. This mighty river carries between five and 24 million acre feet of water per year, with an average of 15 million acre feet. (An acre-foot is the amount of water that it would take to submerge an acre of land, which is about the size of a football field, to a depth of one foot.) It touches seven states before reaching Mexico, and its watershed covers one twelfth of the continental United States.

For several centuries, people have used water from the Colorado to transform the landscape of the American West. Water grows not only crops, but also cities in the desert; the Colorado irrigates 3.5 million acres of agricultural land and provides water to 25 million people, including residents of Denver, Salt Lake City, Las Vegas, Phoenix and Los Angeles. The river runs through six national parks and recreation areas, and both free-flowing and dammed areas provide a variety of opportunities for outdoor recreation. The 11 federal hydroelectric plants on the river use dams to provide power to about three million people.

But these benefits come at a price: all of the states, Mexico and several Native American reservations are allowed to use a portion of the river, and except in the wettest of years, the Colorado dries up about 10 to 20 miles before it reaches its historic mouth at the Gulf of California. Because of dams, native species of fish can't swim upstream to spawn, and they are crowded out by species introduced because of their appeal to anglers. Reservations may soon be able to lease any excess water they save through conservation measures, which may make water a considerably more expensive commodity for the cities and farms downstream.

Procedure:

1. Divide the class into groups of seven to ten students. Some students in each group will form a panel of judges assigned to arbitrate conflicting demands on the Colorado River. (Groups may have two to five judges if numbers are uneven.) Up to five students will represent the various groups competing for water. Have students make nametags to identify their roles. These students are the parties in the arbitration, and their positions are described below:

a) *Sugar beet farmer in Colorado.* You need water for irrigation to grow your sugar beets. Producing sugar in Colorado is an important farm industry and supports many jobs. Without water for irrigation your farm would be worthless and you would have to move to the city to find work.

b) *Planner for the Southern Nevada Water Authority (SWNA).* This is the agency that regulates water for southern Nevada, including Las Vegas. You must provide water for a large tourist industry as well as a booming population. At current growth rates, you can meet the water needs of your region until 2015.

c) *Biologist for the Recovery Implementation Program for endangered native fish.* In 1994, the U.S. Fish and Wildlife Service designated 1,980 miles of the Colorado River as critical habitat for four species of fish under the Endangered Species Act. Your job is to make sure the flow of water through the dams is regulated to sustain fish stocks, which is not the most efficient flow for operating hydroelectric plants and may affect recreation on some sections of the river.

d) *President of an electric utility company in Los Angeles.* Most of the power you supply to your customers comes from the hydroelectric plants on the Colorado River. With new restrictions on the amount of water that can be used to generate electricity, you may have to purchase power from a more expensive or environmentally damaging source and pass along the new costs to your customers.

e) *Representative of a Native American tribal government.* You use 80-90% of the water allocated to your reservation, but a new federal government policy may allow you to lease to other users any water you save through new conservation measures. This could bring much-needed income and jobs

Concept:
Increasing demands on U.S. water supply and diminishing amounts of unpolluted water cause groups to compete for their "share" of the available supply.

Objectives:
Students will be able to:
• Research and understand the position of a stakeholder in competition for a natural resource.
• Present a position on an issue to a panel of peer judges.
• Design a plan to equitably distribute a resource among several competitors.

Subjects:
Environmental science, social studies

Skills:
Public speaking, debate, library research, decision making, problem solving

Method:
By investigating water use along the Colorado River, students get a first-hand look at the complexity and frustration surrounding water use problems in arid and semi-arid regions.

Materials:
Note cards for arguments and questions (optional)
Poster board for charts and evidence (optional)

Roll on Mighty River

to the reservation. Currently, water savings such as this are available for free use by others downstream.

2. Allow the parties time to research their positions in the library and on the Internet. This should take one or two class periods. Advise them of the points they should cover and encourage them to use charts and posters to summarize their positions. The judges will also need to spend time in the library in order to prepare for the trial. They should make a list of questions to ask the different sides during the arbitration, based on their own research. Some good sites to start with are the Water Education Foundation at http://www.water-ed.org and the Southern Nevada Water Authority at http://www.lvvwd.com/snwa/html.

3. When everyone is ready, hold the arbitrations. To avoid distraction, separate the groups as much as possible, ideally in different rooms. During each arbitration, the parties present their cases, using visual aids and note cards when needed, and then answer questions by their panel of judges.

4. After the presentations, the judges need to make decisions and design a plan of action. Each plan should then be presented in front of the class by one of the judges. The plan may include a specific course of action, such as giving more or less water to one of the parties. It could require that the parties conserve water. Or it could recommend technological solutions such as better irrigation equipment or fish elevators. The plan should clearly set priorities for water use in the area, justify these priorities, and indicate how conflicting demands might be met in the future.

Follow-up Activities:

1. As this activity illustrates, short of impractical or extremely expensive methods, it is almost impossible to create more water. The only way to make more water available is to conserve it.

There are many ways to save water in students' everyday lives. For example, they can:

- take short showers instead of baths;
- turn the water off when brushing their teeth;
- wash the car from a bucket rather then letting a hose run;
- collect rain water to water house plants;
- replace old showerheads with low flow models;
- and place plastic bottles of water and rocks in toilet tanks.

Have students come up with their own list of the many possible ways to conserve water. Make a poster listing all of the conservation ideas and hang it in the classroom.

One systematic way to save water is to conduct a water audit of the school or individual homes. Have students work through the water audit in *Student Activity 10: Water, Water Everywhere.*

2. Find out where the water for your school comes from, and trace its path from the original body of water to its end location after wastewater treatment. Discover other uses of the same water source and identify any scarcity or pollution problems for your water source.

Sources: Layperson's Guide to the Colorado River and Colorado River Water Map, *Water Education Foundation, Sacramento, California, 1995.*

Deforestation

Deforestation: The Unkindest Cut

The Earth is made up of many different ecosystems, but perhaps none more spectacular and life-sustaining than the forests. We depend upon the world's forests to regulate climate, clean air and water, conserve precious soil and provide habitat to much of the planet's wildlife.

Forests of all types are giving way to population pressures, causing irreversible damage to an integral part of our biosphere. The Earth's forests today cover about 3.5 billion hectares, a 23 percent decrease from the forest area in 1700. The total forested area continues to decrease by about 13.7 million hectares per year, an area about the size of Florida.[1]

Trouble in the Tropics

Of primary global concern is the loss of the Earth's tropical rainforests. **Tropical rainforests** are defined primarily by two factors: location (between the Tropics of Capricorn and Cancer) and level of rainfall. Rainforests receive from four to eight meters of rain each year. The five meters of rain that falls on Borneo each year represent five times the rain that annually falls on New York City. Due to a constant climate, tropical rainforests grow all year long.

The effects of rainforest destruction are felt by every community in the world. Although tropical forests cover less than seven percent of the global land surface, they are home to more than half the species of all living things. Rainforests are a treasure house of foods, medicines, and other resources we have only begun to discover. Less than one percent of rainforest species have even been studied for their potential usefulness.

Tragically, 150 acres of tropical forests are destroyed every minute.[2] The Rainforest Action Network estimates that the planet loses 78 million acres of rainforest (an area about the size of New Mexico) every year to agriculture, ranching and timbering in Southeast Asia, Africa, and Central and South America. In fact, all the primary rainforests in India, Bangladesh, Sri Lanka and Haiti have been destroyed; the Ivory Coast rainforests have been completely logged out; and the Philippines and Thailand have depleted half of their rainforests since 1960. Of the 8 million square miles of tropical forests that once circled the globe, less than half remain, and these are being destroyed at an ever-increasing rate.

A Deep-Rooted Problem

What drives humans to deplete this precious ecosystem? The causes of rapid tropical deforestation are many and often interconnected. The initial and probably most devastating cause has been the lack of knowledge concerning the rainforest. A case study in Brazil illustrates this point. In 1969, Brazil enacted a National Integration Program with the goal of populating Amazonia with thousands of landless and unemployed people. This was in response to overpopulation and inequitable distribution of land and wealth. Another goal of the program was to get wealthy investors to clear the forest lands and raise cattle for export to the industrialized world. The program proved a disaster because the people implementing the project failed to realize that the richness of the once-vast Amazon forest is in its trees, not its soil.

Tropical rainforest land cleared by slash and burn techniques will support a farmer for a year or two before the soil erodes and the

Deforestation: The Unkindest Cut

farmer is forced to relocate elsewhere to continue this destructive process. With some previous research, this program might not have been implemented, and vast amounts of Amazonian forests could have been saved. Because of this oversight, the Brazilian government's goals to create additional habitation and grazing land were not realized. This scenario has been repeated in different regions of the world.

Another leading cause of **deforestation**, particularly in parts of Africa and Asia, is the need for fuelwood. Two in five of the world's people depend on wood for fuel to cook and to heat their homes. The Food and Agriculture Organization of the United Nations estimates that nearly two billion people face fuel shortages, and that 100 million people suffer a "fuelwood famine" and are unable to meet their minimum fuel needs.[3] The endless search for wood dominates the lives of millions of women and children who spend anywhere from 100 to 300 days each year looking for fuelwood.

Timber cutting is yet another major contributor to tropical deforestation. Tropical forests provide about one-fifth of all the wood exported worldwide for industrial uses. In the process of harvesting timber, industries build roads to facilitate retrieval of the wood deeper in the rainforest. These roads open once impenetrable forests to exploitation by miners, hunters, ranchers and farmers.

Some processes of cutting timber have more harmful impacts on the environment than others. When timber is **clear-cut**, all the trees on an area of land are cut down, and the habitat of all species living there is destroyed. Even if the land is replanted, it is usually with only one or two species of trees. The former wealth of **biodiversity** never returns.

Frequently, timber is harvested by selective cutting. That is, harvesters cut only the trees they wish to sell, leaving the rest of the forest intact. This process, while still destructive, is less harmful to the forest ecology than clear-cutting. Moving the fallen trees to the roads without disturbing the soil, carefully planning the roads that carry trees out of the forest, tak-

ing the time to cut all vines off of the selected trees, and directing which way they should fall can all help to reduce the impact of logging on the surrounding forest in addition to reducing waste for the harvesters.

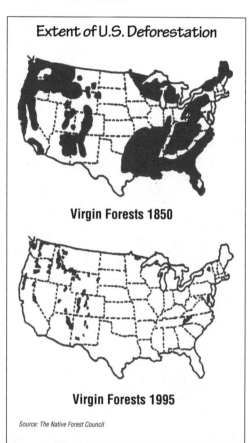

Extent of U.S. Deforestation

Virgin Forests 1850

Virgin Forests 1995

Source: The Native Forest Council

Deforestation North American-style

While tropical rainforest destruction is a globally significant issue, the cutting down of **temperate rainforests** in North America, which are found in the pacific northwest from California through Canada and into Alaska, has developed into a serious controversy on this continent. Since the turn of the century, the U.S. Forest Service has been managing National Forests in the U.S., with a total of 155 national forests, covering 187 million acres.[4] The Forest Service is mandated to manage the forests for multiple, often conflicting, uses, including timber harvest, recreation, wildlife habitat, wilderness, watershed

Deforestation: The Unkindest Cut

protection and range management. However, it has been criticized for focusing too heavily on timber yields.[5]

Much of the bitter controversy between environmental groups, the timber industry and the federal government has been directed toward the fate of the most ancient of the rainforests, also called **old growth**. At one time, old-growth rainforest covered some 15 million acres in the Pacific Northwest. Today, less than one-sixth of this original forest remains.[6] Some areas included trees ten feet wide, 275 feet tall, and 1,120 years old. But, because of their size and the quality and strength of their wood, old-growth trees represent valuable lumber to loggers. An estimated 90 percent of North America's temperate rainforest forest has been logged at least once, leaving only around 10

The Rainforest in Dollars and Cents

A scientific team from the New York Botanical Garden assessed, in U.S. dollars, the profits that could be made over a 50-year period from harvesting and selling the natural products of trees and plants found in an untouched hectare (2.471 acres) in the Amazonian rain forest in Mishana, Peru. Compared to the potential profits from using an equivalent area for cattle ranching or for timber production, the rain forest is twice as valuable if left standing.

One Hectare of Rainforest Can Be Used For

Timber Production	Harvest of Naturally Occuring Produce	Cattle Ranching

Annual Yield

- $391.02 Palm Fruits (70 plants)
- Wild Chocolate and Legumes (12 plants) $49.50
- Rubber Plants (24 plants) $57.60
- $199.67 Other Fruits (11 plants)

Over 50 years, the total value of the yield from one hectare is

$3,184	$6,330	$2,960

Deforestation: The Unkindest Cut

percent of the original virgin forests.[7] Furthermore, less than one percent of the nation's native forests are protected from logging.

The Canadian province of British Columbia has lost 65 million acres (26.3 million hectares) of forest since 1950, and logging continues at the rates of 568,000 acres (230,000 hectares) per year.[8] Old-growth hardwoods once covered most of Canada's Atlantic zones, but today only a few pockets remain.[9]

After the Fall

Both tropical and temperate rainforests are rapidly disappearing because they are being logged and burned far faster than they are being replenished. Many of the effects of deforestation are the same for all types of forests. One of the catastrophic consequences of continued deforestation is mass species extinction, especially in the tropical rainforests, home to 50 to 70 percent of all the species on the planet. An estimated 20 to 75 species become extinct every day due to rainforest destruction. By 2015, six to 14 percent of all species on the planet today are expected to be extinct.[10]

Additionally, since the roots of trees and smaller forest cover stabilize the soil, deforestation allows potentially severe local damage from rainfall including erosion, flooding and landslides. Globally, deforestation affects the world's climate. A broad uprising of air follows the rainforests around the equator, driven, in part, by heat absorbed by tropical forests. This massive uprising helps drive the circulation patterns of the entire global atmosphere. Tropical deforestation can disrupt this process, resulting in reduced rainfall and altered weather conditions over a large portion of the globe.

All deforestation adds to the atmospheric pool of rising carbon dioxide emissions, hastening the onset of global warming. An intact forest naturally removes carbon dioxide from the air and stores it through the process of photosynthesis. When trees are cut down, this carbon dioxide is released into the atmosphere. Tropical deforestation releases 1.5 billion tons of carbon dioxide every year — that's 19 percent of the total global CO_2 emissions.[11]

Pleas for the Trees

Old growth forests, as well as tropical rainforests, play significant roles on Earth. Fossil records show that the forests of Southeast Asia have existed for 70 to 100 million years. This all stands to be drastically changed if nations continue to sacrifice the Earth's long-term health for short-term profits.

Unless actions are taken soon to end the steady assault on the world's old forests, little of these ecosystems will remain for the next generation. Given the pressures of population growth, poverty and debt, saving these forests will pose a number of challenges. International cooperation is required to reduce wood demand and implement sustainable forest management. Solutions might include distributing forest land more equitably among indigenous people, reducing population growth, or harvesting only the forest's naturally occurring produce, such as fruit, chocolate and rubber. Over $11 billion of these products are already traded internationally each year.[12] In the long term, this sort of forest management will reap greater profits than the limited returns of timber production and cattle ranching.

Governments and individuals need to educate themselves about the dangers of forest destruction, or ignorance will lead to further disaster. Above all, we need to realize that every acre of virgin forest that is destroyed takes centuries to replace.

Endnotes

[1] Cheri Sugal. "Forest Loss Continues." *Vital Signs 1997*. Washington D.C.: Worldwatch Institute, 1997. Original source: *State of the World's Forests 1997*. U.N. Food and Agriculture Organization.

[2] Rainforest Action Network homepage: www.ran.org.

[3] *State of the World's Forests 1997*. U.N. Food and Agriculture Organization.

[4] National Forest Service homepage www.fs.fed.us.

[5] *Environmental Almanac*. World Resources Institute. New York: Houghton Mifflin Co., 1993.

[6] Ibid.

[7] "What Is So Important About Rainforests?" National Audubon Society Fact Sheet.

[8] Op. cit. note 5.

[9] Environment Canada homepage www.doe.ca.

[10] Op. cit. note 5.

[11] Cheri Sugal. "Forest Loss Continues." *Vital Signs 1997*. Washington D.C.: Worldwatch Institute, 1997.

[12] Op. cit. note 3.

To Log or Not to Log

Introduction:

As the U.S. population increases, so does the demand for lumber. Each year, every person in the United States uses in wood and paper products the equivalent of one 18-inch diameter, 100-foot tall tree. The need for more timber has led to a debate concerning the remaining **old-growth** forest. Old-growth refers to native forest land which has never been logged, where trees can be as much as 10-feet wide, 275-feet tall and 1,120 years old. Currently, only two percent of U.S. forest area has never been logged, and these remaining virgin forests are disappearing at an alarming rate. This course of action alarms environmentalists who see the old-growth forests as a biologically rich area, valuable to both our country and planet. Of special concern is the logging practice known as clear cutting, when all trees in a region are cut down at once, which leads to soil erosion, silted rivers and an altered wildlife habitat. The following scenario illustrates how interests conflict when attempting to regulate land use.

The situation concerning this trial occurs in Pineville, an imaginary small mill town in Northern California. Pineville is surrounded by a vast amount of virgin forest land, most of which is owned by Logs-R-Us, a large logging company. Of the 9,000 Pineville inhabitants, 40% have jobs connected to the lumber industry. In addition to the loggers, many town members work in the mill, refining lumber to be shipped to other areas of the state to accommodate the growing housing needs. A final consideration is that the area is known for its excellent hiking and fishing spots. Some of the town merchants depend on out-of-towners stopping for supplies before heading into the wilderness.

Some time ago, Logs-R-Us obtained a cutting permit from the State Department of Forestry and began felling trees in order to keep up with the growing demand for lumber from other parts of the state. However, Green Rage, a national environmental group, has filed a suit requesting an injunction to cease the logging immediately. According to Green Rage, the land should be designated a natural treasure and allowed to exist in its pristine condition. The group cites a state statute which stipulates that, "private land owners shall manage their land responsibly in such a manner as to minimize negative impacts on the greater community and environment."

In an effort to be realistic while still pushing their ideal goal, Green Rage has filed their injunction in such a way that it could be accepted on either of two different levels. Their first claim for relief is to ban all commercial logging. If this claim is denied, their second claim for relief is to ban clear cutting, the most destructive kind of logging. It will be up to the jury to decide which option, if either, seems most reasonable and in accordance with the statute cited. (Note: Such a civil trial would not usually have a jury, but in the interests of involving as many class members as possible, normal legal procedure has been modified for this activity.)

Procedure:

1. To begin, explain that the class will spend the next week participating in a mock trial about a case involving the fate of part of the U.S. native forest. Tell students that they will each participate in the trial and will have to research their roles in order to accurately play their parts. Then read the scenario in the introduction aloud to the students. You may also wish to distribute copies of the scenario and procedure for students to refer to during the activity.

   Assign each class member a role to play during the mock trial and give each an applicable player's card. The activity is designed for 28 students. However, if you have more, you can add a bailiff, court reporter and members of the media. If you have fewer students, you can either reduce the numbers of lawyers by having one from each side question all witnesses or limit the number of witnesses, keeping the numbers for each side even, if possible. Ask students to read their roles and make a list of what they will need to do to prepare for their role. Encourage students to ask questions about their roles or the scenario.

2. Students should spend the next day or two researching their parts. Encourage students to make use of the Internet, library

Concept:
Competing interests are vying to control the future of the remaining native old-growth forests, a rapidly diminishing resource in the United States.

Objectives:
Students will be able to:
• Conduct research into an assigned role for a mock trial.
• Represent the interests of their selected role in a mock trial.
• Work with others to find mutually compatible solutions to difficult problems.

Subjects:
Social studies, environmental science, language arts, economics, government/civics

Skills:
Research, public speaking, persuasion, evaluation, critical thinking

Method:
By conducting a mock trial concerning the use of old-growth forests, students research perspectives of various parties in the case and learn about the complexities of trying to save forests for the "greater good."

Materials:
Role playing cards (duplicated from this activity)

Optional: A judge's gown and gavel

Optional: An instructional guide for mock trials, such as *Putting on Mock Trials*, published by the American Bar Association (see the "Mock Trial Resources" section on the next page for other titles). These guides offer hints on setting up a mock trial and provide simplified rules of evidence and court procedure for students to follow.

To Log or Not to Log

Mock Trial Resources:

Putting on Mock Trials, compiled by the American Bar Association, is available for $5.00 from the Special Committee of Youth Education for Citizenship, 750 North Lake Shore Drive, Chicago, IL 60611; 312/988-5555.

Street Law Mock Trial Manual by the National Institute for Citizen Education in the Law. Available for $12.95 through the Social Studies School Services Catalog, 10200 Jefferson Boulevard, Culver City, CA 90232-0802; 800/421-4246.

resources, community members and/or relevant organizations. Lawyers need to formulate their opening statements and prepare their witnesses. (Closing statements are flexible since they should also sum up weaknesses in the other side's arguments). Witnesses need to research their parts so that during the trial they can speak with authority in their area. For example, the biologist should know the arguments concerning loss of biodiversity and ecosystems related to the destruction of old-growth forests. Members of the jury will not need as much time to prepare and may need to be kept occupied with another assignment; much of their work will be after the trial when they need to deliberate and report back to the court.

(Optional: you may wish to bring a local judge, lawyer, or law student in to speak to the students about legal procedure, or possibly serve as judge during the trial. It is important to get someone who is comfortable around young people and understands that the main goal of the trial is to learn about the old-growth forest debate, not memorize courtroom procedure to the letter. If you do use a guest judge, make sure to provide him or her with a copy of the scenario and role cards before the trial, and have the students contribute to the thank you note afterward.)

3. The mock trial itself will probably take between two and three class periods. If possible, move the desks and chairs in the room to resemble a real courtroom. For an added touch of authenticity, encourage students to dress for the parts that they will be playing in the case.

After the judge is seated, the lawyers for the plaintiff and then defendant make their opening statements. In the opening statement, each lawyer explains what he or she intends to prove during the trial and outlines the key facts which will support his or her side. They speak without interruption from the opposing attorneys.

Next, witnesses are called, first for the plaintiff, and then for the defendant. Each witness undergoes direct examination from the attorney on the side he or she is representing and then cross-examination by the other side's attorney. During direct-examination, the lawyers are not allowed to ask questions which suggest the answer (e.g., you can't ask the president of the logging company, "Isn't it true that your company places environmental concerns as a primary goal in planning for the future?") However, during cross-examination, questions of this kind are acceptable.

After all witnesses have been heard, lawyers from both sides make their closing statements. This is when the lawyers really argue the case to the jury. They make a summation of all evidence and give a persuasive pitch for a decision in their favor. Finally, the jury deliberates and reports back to the class (or, for educational purposes, you could have the jury meet in front of the class so other students can see how the decision is made and which evidence is most persuasive). In civil cases, 9 out of the 12 jurors need to agree to have the verdict be binding.

Follow-up Activities:

1. After the trial, have students write reports about whether they agreed or disagreed with the decision of the jury, including what they would have done differently if they were an attorney for the plaintiff or defendant. Discuss ways the case might have been settled and negotiated out of court. Also, students could plan a field trip to the local court and see a real trial in action.

2. Students should look into land use in their area. Find out if there are any conflicts of interests between local parties. Does one party seem to be more concerned about short-term profits while another is concerned about the long-term consequences? How would students feel if one of the main sources of income in their community was shut down? The entire trial could be re-worked, using a different land-use scenario appropriate to the local situation, as a supplement or adaptation of this activity.

To Log or Not to Log

ROLES

Attorneys for the Plaintiff:

Green Rage hired members of the Environmental Legal Defense Group to represent them in this trial. The following lawyers are a part of the team:

Plaintiff Attorney #1: Opening Statement

At the beginning of the trial you inform the jury of the nature and facts of the case, without interruption from the defense. You summarize key facts each witness will bring out in testimony. Finally, you explain what you are asking the jury to decide (e.g., to stop all commercial logging of this old-growth forest).

Plaintiff Attorney #2: Direct Examination

You question all witnesses in favor of banning the logging. Your purpose is to present the evidence necessary to convince the jury to decide in favor of Green Rage. You want to present your witnesses in the best possible light and establish their credibility.

Plaintiff Attorney #3: Cross Examination

You question witnesses called by the defense (i.e., those in favor of logging). Your purpose is to obtain admissions from these witnesses which tend to prove your case and to discredit these witnesses. (Hint: "Yes or no" questions tend to be more effective than questions which ask the witnesses to explain in their own words.)

Plaintiff Attorney #4: Closing Statement

You summarize the highlights of the testimony as it supports your case and undermines Logs-R-Us' case, using actual examples from the trial that you have written down. Persuasively request that the jury decide in favor of Green Rage to stop the logging.

Witnesses for the Plaintiff:

Biologist

As an expert in the field of biology, you need to educate the court about the importance of old-growth forests in the biosphere. You should emphasize the loss of biological diversity when an entire ecosystem is destroyed.

Environmentalist for Green Rage

You believe that people need to look beyond short-term gains and protect the environment for the good of future generations. Try to emphasize the "big picture" loss if old-growth forests are destroyed.

Chairperson of Outdoor Enthusiasts Club

As one who appreciates the exceptional beauty of this wilderness area, your testimony should illustrate an alternate use of the forest which will inflict far less damage than clear cutting the land.

Native American

Your ancestors have lived in harmony with the land for many years before the white man came and began destroying the forests. Your testimony should illustrate that land ownership should not necessarily involve the right to damage something that belongs to everyone.

To Log or Not to Log

Attorneys for the Defense:

Logs-R-Us has hired a prestigious legal firm, Powers and Dinero, from San Francisco to try the case. The following lawyers are a part of the team:

Defense Attorney #1: Opening Statement

You speak at the beginning of the trial after the plaintiff's opening statement. Your purpose is to deny that Green Rage has a valid claim and, in a general way, outline the facts from the standpoint of Logs-R-Us. You will not be interrupted by the plaintiff during this speech.

Defense Attorney #2: Direct Examination

You question all witnesses in favor of continued logging. Your purpose is to present the evidence necessary to convince the jury to decide in favor of Logs-R-Us. You want to present the witnesses in the best possible light and establish their credibility.

Defense Attorney #3: Cross Examination

You question the witnesses called by the plaintiff (i.e. those opposed to logging). Your purpose is to secure admissions from these witnesses which will be favorable to your case and discredit the witnesses. (Hint: "Yes or no" questions tend to be more effective than questions which ask the witnesses to explain in their own words.)

Defense Attorney #4: Closing Statement

You summarize the highlights of testimony as it supports your case and undermines Green Rage's case, using actual examples from the trial that you have written down. Persuasively request that the jury decide in favor of Logs-R-Us and allow the logging to continue.

Witnesses for the Defense:

Developer

You need to fulfill a contract to build new houses in the Los Angeles area and you were counting on this lumber from Logs-R-Us. You should speak of the growing demands for housing and other wood products in the state.

Pineville Chamber of Commerce Representative

Since a large percentage of Pineville's citizens depend on the logging industry, you are concerned for the future of the town's economy if the major source of revenue is removed. You should speak of the numbers of jobs lost, and the probable fate of those who are untrained in other professions.

President of Logs-R-Us

You need to convince the jury that your use of the land is acting for the greater good of the community and environment. You might want to talk about services your company provides to the community and efforts the company makes to replant logged forest areas.

Pineville Mill Worker

If Logs-R-Us is prevented from logging, your mill will undoubtedly close and you will be out of a job. You have a family of five to feed and don't want to go on welfare. Also, since Pineville will be economically depressed, you will probably have to move your family to another town, leaving your neighborhood and friends.

Members of the Jury

Members of the Jury (twelve students)

You need to listen carefully to all points of view represented in the trial since it is your job to determine the facts in the case. After everyone has finished, it will be up to you and the 11 others to decide in favor of either Green Rage or Logs-R-Us and tell your decision to the court. In order to reach a valid verdict, at least 9 of you must agree on the final recommendation to the court. (Hint: Your decision will be influenced by how you interpret the state statute cited in the case, which reads, "Private land owners shall manage their land responsibly in such a manner as to minimize negative impacts of the greater community and environment.")

Go for the Green

Introduction:

Tropical rainforest destruction is an alarming issue, commanding the attention of scientists, environmentalists, and politicians worldwide. There are no easy solutions because deforestation is occurring for many reasons. Governments, banking institutions, indigenous people, loggers and other groups differ on how the rainforests should be used. The pursuit of "green" currency may place the "green" ecosystem in jeopardy. The following game illustrates the difficulty of maintaining an ecological and economic balance when addressing rainforest issues.

Preparation:

The game is best played in groups of 3 to 5 students. You will need to reproduce the game board as well as the Choice and Risk cards so that each group has all three. (Note: Copying the Choice and Risk cards on different colors of paper avoids confusion.) Each stack of cards should then be placed face down on the game board. You also need to decide what you will use as game pieces. This could range from pen caps to something you may have in your room that is related to the subject (i.e., rubber bands, sticks of gum, nuts, etc.).

Rules of the Game:

1. Each player will be responsible for keeping track of his/her points through each round. Before the game begins, make a chart on a piece of paper with two headings —"Environmental points" and "Wealth points."

2. Each player will start with 4 environmental points and 400 wealth points. *The winner of the game is the first player to get 10 environmental points and 1,000 wealth points.*

3. The players may place their markers anywhere on the game board to start. Movement around the board is in the clockwise direction. They can roll the dice to determine the order of the turn.

4. Each player will roll the dice and move around the board for the designated spaces. After landing on a space, follow the directions given on the board.

5. If you are required to pick a Choice or Risk card, pick from the top of the pile and put the card at the bottom of the pile when you are through.

6. A player may not choose an option on a Risk or Choice card which would put him/her into debt. For example, if a player has 300 wealth points and he/she picks a Choice card that has an option to lose 400 wealth points, this option cannot be chosen because the player does not have enough wealth points. But, if a card requires a player to pay 300 wealth points and the player only has 200 wealth points, that player will be in debt for 100 wealth points. In other words, a player cannot voluntarily choose to go into debt.

Note to the Teacher: If you find there is no winner by the end of the allotted time, reward each player 100 wealth points for each environmental point and total each player's wealth points. The player with the highest number of wealth points will be the winner. It is advisable not to tell the students of this rule because it may change their strategy when playing.

Follow-up Activities:

1. Lead a discussion on the outcome of each group's game and what students learned from their choices.

2. Have students research one of the specific areas discussed on the Choice or Risk cards (for example, the effects of rainforest destruction on the indigenous peoples).

3. The class together could choose a specific rainforest of interest and conduct an in-depth study of all the aspects of the controversy. The students could be broken into groups and assigned specific subtopics to research.

Concept:
The earth's rainforests are irreplaceable ecosystems that hold a significant place in the global environment. However, economic interests often pose obstacles to rainforest preservation.

Objectives:
Students will be able to:
• Make decisions based on qualitative criteria.
• Present the rationale behind their decisions to fellow classmates.

Subjects:
Social studies, environmental science, biology, economics

Skills:
Decision making, strategizing

Method:
Through the playing of the board game that accompanies this activity, students are presented with various scenarios that help them gain an appreciation for the complexities of making decisions that serve to protect rainforest lands.

Materials:
Choice and Risk cards and game board (duplicated from this activity)
Dice
Game pieces (be creative)

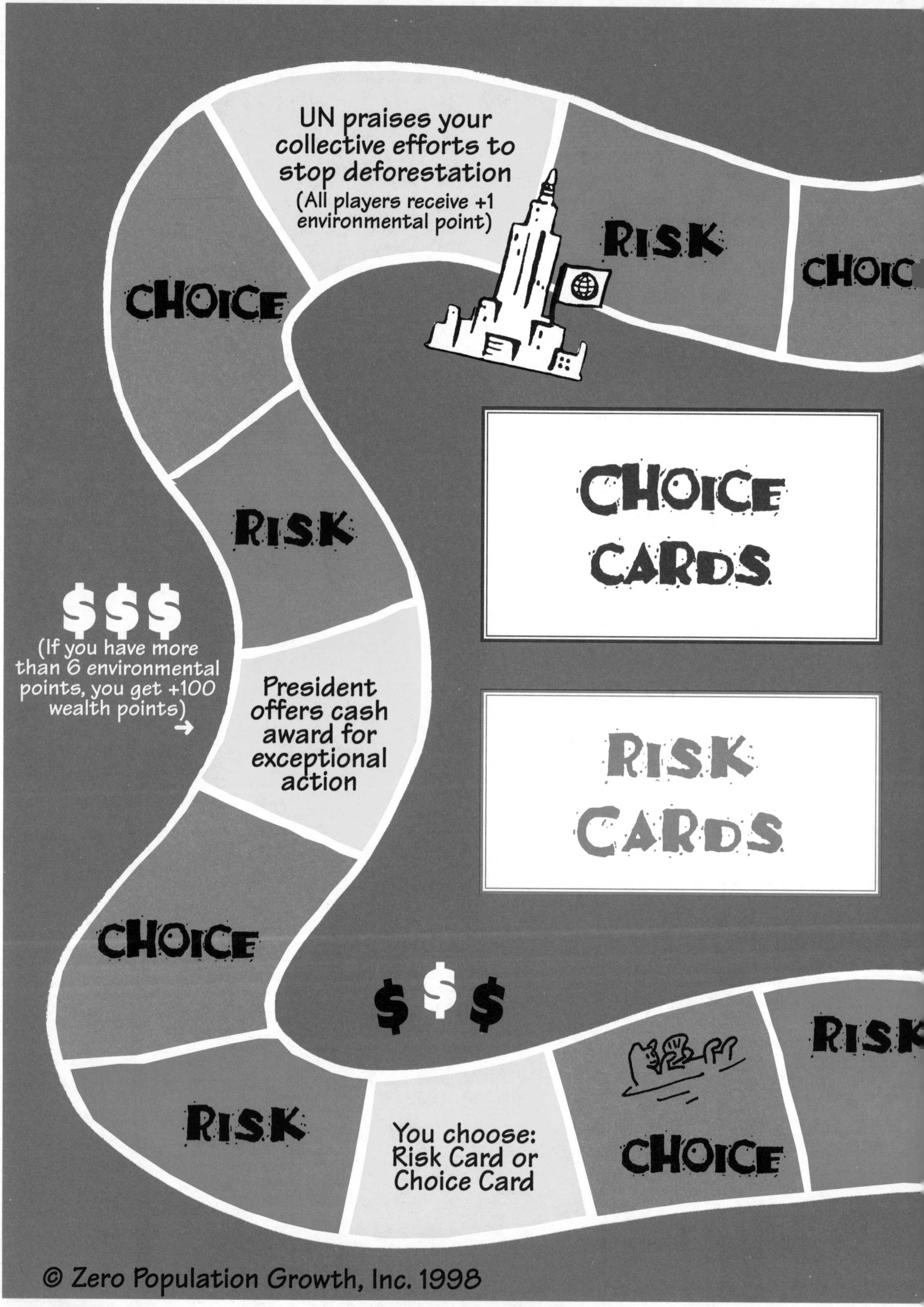

UN praises your collective efforts to stop deforestation
(All players receive +1 environmental point)

RISK

CHOIC

CHOICE

CHOICE CARDS

RISK

RISK CARDS

$$$
(If you have more than 6 environmental points, you get +100 wealth points)
→

President offers cash award for exceptional action

CHOICE

$ $ $

RISK

You choose: Risk Card or Choice Card

CHOICE

RISK

"GO FOR THE GREEN"

Heavy rains and soil erosion cause a destructive mud slide (-75 wealth points)

RISK

CHOICE

Time Magazine prints your article on rainforest destruction (+1 environmental point)

CHOICE

RISK

International Holiday-no activity (Miss a turn)

Record Nut Harvest (+100 wealth points)

RISK

CHOICE

RISK

Go for the Green

Choice Card

You are the Minister of Agriculture for Thailand. Your job is on the line due to the lack of progress your country has made in dealing with the problem of feeding an increasing population. You can:

• Decide to tear down rainforest land as a desperate measure to plant more crops for food (- 1 environmental point, + 250 wealth points) **or:**

• Make a controversial political move and propose seeking assistance from industrial countries and thereby going deeper into debt (+ 100 wealth points) **or:**

• Make a stand for the environment and resign from the job, stating your opposition to destroying more rainforest and emphasizing the need for a comprehensive population policy (+ 3 environmental points, - 200 wealth points).

Choice Card

You run a small-scale mining operation in the Amazon region, bulldozing and dredging stream banks in search of gold ore. The government has recently enacted new environmental regulations on mining practices in your region. In order to comply with these regulations your company would have to forfeit almost one year's profit. You can:

• Follow the regulations to the letter and write your money off (+ 2 environmental points, - 250 wealth points) **or:**

• Use a favor you have with local officials to postpone an inspection of your operation, giving you a year or so leeway (+ 1 environmental point, - 100 wealth points) **or:**

• Go deeper into the forest and set up a secret mining operation illegally, disregarding all environmental or health regulations (- 2 environmental points, + 250 wealth points).

Choice Card

You are aware of the increased energy needs created by a rapidly growing population. As a graduate of a prominent Brazilian engineering university, you have two job offers in the energy field. You can:

• Work with a low-paying, non-profit group, designing and building an experimental solar energy system resting in the rainforest canopy (+ 2 environmental points) **or:**

• Work on the operation and maintenance of a hydroelectric dam which generates large amounts of electricity, but also damages the surrounding rainforest (- 1 environmental point, + 350 wealth points).

Choice Card

Giggley's Gum, Inc. has offered to double its order for chicle latex (used to make chewing gum) next year. However, your land is currently producing as much chicle latex as possible and you are unable to fill the order. You can:

• Tell Giggley's you are unable to provide that amount of product (+ 1 environmental point) **or:**

• Slash and burn surrounding rainforest to cultivate new plants and promise Giggley's you will fill the order within a year or two (- 1 environmental point, + 200 wealth points).

Go for the Green

Choice Card

Due to an increased number of espresso drinkers worldwide, demand for the coffee beans from your land has risen dramatically. You can:

• Meet the demand by over-planting and cutting down surrounding land. Although this process will destroy the land within five years, you will have made enough money to retire (- 2 environmental points, + 300 wealth points) **or:**

• Maintain production schedule, hoping that the demand will continue indefinitely, and allowing the land to survive for other uses (+ 2 environmental points, - 150 wealth points).

Choice Card

You go to the grocery store for your weekly items. You see that many of the store brand products are cheaper, but you usually shop environmentally by paying attention to packaging and looking for products harvested from the tropical rainforests. You can:

• Purchase the store brand items to save some money (- 1 environmental point, + 50 wealth points) **or:**

• Spend the extra money on the sustainable products and support the rainforest region (+ 1 environmental point, - 50 wealth points).

Choice Card

You live in North America and raise exotic birds. Much of the rainforest habitat of your favorite species has been destroyed, due to increased demands on the forest caused by overpopulation and irresponsible practices. The bird is in danger of becoming extinct. You can:

• Stop importing the birds from the rainforest where they have been captured and removed from their natural habitat (+ 1 environmental point) **or:**

• Create a private bird sanctuary and continue importing and breeding these birds, figuring you can provide a safer environment than the decreasing forest (+ 2 environmental point, - 150 wealth points) **or:**

• Capitalize on their increasing rarity by importing and breeding the birds to sell for profit (- 1 environmental point, + 200 wealth points).

Choice Card

You own a small cashew plantation. The large American company Nifty Nuts, Inc. has decided not to renew your contract for cashew shipments. You can:

• Hold on to your land, forgo the money from this year's harvest, and hope for better luck next year (+ 1 environmental point, - 150 wealth points) **or:**

• Join forces with several other small farmers, combining land so that you can share profits and losses (+ 50 wealth points) **or:**

• Sell the land to a big cattle rancher who needs more grazing room (- 1 environmental point, + 150 wealth points).

Go for the Green

Game Cards

Choice Card

You are a manufacturer of rubber wetsuits in Los Angeles. You have two options for sources for the raw rubber. You can:

• Buy from small farmers, who extract the rubber sustainably, at a higher price (+ 1 environmental point, - 100 wealth points) **or:**

• Buy from large plantations who have cleared forest for their rubber crops (- 1 environmental point, + 150 wealth points).

Choice Card

The government of the Democratic Republic of Congo has offered you a contract to build a road into one of the rainforests to facilitate commercial game hunting. You can:

• Refuse the job, explaining that large-scale commercial hunting leads to extinction and that the road construction will completely disturb the ecosystem (+ 2 environmental points, - 300 wealth points) **or:**

• Accept the job, reasoning that otherwise someone else will do it, and people need to eat (- 2 environmental points, + 300 wealth points).

Choice Card

A new plant species has been discovered on land you own in the rainforest. Scientists believe the plant may have healing powers. You can:

• Sell the land to the government who intends research this plant — although you cannot be assured this government will stay in power to conduct the necessary research (+ 150 wealth points) **or:**

• Keep the land in its natural state and receive a small stipend from an international science group to conduct its own research (+ 1 environmental point, + 50 wealth points) **or:**

• Continue to slash and burn the land for profit (- 2 environmental points, + 300 wealth points).

Choice Card

As a National Geographic photographer assigned to capture the beauty of Indonesia's rainforest, you are determined to travel deep into the heart of the forest. When making travel plans you can:

• Take a plane operated by a large-scale developing company, lasting about an hour (- 1 environmental point, + 1 extra turn) **or:**

• Hire a guide, buy provisions, and travel the distance by river and on foot, taking two extra weeks (+ 1 environmental point, - 75 wealth points).

Go for the Green

Choice Card

You are a leader of a group of migrant peasants in the Ivory Coast. Due to population pressures and overuse of rainforest land, your people are forced to travel from area to area within the forest for fuel, food and shelter. Now environmental and government groups are pressuring you to give up your lifestyle so the land can be preserved. You can:

• Accept their arguments that your practices are harming the rainforest and move your people to an area where you do not know how to survive (+ 2 environmental points, - 300 wealth points) **or:**

• Continue to live off the land as long as you possibly can and petition to continue your way of life (- 1 environmental point, + 150 wealth points).

Choice Card

You are the president of Sunny Drinks, Inc. Your company's product, Truly Fruity, is not selling because it doesn't have enough tropical fruit flavor. You can:

• Use "incentives" to encourage his tropical fruit supplier to triple the output of their crops without having to purchase extra land (- 2 environmental points, + 250 wealth points) **or:**

• Spend the extra money on fruit which is sustainably harvested, basing a new ad campaign about the rainforests and the need to preserve them (+ 1 environmental point) **or:**

• Cut your losses and abandon the line altogether, concentrating on your popular Prunetta Punch (+ 50 wealth points).

Choice Card

You are a young entrepreneur and have successfully opened a small furniture shop. A salesman comes into your shop with beautifully made mahogany desks, asking an unbelievably low price. You can:

• Refuse to purchase the items because mahogany comes from the rainforest and you boycott such products (+ 1 environmental point, - 100 wealth points) **or:**

• Purchase many of the desks to sell in your store (- 1 environmental point, + 200 wealth points).

Choice Card

You are a cocoa supplier for Sweet Dreams, Inc. which is coming out with a new product called Choco-Caramel Delight. The company has strong indicators that this will be a smash so they want to increase production. You can:

• Increase land for planting cocoa by destroying an area of rainforest you had set aside for public relations reasons (- 2 environmental point, + 250 wealth points) **or:**

• Continue to produce the same amount of cocoa and send Sweet Dreams elsewhere for the additional need (+ 1 environmental point).

Go for the Green

Choice Card

You have handled guns your whole life. One day at the shooting range, you are approached by two businessmen who proposition you to go to Central Africa and commercial game hunt. You can:

- Decide to go because the money is good and you love hunting. However, the numbers they are asking you to kill could have a detrimental effect on the survival of several species (- 2 environmental points, + 300 wealth points) **or:**

Strike a bargain with the businessmen and agree to kill a certain quota of game that will allow the species to continue to survive (+ 1 environmental point, + 50 wealth points) **or:**

- Decide to decline the offer in hopes of stopping the possible wholesale slaughter of several game species. (+ 3 environmental points, - 300 wealth points)

Choice Card

You have won the state lottery and decide to go on your dream vacation to the Malaysian rainforests. When making your travel arrangements you have two options. You can:

- Take advantage of a "budget deal" offered by your local travel agency , which charters an American plane and uses American guides (- 1 environmental point, + 150 wealth points) **or:**
- Pay more for an "eco-tour" which emphasizes learning about the environment and ensures money goes to the local economy, lessening economic pressures to cut down the forest for natives (+ 1 environmental point, - 150 wealth points).

Choice Card

A world-famous Indian chef has realized the missing ingredient in one of her new specialties. All she needs is a spice that is found in a plant indigenous to the Madagascar rainforest. This plant is on your rainforest land, but has been preserved because a specific species of lemur feeds only on this plant. You can:

- Let your stomach do the talking and extract the spice from the plant at the expense of the lemur (- 2 environmental points, + 300 wealth points) **or:**
- Send the chef elsewhere which will certainly please the lemur (+ 2 environmental points) **or:**
- Allow the chef to extract the spice from a portion of your land, thereby preserving the lemur (+ 1 environmental point, + 100 wealth points).

Choice Card

You have received a large sum of money from a film distributor for a documentary you made about the plight of the tropical rainforests. You can:

- Give the money back to the countries where you shot the film, by setting up conservation and service groups (+ 3 environmental points, - 200 wealth points) **or:**
- Keep the money and buy yourself some well deserved treats (+ 200 wealth points)

Go for the Green

Risk Card

You are a subsistence farmer struggling to make a living off your plot of rainforest. A large cattle rancher is urging you to sell your land in order to tear down your plot for grazing. If you have 500 wealth points, you are able to resist (+ 1 environmental point). However if you have less than 500 wealth points, you are forced to sell out (- 1 environmental point).

Risk Card

Due to improper maintenance, a fuel storage tank for logging equipment leaks toxic substances into the water supply. You lose 2 environmental points unless you have 500 wealth points to take care of the problem before significant damage is done.

Risk Card

A huge forest fire is raging throughout Indonesia's East Kalimanton. If you have virgin/unlogged forest (5 environmental points or more), you are okay. If you have logged forest, you lose it all (- 300 wealth points).

Risk Card

A North American zoo would like to find a mate for their female macaw. They want to breed the species because it is considered endangered. If you have enough unlogged forest (5 environmental points or more), you can take advantage of the zoo's offer to pay 400 wealth points for a male macaw.

Risk Card

A heavy rainfall floods your land and causes tremendous erosion because you were forced to live on marginal ground due to overpopulation. You lose 150 wealth points.

Risk Card

An International Global Warming Coalition is offering financial assistance to those who have demonstrated dedication to preserving the rainforests. If you have 5 or more environmental points, you get 200 wealth points.

Risk Card

An elderly, eccentric landowner is offering to sell a large tract of rainforest to someone willing to commit to preserving the land. You may trade 150 wealth points for 2 environmental points, if you want to do this.

Risk Card

Large amounts of curare are found on your segment of the rainforest. (Curare is used as a muscle relaxant for surgery). A hospital chain from Europe gives you 150 wealth points for your supply.

Risk Card

A wealthy European perfume manufacturer is interested in extracting oils from some rainforest plants (bay oil, camphor oil, eucalyptus oil, patchouli oil, rosewood oil, sandalwood oil, and ylang-ylang). If you have 5 or more environmental points, you receive 100 wealth points from this company.

Risk Card

You are throwing a large party and want to serve some ecologically sound food, however you have financial concerns to consider. If you have 400 or more wealth points, have a "rainforest caterer" deliver nuts, dried fruits, palm hearts, etc. (+ 1 environmental point) or: if you have under 400 wealth points, forgo the environmental snacks and buy pretzels.

Go for the Green

Risk Card

You and your family are attacked by guerrillas fighting civil war in Mozambique. Unfortunately, your son is severely hurt. If you have 400 wealth points, he can get the necessary medical attention. However, if you do not and he should die, your number of laborers will be too low and you will be forced to sell your rainforest land to the loggers (- 2 environmental points).

Risk Card

Your deforestation practices in the Himalayan mountains helped contribute to the 12 million acres of damaged land in India (- 1 environmental point).

Risk Card

This is your lucky day! On your way to an important conference on saving the rainforest, you are seated next to a famous rock star on the plane. You convince her not only to attend the conference, but to promote your cause on her next album (+ 2 environmental points).

Risk Card

Your new line of "rainforest cosmetics" is a big hit. Not only is it selling well (+ 100 wealth points), but it is raising awareness of rainforest destruction and promoting sustainable harvesting (+ 1 environmental point).

Risk Card

As a wealthy alumnus of an Ivy League university, you are approached by a group of students trying to start a conservation biology program. If you want to support their efforts, you may trade 150 wealth points for 2 environmental points.

Risk Card

You have clear-cut the rainforest to provide pastures for your cattle. However, within a year, the land is invaded by toxic weeds which kill all your cattle (- 1 environmental point, - 100 wealth points).

Risk Card

Congratulations! Your proposed "debt for nature" trade between a U.S. bank and the government of the Democratic Republic of Congo was adopted (+ 1 environmental point).

Risk Card

You have developed a series of rainforest preservation T-shirts which have become a huge success with teenagers (+ 1 environmental point, + 100 wealth points).

Food and Hunger

Feeding the Global Family

Anyone who has ever driven through the endless amber waves of grain in America's Midwest may find it difficult to believe that we may soon be in the midst of a global food shortage. Presently 841 million, or one out of seven, people worldwide do not have enough food to sustain a normal, active life.[1] Around two billion people, or one out of three, are **malnourished**, That is they do not receive the proper balance of nutrients; many do not receive enough protein.[2]

Today if a person or family goes hungry, whether in North America or sub-Saharan Africa, it is usually because of poverty; they do not have money to buy enough food. Poverty and restricted access to food can arise from many different causes, including unequal distribution of wealth or economic opportunities, environmental degradation, or discrimination based on race, gender or age.[3] However, if the world's population continues to grow faster than food production (as it does right now), not having enough food to go around may become a significant cause of hunger in generations to come. As more and more people must be fed on the food produced each year, what people eat, and how food is distributed will play a larger role in whether there will be enough for everyone.

According to Lester Brown, president of Worldwatch Institute, the world could support 2.5 billion people on a North American-style diet high in animal protein (well below half of the world's present population), five billion on a "Mediterranean" diet, heavy in fruits, vegetables and grains, and ten billion people on an Indian-style diet, which consists mostly of a starchy staple food.[4] Brown states that the healthiest of these three diets is the Mediterranean — however, at current grain production levels, world population has already outstripped the Earth's ability to provide the amount of grain to allow all the world's inhabitants to eat such a diet.

People Outpacing Food

Annual grain harvests have more than tripled since the 1950s, and recent years have seen record grain harvests.[5] That's the good news. What's the bad news? Over the last decade, growth in the amount of grain harvested each year has slowed significantly, and is not increasing as fast as the world's population. This means that the amount of grain per person is falling. In 1996, the amount of grain per person was 313 kilograms, down from the peak of 346 kilograms per person in 1984.[6] Population growth is the primary cause of this drop.

Food to feed the Earth's people comes from two sources: the land and the sea. Since 1988, the total pounds of fish taken out of the oceans each year has remained fairly constant, and no longer increases with increased investment.[7] This indicates that we have reached the sustainable limit for harvesting fish. Since the human population is still growing, the amount of fish per person is already declining. We cannot count on this resource to meet the multiplying demand for food.

Meeting the increasing demand for food created by the 84 million people added to the world each year will depend on increasing grain yields, the amount of food that comes from the land. This depends on two primary resources — land and water, both of which are themselves strained by the pressures of a growing population.

Gene Basset reprinted by permission of NEA, Inc.

The Production Equation

Mathematically, the amount of grain produced in the world each year depends on two variables: the area of land harvested and the amount of grain harvested per unit of land. In 1981, the amount of land harvested reached a peak at 732 million hectares. By 1996, the

Feeding the Global Family

amount of land area harvested had dwindled to 696 million hectares, a decrease of 3.7 percent.[8] When taking population growth into account over the same time period, the decrease amounts to a 25 percent drop in land area harvested per person. Why is the total amount of farm land decreasing each year? The two major causes are **urbanization** and **soil degradation**.

Urban Growth

Not only is the world population growing, but each year a larger and larger percentage of those people are living in cities. All over the world, valuable cropland is being paved over as cities grow outward. For example, more than half of all U.S. agricultural production comes from counties on the edge of expanding cities. For each person added to the U.S. population,

about one acre of land is required for urbanization and highways.[9] An area the size of two New York Cities was paved over each year between 1982 and 1992.[10] On the Indonesian island of Java, enough cropland was lost to urban expansion in 1994 alone to supply rice to over 300,000 people.[11] Around the world, an area of cropland between the size of Virginia and Oregon is lost to urbanization each year.[12] The ongoing trend of urbanization will continue to take more and more cropland out of agricultural use.

Blowing in the Wind

Soil degradation also reduces the area of land available for agriculture. The most common cause of soil degradation is **erosion**, the carrying away by wind and water of the thin layer of topsoil which holds all the nutrients

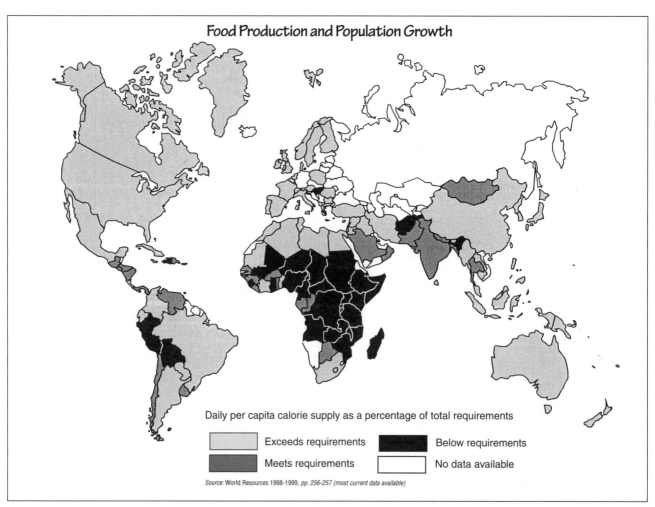

Food Production and Population Growth

Daily per capita calorie supply as a percentage of total requirements

- Exceeds requirements
- Meets requirements
- Below requirements
- No data available

Source: World Resources 1998-1999, pp. 256-257 (most current data available)

Feeding the Global Family

necessary to grow crops. Eleven percent of the world's cropland in 1989 was "strongly eroded" and was not able to be used for production.[13] During the past 40 years, about 30 percent of the world's arable land had been lost through erosion.[14] Erosion is frequently caused by overgrazing, deforestation, agricultural mismanagement, and overharvesting of fuelwood. These activities, in turn, are frequently the result of poverty and the unequal distribution of land. As population growth increases the demand for land, poor farmers are forced to work marginal land, such as hillsides and land cut from tropical forests, which erodes easily.

Increased irrigation, which has allowed for greater crop production in past years, is also a cause of cropland damage. Whereas rainwater is essentially distilled, irrigation water contains salts which are left in the topsoil upon evaporation. This process, called **salinization**, removes 1.5 to 2.5 million hectares per year from agricultural production (an area larger than Connecticut). The remaining salinized area still used produces lower yields, and will continue to produce even lower yields as salinization gets worse.[15]

Wade in the Water

The yield per acre part of the production equation depends largely on the percent of land area under irrigation. The tripling of the world grain harvest since 1950 has been due not to great increases in land area harvested, but to the spread of irrigation.[16] Irrigation improves yields in itself, but also enables crops to get the most nutrients from the fertilizers applied to them.

However, the amount of irrigated land per person has been falling since 1979. The major reason for this is that the amount of water available per person to use for irrigation is diminishing.[17] More and more water that could be used for agriculture now has to be diverted to cities in response to rapid population increases in urban areas. Irresponsible use of water for irrigation, such as drawing water out of aquifers faster than it is being replaced, is another cause of diminishing water supplies.

Slow growth of both land area used in agriculture and grain yields per acre will make it increasingly difficult for increases in food supply to keep up with the rapid increases in world population.

An Unhealthy Diet

In order to satisfy the North American demand for meat and dairy products, much of the prime agricultural land in the U.S. is used inefficiently, feeding animals, rather than providing food for the world's growing human population. One acre of prime land can produce 20,000 pounds of apples, 40,000 pounds of potatoes or 250 pounds of beef.[18] American livestock consume 80 percent of the corn grown in the United States.[19] It is estimated that 100 million people could be adequately nourished using the land, water and energy that would be freed from growing livestock feed if Americans reduced their intake of meat by just ten percent.[20]

This reduction in meat consumption would save water as well, since about 1,000 liters of water are required to produce one kilogram of grain, versus 100,000 liters of water to produce one kilogram of beef.[21] All of these facts amount to a compelling case that our diet choices have a substantial impact on land and environmental degradation, health, worldwide hunger and food distribution.

Rich farmland is also misused in many developing countries where large landowners grow **cash crops**, such as cotton, coffee or tobacco instead of food. To the owners, land becomes an investment, not a source of food for the people who live on it. Meanwhile, an estimated 40,000 people die each day in the world due to hunger or hunger-related causes.[22]

Environmental Threats

Virtually all forms of global environmental degradation are adversely affecting food production. Damage to crops from air pollution and acid rain can be seen in industrial and developing countries alike. Global climate change, brought on by the production of greenhouse gases, poses other threats to crops. Scientists predict hot, dry summers ahead for America's breadbasket in the Midwest as a result of climate change.

Just as industrial practices threaten farmland, modern agricultural practices often pose

Feeding the Global Family

threats to other ecosystems. The water pollution attributable to U.S. agriculture, including runoff of soil, pesticides and chemical fertilizers, is greater than all municipal and industrial sources combined.[23] A growing demand for chemical-free produce in this country has led some farmers to experiment with **organic farming** practices.

Although the definition of **organic** varies from country to country, use of more sustainable farming practices has increased across the globe. Between 1987 and 1993, organically farmed area expanded fourfold in the European Union. In the United States, sales of organic produce doubled between 1990 and 1994, and in India, the Karnataka Farmers Association has formed an International Institute for Sustainable Agriculture representing one-third of farmers in the state in an attempt to decrease the use of chemical pesticides.[24]

A Sustainable Future

If we hope to prevent a world food crisis, we must commit ourselves to sustainable agricultural practices. Sustainable agriculture means using the land in such a way as to safeguard its natural productive capacity for generations to come. It is not enough to focus on the most efficient and profitable way to grow food today. Ensuring that an ample amount of land will remain for tomorrow's food supply must also be our concern. For example, destroying rainforest to create cropland provides productive land for only a few years before topsoil erodes. Leaving the rainforests intact and harvesting renewable products, such as fruits and nuts, ensures a steady stream of produce indefinitely.

With such finite cropland, we must use this precious resource judiciously. Diversification of crops, moderate irrigation and responsible land management are just a few ways to produce food more sustainably. Eating a wide variety of foods and not depending heavily on animal products (as recommended in the USDA's Food Pyramid), will allow us to use land more efficiently to feed more people. Better distribution of available food is also essential in preventing mass starvation in poor countries.

While there are multiple ways to address the problem of global hunger, most experts agree that unless population pressures ease, a lasting victory over hunger will not be achieved. Feeding people adequately into the 21st century will depend on slowing world population growth to bring it in line with food production.

Endnotes

[1] *Hunger in a Global Economy: Hunger 1998.* Silver Spring, MD: Bread for the World Institute, 1997.

[2] *Bridging the Gap.* Geneva: The World Health Organization, 1995.

[3] Op. cit. note 1, p. 13.

[4] Lester R. Brown. "Facing the Prospect of Food Scarcity." *State of the World 1997.* Washington, DC: Worldwatch Institute, 1997. p. 35.

[5] Lester R. Brown. "World Grain Harvest Sets Record." Vital Signs 1997. Washington DC: Worldwatch Institute, 1997. p. 26.

[6] Ibid.

[7] Op. cit. note 4, p. 24.

[8] Op. cit note 4, p. 40.

[9] Personal communication, David Pimentel, Professor of Agriculture and Life Sciences, Cornell University. April 27, 1998.

[10] Gary Gardner. "Preserving Global Cropland." *State of the World 1997.* Washington, DC: Worldwatch Institute, 1997, p. 47.

[11] Ibid., p. 45-46

[12] See note 9.

[13] Op. cit. note 10, p. 50.

[14] D. Pimentel, et al. "Environmental and Economic Costs of Soil Erosion and Conservation Benefits." *Science,* 267: 1117-1123, 1995.

[15] Op. cit. note 10, p. 50.

[16] Op. cit. note 4, p. 28

[17] Ibid., pp. 29, 31.

[18] Earthsave homepage. Original source: Tom Aldridge and Herb Schlubach, "Water Requirements for Food Production," *Soil and Water,* no. 38 (Fall 1978), University of California Cooperative Extension, 13017; Paul and Anne Ehrlich, *Population, Resources, Environment* (San Francisco: Freemen, 1972), p. 75-76.

[19] Earthsave homepage: http://www.earthsave.org. Original source for corn: USDA, Agricultural Statistics 1989; p. 31, table 40 "Corn Supply and Disappearance US, 1974-1988."

[20] Earthsave homepage. Original source: Lester Brown, as quoted by Resenberger, "Curb on US Waste Urged to help the World's Hungry," *New York Times,* November 14, 1974, adjusted using figures from USDA, Agricultural Statistics 1989, table 74, "High Protein Feeds," and table 75, "Feed concentrates Fed to Livestock and Poultry."

[21] D. Pimental, et al. "Water Resources: Agriculture, the Environment, and Society." *BioScience,* 47(2): 97-106, 1997.

[22] Earthsave homepage. Original source: Patricia Allen, "The Human Face of Sustainable Agriculture," Issue Paper No. 4, November 1994, University of California, Santa Cruz, Center for Agroecology and Sustainable Food Systems.

[23] Earthsave homepage. Original source: Jim Mason, "Fowling the Waters," *E Magazine,* Sep/Oct 1995, p. 33.

[24] Gary Gardner. "Organic Farming Up Sharply." *Vital Signs 1996.* Washington, D.C.: Worldwatch Institute, 1996. pp. 110-111.

The Hunger Banquet

Introduction:

This luncheon-game is meant to simulate for students some of the inequities of the present socioeconomic world situation and some of the feelings of helplessness and frustration that result from these inequities. By enabling the participants to deal with a concrete experience of purchasing power, the exercise becomes a learning tool that explores global imbalances. Through this luncheon, students will become more familiar with the disparity of resources around the world and may then make the links to the disparity of resources in the United States.

Procedure:

Set-up:

The game is best played with at least 30 people in order to have a visible proportion of rich and poor. It is a good exercise to coordinate with other classrooms during lunch period or on activity night. You might use the following figures in proportioning your players and resources.

Area	Population Distribution	Players	Resources Distribution	Chips
Industrial/ First World*	15%	4	80%	40
Transitional/ Second World*	10%	3	15%	8
Developing/ Third World*	75%	23	5%	3

Economic classification based on per capita GNP as listed in the World Bank, World Population Projections 1994-95 (First World: $8,356 or more; Second World: $2,696-$8,355; Third World: below $2,695).
+Wealth distribution based on a comparison of per capita GNP averages as outlined above and as differentiated by reliance on the export of raw materials to earn foreign exchange. The classifications and income concentrations are cited from World Resources: A Guide to the Global Environment 1996-97.

You will have to adapt these figures if you have more or fewer players, but you can base this on the population distribution. The above figures are estimates drawn from multiple sources and therefore you may want to draw more precise figures on particular countries from the cited sources.

There should be two persons available for selling food and visas.

The game is prepared around the setting of a luncheon buffet. Feel free to adapt the menu provided.

The food or buffet table should be made to look as attractive as possible. A beautifully furnished table and chairs should be placed in a corner of the room for the Industrial/First World players. Provide a modest table and chairs for the Transitional/Second World players. The Developing/Third World players should be confined to a small unfurnished section of the room, providing only chairs or sitting room on the floor. There should be a clear difference in the three settings.

Prepare envelopes for each student, including a role-identity sheet and the proper number of chips according to the table above. Also, you might include a menu in each envelope. Extra chips can be used by the food and visa sellers for change.

Facilitating the Activity:

1. Give each player his or her materials. If you know the students, it might be a good idea to place a vocal individual in each of the three "worlds." Should you not know the players, simply give a set of materials to each player at random.

2. Tell the participants that:

   a) This is a simulation game approximating the distribution of wealth, population and food as it is in the real world.

   b) They are to deal with the situation as they see it, and enjoy the meal.

   c) There are no rules other than those on their role-identity sheet.

3. The dilemma of how to deal with the inequities of the food and wealth distribution may take various forms. The group may immediately take on a "just and humane" style and work toward providing every player with an equal or adequate share of food. This is "the ideal" and will not necessarily happen. It might happen that the game results in "confrontation" or "revolution." In that case,

Concept:

Much of the world suffers from chronic hunger and malnutrition due to population pressures and the inequitable distribution of food and wealth.

Objectives:

Students will be able to:
• Discuss their reactions to the inequities of the luncheon in a debriefing session.
• Express their values as they respond to the global distribution of population, wealth and food.
• Understand the global disparities of resources as well as the disparity of resources within their own communities.

Subjects:

Social Studies, Family Life Education

Skills:

Communication, negotiation, conflict resolution, strategic planning, writing

Method:

Students participate in a luncheon-game which simulates inequities in the global distribution of food and wealth.

Materials:

(For a class of 30 students)
Food (see menu for items needed — you will need larger quantities of the cheaper items, since most students will only be able to afford those)
3 tables (one buffet-style for food, two for eating)
1 tablecloth and table furnishings (centerpiece, etc.)
10 chairs
200 "chips" (small squares of cut paper)
30 "1/2 chips" (small squares of a different color cut paper)
15 visas (small cards marked "visa")
4 Industrial/First World role-identity sheets*
3 Transitional/Second World role-identity sheets*
23 Developing/Third World role-identity sheets*
30 menus (or one large menu posted for the class)*
*= master is provided with this activity

The Hunger Banquet

it should be resolved by having the sides draw up a statement of "grievance" or "justification," etc. This should express both their feelings and their plan to resolve the situation.

The facilitator should judge when the game has been played out and declare it over. At the finish, it is important to invite the players to drop the rules and share the food. However, you might want to let the inequality go unresolved. This would not be recommended if the session were to be lengthy. This is an exercise in exploring difficult issues, not frustrating students.

Debriefing:

The debriefing session is very important and the facilitator needs to draw out students' reactions and synthesize their perceptions and insights. Also, after the group debriefing session, have students write about their personal experience and response. This should be a non-graded exercise that could either be handed in or shared in small groups. The debriefing should motivate students to study the complex problems of the global and local situations.

Discussion Questions:

1. What was your emotional reaction to the rules? To the rules of the other groups?
2. How did you feel toward the people in the other groups?
3. Did you agree with the manner in which your group resolved the problem? Do you think it was "realistic?"
4. Did your feelings change significantly during the experience? If so, when? Why?
5. Does the global situation make you think about your own community?
6. Is the distribution of resources in the North America equal?

Follow-up Activities:

1. Have students list 3 things they can do as individuals to work toward more equitable food and resource distribution worldwide. Have students extend this list to 3 more things they can do as individuals within their own communities.

2. Design an extra credit project for students to volunteer at a soup kitchen or at other community service projects.
3. Celebrate World Food Day on October 16th by facilitating this exercise in order to engage students with the issues and to heighten awareness around your campus. Contact the U.S. National Committee for World Food Day at 1001 22nd Street, Washington, DC 20437, phone (202) 653-2404.

Adapted with permission from the Americans Friends Service Committee. The original activity, "Simulation Game," appears in Hunger on Spaceship Earth, The American Friends Service Committee, *New York Metropolitan Regional Office.*

The Hunger Banquet

Welcome to the First World...

You are a privileged citizen of countries such as Japan, Germany, Australia and the United States. You are part of the 15% of the world's population who lives in the industrial world and you have an almost unlimited access to the goods of the Earth.

You are invited to enjoy the luncheon we have prepared for you. You have been given 40 chips, which entitle you and your fellow First World citizens to enjoy most of all that is being served because as a citizen of a high income nation you have control of almost 80% of the world's wealth.

Because you enjoy a high level of well-being, health, literacy and wealth, you are granted an unconditional visa to travel anywhere you choose. However, each time you visit the Second World, you must donate 1 chip to the country, and each time you visit the Third World, you must donate a 1/2 chip.

Welcome to the Second World...

You are a member of the "transitional" peoples of the world, a citizen of one of the progressing industrialized countries — such as South Africa, Slovenia, Malaysia and Brazil — where you enjoy 15% of the world's wealth. You are part of the 10% of the world's people who have been given a relative buying power in your packet of 8 chips. Please feel free to purchase whatever you can from the luncheon table.

Since you enjoy a growing level of literacy, good health and wealth, you are free to travel to the countries of the First or Third World under these conditions:

1) You must travel in pairs.
2) Visa must be purchased at luncheon table. One chip must be deposited at luncheon table for each visa, and no more than 2 people may be issued visas at a time.

The Hunger Banquet

Welcome to the Third World...

You are hereby classified as a citizen of the developing world. Unfortunately, that will be of some disadvantage to your participation in this luncheon for you have only 5% of the world's wealth.

Since you make up 75% of the world's population, it is not quite possible for you to have full freedom in consumption of the Earth's resources, or in fact, of our luncheon. You are entitled to a small fraction of the Earth's goods and have been given a relative buying power of 3 chips. We encourage you to be creative in your efforts to increase your buying power, perhaps through combining your chips.

Due to your high level of disease and illiteracy as well as your lack of wealth, we regret to inform you that your ability to travel is restricted.

Cost: Visa to Second World - 7 chips
          Visa to First World - 9 chips Visas may be purchased at the
          luncheon table.

MENU

Item	Size	Cost
Meat	1 slice	4 chips
Cheese	1 slice	4 chips
Salad	1 portion	3 chips
Bread	1 slice	1/2 chip
Pastry	1 portion	5 chips
Rice dish	1 portion	1 chip
Raisins	1 portion	1/2 chip
Cracker	1 portion	1/2 chip
Fruit	1 portion	3 chips
Tea	1 cup	1 chip
Juice	1 cup	2 1/2 chips
Milk	1 cup	1 chip
Sugar	1 teaspoon	1/2 chip
Condiments	1 teaspoon	1/2 chip

Good News, Bad News–Where Do We Stand?

Introduction:

We hear all sorts of information about food issues from the media. Depending on what you read or hear at any one time, the situation related to population and food may seem good or it may seem bad. This activity allows data to be categorized as "good news" or "bad news." Then, comparisons are made to determine some of the relationships between the data we often only evaluate piecemeal.

Procedure:

1. Ask the students if they are pessimistic or optimistic about the chances of feeding the world and slowing rapid population growth.

2. Tell them that you would like them to rate some statements of fact. Have them decide whether the statement is, in their own judgment, "good news" or "bad news." Have students draw a line down the middle of a piece of paper and label one column "Good News" and the other column "Bad News." They should then copy each statement or statement number in the appropriate column.

3. Have students discuss the ratings. You might identify some statements and discover to what degree the students agreed on the rating for that statement. Then, discuss these questions:

   a) Are there statements in one column that make another statement seem better or worse?

   b) What other statements make a statement seem much better or much worse?

   c) Take a statement and draw lines to the other statements on the list which affect it.

   d) Does the data confirm your pessimism or optimism? Why?

4. Ask the students if they have changed their minds about the ratings. Encourage them to collect more information that will help them evaluate the prospects for positive solutions to the population/food dilemma.

Follow-up Activities:

1. Have students write an opinion paper on the following statement: *With modern technological know-how, the world will/will not succeed in feeding its people in the future.*

2. Make a bulletin board with two sections — "Good News" and "Bad News." Have students bring items such as articles and graphics to place on the board. Let the group discuss the new information as it becomes available. This points out the continual process of data collection and attitude evaluation.

Adapted by permission from University of Denver Center for Teaching International Relations. The original activity, "Good News, Bad News," appears in Teaching About Population Issues *by George Otero, Jr. and Richard Schweissing, Center for Teaching International Relations, University of Denver, CO 1977.*

Concept:

When studying global issues, such as population growth and food availability, we must refer to a number of data resources to get a clear picture of the situation.

Objectives:

Students will be able to:
• Identify current events which have implications for food availability.
• Develop a better understanding of issues by balancing opposing facts and information.
• Defend a position on an issue using relevant facts.

Subjects:

Social studies, environmental science

Skills:

Evaluating and ranking data, critical thinking, research, writing

Method:

Students determine whether given statements on population growth and food issues are "good news" or "bad news." They then compare data to identify relationships and shape their evaluation of population/food issues.

Materials:

Duplicate the list of statements on the following pages for each student.

Good News, Bad News-Where Do We Stand?

Statements

1. Some countries are paying their farmers not to produce food.

2. Fifty-one nations are more than three times as crowded as the United States.

3. Much potentially arable land must be irrigated.

4. Tropical land receives greater solar radiation and multiple crops could be raised each year on this land.

5. The soil in many tropical areas is very poor and erodes easily.

6. Infant death rates are dropping in almost every country in the world.

7. Most nations of the world now have family planning programs.

8. Many of the new high-yield varieties of grains have lower protein content than pre-World War II varieties.

9. Research is now concentrating on developing and testing grain varieties with higher protein content as well as possible additives to enrich the present varieties.

10. One out of every seven people worldwide do not have enough food to sustain a normal, active life.

11. Life expectancy has increased in most parts of the world.

12. There are more hungry mouths in the world today than ever before in history.

13. The use of improved seed lines, water control, more fertilizer, and disease and pest controls have together brought about sharp increases in grain production around the world.

14. The United States has less than five percent of the world's people and consumes almost 30 percent of the world's resources.

15. A map of the cultivated land on our planet shows the Eastern and Central United States, Europe, the Russian plains, India and China to be the major cropland areas; the most adequate soils, by far, are those of the American Midwest.

16. Most countries, including the United States, are running out of land that can be converted to cropland.

17. Land not under cultivation will require immense inputs of money for clearing, irrigation, and fertilization to make it productive.

18. Much productive land is diverted to non-nutritive crops such as tobacco and coffee.

19. The food that is annually lost in India to pests, poor storage and bad transportation could feed 50 million persons.

20. Less than five percent of the soils of the tropics are potentially fertile cropland.

21. Worldwide usage of fertilizers began to decline in 1989.

22. There's a booming trade in the United States in vegetarian and low-meat cookbooks.

23. It takes 400 billion dollars to build up an inch of topsoil.

24. If Americans reduced their intake of beef by 10 percent, 100 million people could be fed using the land, water and energy that would have been used for livestock feed.

25. 70 percent of U.S. grain production is fed to livestock.

Good News, Bad News-Where Do We Stand?

Statements

26. From 1950 to 1990, world grain production nearly tripled.

27. Between 1990 and 1996, the grain harvest per person dropped 10 percent.

28. In China between 1987 and 1992, 60 percent of farmland was returned to forest and pasture.

29. Cropland expansion will most likely come at the expense of rangeland, forests, wetlands and other areas that are both economically important and ecologically fragile.

30. Average global grain consumption per person, per year is 300 kilograms. In the United States, it is 800 kilograms.

31. 21 percent of U.S. irrigated cropland is being watered by drawing down underground aquifers.

32. Some U.S. farmers are cutting back on chemicals and adopting alternative farming practices that are both economically and environmentally beneficial.

33. The total annual marine catch has remained constant since 1988.

34. India more than tripled its grain harvest between 1965 and 1983. Since then grain production has not increased.

35. By the year 2000, India is expected to have approximately one billion inhabitants.

36. Waterlogging and salinity are lowering productivity of one-fifth of the world's irrigated cropland.

37. Each year, the world's farmers lose an estimated 24 billion tons of topsoil from their cropland in excess of new soil formation.

38. Many widely used pesticides and herbicides are toxic. The runoff of these chemicals can contaminate groundwater and endanger wildlife.

39. Cropland lost to urban growth on the Indonesian island of Java in 1994 could grow rice for 300,000 people.

40. 40,000 people die each day due to hunger or hunger-related causes.

Waste Disposal

What A Waste!

When it comes to garbage, Americans hold the singular distinction of producing more garbage per person than people in any other country in the world. In 1960, the average American produced two and a half pounds of garbage per day. Since then, the population has increased by almost 90 million, and we have developed into a "disposable society" that now produces more than four pounds of garbage per person per day.[1] Canada runs a close second at about three and a half pounds per person per day.[2] Disposal of solid waste is a global problem. Several methods have been created to alleviate the disposal situation, but few have been implemented without opposition due to hazardous environmental side effects.

According to the Census Bureau, the U.S. population will grow by nearly 30 million by 2010. At the current level of 4.3 pounds of garbage per person per day, the people added each year will produce more than an extra 150 million extra tons of trash between 1998 and 2010. This is enough to fill a convoy of ten-ton garbage trucks wrapped around the Earth almost six times!

Another way to look at it is that by 2010, the amount of garbage produced every year by the United States is expected to increase to 253 million tons, 17 percent over current levels.[3] Since there will be ten percent more people in 2010 than there were in 1997, population growth will account for more than half of that increase in waste generated. In other words, the United States would have to decrease its production of waste per person by ten percent just to maintain the same levels of waste generation. But the average amount of trash generated by each person every day has been growing steadily. The waste problem in the United States is made worse not only by our growing population, but also by the fact that each member of that population is producing more and more trash.

While the United States and other industrialized countries have relatively good garbage disposal and sanitation, the waste must still go somewhere. **Landfills** and **incinerators** are the two most common methods of disposal for waste that is not recycled, but regardless of whether it is burned, recycled or buried, the fate of garbage has major impacts on health, the environment and the economy.

All Full Up

Landfills manage about 57 percent, or 118 million tons, of U.S. garbage generated each year.[4] In 1995, there were about 2,500 landfills operating in the United States.[5] Although there are fewer landfills now than in the past, total landfill capacity has remained about the same since new landfills tend to be much larger than older ones.

One Person's Garbage
in selected cities (lbs. per day)

High Income Countries

New York, USA	3.8
Toronto, Canada	3.1
Paris, France	2.9
Athens, Greece	2.4

Middle Income Countries

Rio de Janeiro, Brazil	2.4
Moscow, Russia	1.8
Windhoek, Namibia	1.5
Manila, Phillipines	1.5

Lower Income Countries

Tirana, Albania	1.5
La Paz, Bolivia	1.1
Lagos, Nigeria	0.7
Dhaka, Bangladesh	0.2

Source: World Resources 1998-1999, *pp. 278-279 (1993 data).*

Landfills are holes in the ground, consisting of a liner made of clay or plastic to contain the wastes; pipes and pumps to remove water and other liquids that collect in the landfill; and a cover to keep out water and to prevent the wastes from spilling over the sides. Over the last two decades, several environmental problems related to landfills have developed. Experts now argue whether it is possible to build a landfill that will not leak and expose the

What A Waste!

surrounding environment and groundwater to hazardous contaminants.

One environmental problem of landfills is that the liners and covers are subject to cracking and deterioration from weather or chemicals. The most dangerous potential problem with landfills, though, is the failure of the pumping system. When a liquid (such as rainwater) filters through a landfill, it becomes contaminated by the waste it touches. This liquid, called **leachate**, is piped out of the landfill and into a storage container. If it is not pumped out, the leachate can leak into surface or groundwater supplies, contaminating them. Landfills can also emit hazardous, and sometimes highly flammable, gases such as methane. New environmental regulations have been created to counter the problems. But this legislation has made landfills more expensive to build and manage.

As of 1995, New Jersey and Massachusetts had less than five years of capacity remaining in their landfills. Nine additional states across the country had between five and ten years of

capacity remaining.[6] As the population continues to grow, the demand for land for other purposes — housing, parks and roads — increases, and finding space for new landfills will become more difficult. Some states have tried to deal with the problem of waste disposal by attempting to send garbage to other states for disposal. This practice is becoming less successful as many communities are unwilling to accept garbage. In the mid-1980s, a barge carrying 3,186 tons of Long Island waste was rejected by six states before it was finally incinerated several months later.

Burn It Away

Incineration, the burning of wastes into gases and ash, has been in existence since the Industrial Revolution. During the 1960s and early 1970s, many incinerators were forced to shut down due to the lack of pollution control equipment. In the 1980s, incinerators experienced a growth spurt after the development of "cleaner burning" technology. Today, in the United States, approximately 16 percent of solid waste, or 33.5 million tons, is incinerated each year.[7]

Incinerators do not completely "burn away" all solid wastes. All incinerators must still send left-over waste, in the form of ash, to a landfill. One advantage of incinerators is that the process of incineration does reduce the amount of waste to be put in a landfill. The left-over ash, as a general rule, is about 25 percent of the weight and 10 percent of the volume of the garbage put into the incinerator.[8] This ash, however, contains high concentrations of toxic metals such as lead, and can cause problems in landfills if not properly taken care of. It is often more hazardous to public health and the environment than the original garbage. In addition, not all garbage can be incinerated. Waste that is non-combustible must be separated out and landfilled before incineration.

With the combustion of waste, most municipal incinerators not only reduce the volume of the waste, but they also generate energy. In this process, called waste-to-energy combustion, the energy created by burning the waste at very high temperatures is sold to electric utili-

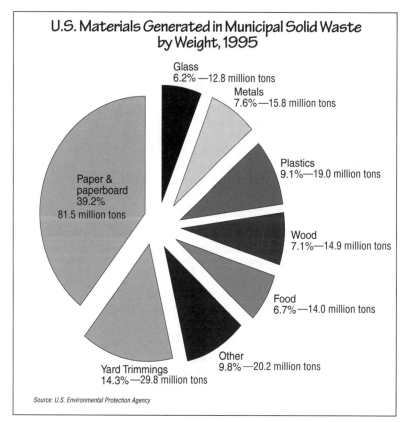

U.S. Materials Generated in Municipal Solid Waste by Weight, 1995

Glass 6.2% —12.8 million tons
Metals 7.6% —15.8 million tons
Plastics 9.1% —19.0 million tons
Paper & paperboard 39.2% 81.5 million tons
Wood 7.1% —14.9 million tons
Food 6.7% —14.0 million tons
Other 9.8% —20.2 million tons
Yard Trimmings 14.3% —29.8 million tons

Source: U.S. Environmental Protection Agency

What A Waste!

ties who distribute it to local homes and businesses. Using this energy in place of energy generated by burning fossil fuels such as oil and coal can help the environment by reducing emissions of carbon dioxide, the primary greenhouse gas. However, garbage is not a very efficient fuel, and putting it through a waste-to-energy incinerator does not generate as much energy as would be saved through recycling.[9]

Finally, despite careful pollution controls on what incinerators release into the air, gaseous emissions frequently include toxic compounds called dioxins, as well as carbon monoxide and sulfur dioxide, all of which can be harmful to humans and the environment.

It is important to note that many of the municipal waste incinerators and landfills in the United States are located in or near lower income communities and communities of people of color. These groups have been found to suffer more health problems related to environmental causes than the general population. People who fight to raise awareness of these issues and give a voice to the disadvantaged groups make up the Environmental Justice Movement.

Reduce, Reuse, Recycle

The only safe, clean way to reduce the garbage problem is to first use fewer materials, and then reuse and **recycle** the materials you do use, thereby decreasing the amount of waste that needs to be stored or incinerated. Reducing the amount of waste to be disposed by encouraging people to buy and use fewer things (a strategy called **source reduction** or **waste prevention**) is now one of the primary efforts many cities are making to alleviate their waste disposal problems.

Individuals can reduce solid waste by exercising their environmental purchasing power. Packaging accounts for 38 percent of all municipal waste.[10] By selecting items that are efficiently packaged, especially with recyclable or reusable materials, people can substantially reduce levels of waste they generate.

Recycling is the separation from the waste stream of certain types of products such as glass or aluminum that can be converted back

into useful raw materials and reintroduced into the marketplace. The overall aim of recycling is to decrease the amount of materials that enter and exit the economy. As available landfill space continues to shrink, recycling is becoming an economically as well as environmentally sound method of waste management.

Most materials used today are discarded after one use. Many do not realize the amount of energy saved by reusing and recycling materials. Recycling is more energy efficient than producing goods from raw materials because recycled materials are not extracted from the environment, and they usually need less processing than raw materials. Recycling saves more than three times as much energy as is generated by using raw materials and disposing of them through waste-to-energy combustion, and it requires 33 times less energy than using raw materials and then placing them in a landfills after use.[11]

What A Waste!

Recycling reduces air pollution by reducing emissions of gases such as carbon dioxide, the primary greenhouse gas, and sulfur dioxide and nitrogen oxides, the primary causes of acid rain. Landfills are the main source of methane gas emissions in the United States. Recycling reduces the amount of trash in landfills and the number of landfills needed. At present rates, recycling reduces methane emissions by an amount equal to almost a quarter of the methane emissions from all the landfills in the country. Recycling also reduces the amount of pollutants released into our surface and groundwater.[12]

In the United States, 27 percent of all municipal waste, over 50 million tons, is "recovered" through recycling and composting.[13] Although this is the highest percentage of any industrialized country, the United States still burns and buries more waste than any other country. Paper and cardboard, the single largest component of municipal solid waste, comprising nearly 40 percent, could be recycled easily and efficiently, but instead, about half is thrown away.[14] By contrast, Spain and the Netherlands recycle more than 60 percent and Japan recycles about 55 percent of their paper products,[15] including 93 percent of its newspapers. Each ton of recycled paper keeps 17 trees from being used to produce paper and saves 25 barrels of oil, 7,000 gallons of water, and three cubic yards of landfill space.

Along with recycling glass, metals and paper, a sustainable society also recycles nutrients. Individuals can recycle nutrients by **composting** their yard waste, food scraps and other kitchen waste. Composting reduces waste while producing a rich fertilizer.

Wasting Away

It is important to realize that when we dispose of waste, we are not really throwing it "away." We are only displacing it from one area (our homes) to another (landfills or incinerators).

In the long run, source reduction produces the most environmentally sound and cost-effective way of dealing with our growing solid waste problem. Successfully reducing waste requires a change in our lifestyle. Yet even our most aggressive efforts to reduce, reuse or recycle waste will be continually undermined unless steps are taken to stabilize population size.

Endnotes

[1] *Characterization of Municipal Solid Waste in the United States: 1996 Update*. Washington, D.C.: U.S. Environmental Protection Agency, 1996, p. 2.

[2] U.S. Environmental Protection Agency. Office of Solid Waste Webpage; www.epa.gov/osw. "International Solid Waste Practices."

[3] Op. cit. note 1, p. 3.

[4] Op. cit. note 1, p. 10.

[5] Edward W. Repa and Allen Blakey. "Municipal Solid Waste Disposal Trends in the U.S." *Waste Age*. May, 1996. pp. 171-180.

[6] Ibid.

[7] Op. cit. note 1, p. 10.

[8] Keep America Beautiful Website: www.kab.org; "Fine Particles—Part 5: Incineration Worsens Landfill Hazards." *Rachel's Hazardous Waste News #362*." January 3, 1990.

[9] Ruth Caplan, et al. *Our Earth*. New York: Bantam Books, 1990. p. 174.

[10] Op. cit. note 1, p. 8.

[11] Richard A. Denison. "Environmental Life-Cycle Comparisons of Recycling, Landfilling, and Incineration: A Review of Recent Studies." *Annual Review of Energy and the Environment*. Vol. 21, pp. 191-237, 1996.

[12] Ibid.

[13] Op. cit. note 1, p. 10.

[14] Op. cit. note 1, pp. 5,8.

[15] Op. cit. note 2. Original source, Pulp and Paper International.

Talkin' Trash on Tropico

Introduction:

Disposing of the solid waste created by an expanding population has become a dilemma facing many communities today. The average American generates four pounds of garbage a day, which quickly adds up to a storage problem, especially in urban centers and areas with a high concentration of people. Simply carting everything off to the local landfill is no longer a feasible option for much of the country. In the following activity, students will set goals for a waste disposal program, form committees to research options, and then meet together to work on an acceptable implementation plan.

Procedure:

1. Explain that students will represent a steering committee for Tropico, an island faced with waste disposal problems. The island's population has been growing at a rapid rate, doubling in the last 25 years from 28,000 to 56,000. Simultaneously, the consumption patterns have risen due to an increased standard of living and greater use of disposable products. The modest local landfill could not keep up with the ever-increasing flow of trash and was forced to close because of health hazards and an overflow problem.

   The class must first outline the goals they want to achieve for their plan. Emphasize that they will need to plan for the long term (at least 10 years) and should try to balance environmental and economic concerns. Also, remember the amount of garbage generated may increase from continued population growth or decrease from better habits by individuals and businesses.

2. The students should break into groups to research different parts of an effective waste disposal plan. Each group should fill out the student worksheet and make a final recommendation about the role their method should play in the final program. Research may be done in the library, by contacting local waste disposal services and organizations such as Keep America Beautiful for additional information (see "Resources" section at the end of the activity for a list of potential sources). To decrease the amount

of class time needed for this activity you may want to collect the information from these organizations a few weeks before the activity begins.

Groups should be formed to research the following areas:

a) Reducing the amount of waste generated (e.g. tax incentives for less trash per household, or restrictions on packaging consumer goods).

b) Various recycling programs, and the feasibility of each. (The success of recycling programs usually depends on a steady stream of the goods to be recycled, and a demand for the end materials.)

c) Composting, and how it might work for a portion of the island's garbage.

d) Incineration, or "waste-to-energy" as an option.

e) Building a new landfill, and using the most environmentally and monetarily sound safety features. (Even if the other options are utilized, a landfill will still be needed for non-recyclable, non-burnable, non-compostable items and ash from incineration.)

3. After the groups complete their worksheets, the class should meet to decide how the recommendations will fit together to form a cohesive program for the island. A spokesperson from each group should report on their findings and give a recommendation. Remember to keep the long-term goals in mind while debating which options to emphasize. If the class cannot agree on one combination of options, you could pick the two or three most popular proposals and have the class vote.

4. Once the program is determined, the class will also have to choose locations for the implementation of different parts of the plan. At this point, some socioeconomic considerations will come into play. The island's indigenous LoLi tribe are in desperate need of money and are willing to host recycling stations, incineration plants or the new landfill on the land allotted to them by the government. The price they are asking is only about half of the price of placing these options in other areas of the island. In

Concept:
As the population increases, so does the amount of solid waste produced, creating a dilemma of how and where to dispose of the garbage.

Objectives:
Students will be able to:
• Develop goals and a long-term plan to meet the resource management needs of a community.
• Identify and weigh positive and negative impacts of a proposed course of action to manage resources.
• Understand how economic factors may affect environmental decision making.

Subjects:
Environmental science, economics

Skills:
Research, writing, evaluation, cooperation, decision making

Method:
Students will weigh the advantages and disadvantages of various waste disposal options when deciding how to manage the waste of a growing island community

Materials:
Research materials about solid waste (see "Resources" list at the end of the activity), Copies of Student Worksheet

Talkin' Trash on Tropico

exchange for the low price, they are asking that the new jobs generated by these options be reserved for their people. However, as the student worksheets indicate, some of the projects involve more health risks to local populations than others. Also of consideration is the potential contamination of the drinking water. Not only do you want to keep the lake free from toxins, but the groundwater needs to be preserved as well. The class will need to weigh the moral, environmental, and economic arguments of the placement of the different facilities.

Follow-up Activities:

1. This activity would have different results if the island had other characteristics. You may want to try a version where groups research varied types of islands. For example, one could be close to Miami, use a lot of plastic, and be able to ship recyclables to the mainland. Another could be a popular tourist spot, with large amounts of waste and income. A third could be far from anywhere, using mostly organic products.

2. Ask students to think of other options to dispose of the waste (e.g., dump it in the ocean, send it to another island). What are the major drawbacks of these? Try to get students to realize that many options only temporarily solve the problem.

3. Remind students that the island's population doubled in the last 25 years. Will their plan be able to incorporate another doubling in the next 25 years? How about the next? How could this problem be handled?

4. Students should also find out about the methods of disposing of solid waste in their community. How much waste does the average person generate in the area? How much of the waste is being recycled? How much longer will the local landfill be able to operate? Are there local, state or federal regulations for waste disposal programs? Students can get a first-hand look at where their garbage goes by taking a field trip to the local landfill and other facilities and speaking with the people who run the programs.

Resources:

Resource Recycling: North America's
Recycling Journal
P.O. Box 10540
Portland, OR 97296
e-mail: resrecycle@aol.com

Tennessee Valley Authority
Waste Technology Program
Forestry Building
Norris, TN 37828
(423) 494-7137

Keep America Beautiful
1010 Washington Blvd.
Stamford, CT 06902
web site: www.kab.org

The U.S. Environmental Protection Agency
Office of Solid Waste
401 M Street, SW
Washington DC 20460
web site: www.epa.gov/osw

Environmental Industry Association
4301 Connecticut Ave.
Suite 300
Washington, DC 20008
(202) 244-4700

The Environmental Defense Fund
257 Park Avenue South
New York, NY 10010
web site: www.edf.org

Talkin' Trash on Tropico

The Island of Tropico

Most of the inhabitants of Tropico live at the end of the island where the freshwater river empties into the sea. A native tribe lives on government land at the other end of the island and tends to have a lower standard of living than the rest of the population. In the center of the island lies a fresh water lake from which the river flows; both the lake and river are used by the islanders for bathing, drinking and washing.

Talkin' Trash on Tropico

   You will be developing a new waste disposal plan for Tropico, a fictitious island community. The island is 22 square miles, has a population of 56,000 and generates an average of 112 tons of solid waste daily. The waste stream is similar in composition to that of the average town in the United States: 37% paper products, 18% yard wastes, 10% glass, 10% metals, 8% food waste, 7% plastics, and the rest "other" wastes. Working in small groups, you need to research the feasibility of the options assigned to you and complete the following worksheet. Whenever possible, find out specific information such as how much land the option you are researching will need to operate, how much of the solid waste stream can be disposed of with your option, how much room the program could save in a landfill, in what kind of area your program should be located.

Disposal plan:

Description of option:

Benefits: Environmental   Economic   Convenience

Drawbacks: Environmental   Economic   Convenience

Recommendation:

It's in the Bag: The Grocery Store Dilemma

Introduction:

"Paper or plastic?" the cashier asks as you place your items on the checkout counter at the grocery store. You know that both bags have costs and benefits associated with their use, and there are so many factors to consider. What are they made of? How are they made? Which is more convenient? Which is easier to recycle? It seems there is no right or wrong answer. Meanwhile, the cashier is waiting . . .

As consumers, our decisions about products and packaging are influenced by many factors, including how those products affect the environment. Especially in North America, we are faced with an incredible variety of products but little information about their true environmental costs. The choice of grocery bags is a relatively new issue for consumers; the first plastic grocery bags were introduced in 1977. Now almost four out of five bags used are plastic. Both the paper and plastic industries formed special groups, the Plastic Bag Association and the Paper Bag Council, to promote the use of their bags. Because of the rapid growth in the popularity of plastic bags, many people concerned with the environment began to wonder — even with new plastic bag recycling program springing up across the country — which bag is better.

Procedure:

1. Divide the class into three groups. Groups #1 and #2 will debate the grocery bag dilemma, with Group #1 supporting plastic and Group #2 supporting paper. Group #3 will decide which bag is preferable after hearing the arguments from both sides and posing questions.

2. Groups #1 and #2 will need facts and evidence to present convincing arguments for their side of this issue. For their research, they should contact individuals and organizations representing each side of the issue. Besides the Plastic Bag Association and the Paper Bag Council, students might seek out local waste management experts, grocers, consumers and environmentalists in their area. Members of Groups #1 and #2 may wish to focus on particular aspects of the debate, such as recycling or energy used in the manufacture of the bags. Group #3 should prepare questions for the debaters in the other groups to elicit information which will help them make their final decision.

3. On the day of the debate, set up a table or podium in the front of the room. Members of Group #3 will be seated in the front row facing the podium. The other groups will be seated together behind Group #3.

4. Groups #1 and #2 will flip a coin to see who will be the first to present their argument. A representative from each group will then have a set time to make an opening statement. Depending upon the length of the class period, two to five minutes should be allowed. After the opening statements are finished, members of Group #3 will pose questions to each of the other groups. Group #3 may use questions from their original list, or they may ask questions in response to facts presented in the opening arguments or other questions. When a question is posed to a group, a representative of that group will have a set time to respond. If the other group wishes to give a rebuttal, one of their representatives may do so. A one to two minute limit is recommended for answers and rebuttals. In order to involve as many students as possible, students in each group should take turns asking, answering and rebutting questions.

5. You may want to limit the questioning to ten or fewer questions. Members of Group #3 should take notes on the answers they receive and on the persuasiveness of the arguments. It might be helpful for Group #3 to divide note paper into two columns to list points and counterpoints.

6. After the debate, Group #3 should convene to decide which bag is the best choice. Their decision should be based more on the facts and strength of the arguments than on the oratorical skill of their classmates. Once a decision has been reached, Group #3 should report this to the class, including a summary of the reasoning on which they based their decision.

Concept:

Environmental issues are often quite complex, with few completely right or wrong answers. Critical thinking skills are essential in determining which practices are the most environmentally-sound and cost effective.

Objectives:

Students will be able to:
• Present and defend an argument for one side of an environmental debate.
• Discern the relative costs and benefits of two actions which affect the environment, and determine which is the better alternative.
• Research an environmental issue from both sides of the argument.

Subjects:

Environmental science, language arts, family life

Skills:

Critical thinking, debate, research, writing, public speaking

Method:

Students learn about the complexity of environmental decision-making by researching and debating the choice between paper and plastic grocery bags.

Materials:

Students should contact the following groups for helpful research materials to prepare for their debate:

Paper Bag Council
American Forest & Paper Association
1111 19th St. NW
Washington, DC 20036
202-463-2700
www.afandpa.org

Plastic Bag Association
1817 E. Carson St.
Pittsburgh, PA 15203
1-800-438-5856
www.plasticbag.com

It's in the Bag: The Grocery Store Dilemma

Follow-up Activities:

1. Many grocery stores are promoting a third alternative to plastic or paper bags – reusable nylon or canvas bags. The bags are usually offered for sale in the grocery stores, and consumers who reuse bags receive a discount of $0.03 to $0.05 per bag. Students can research the costs and benefits of these bags and obstacles to their use, relative to plastic and paper. Students then can devise a plan to increase the use of reusable bags, involving both the grocer and the consumer, and present the plan to a local grocery store.

2. We make personal choices every day which impact the environment. As an alternative to debating about grocery bag choice, students could take on the diaper dilemma (cloth vs. disposables), soda packaging (cans vs. plastic bottles) or even transportation (cars vs. bikes). A series of debates would allow students to explore different issues and take on a variety of roles within the groups.

"Paper or Plastic?"

Waste A-Weigh

Introduction:

The U.S. population constitutes only 5 percent of the world's population, while consuming 28 percent of the world's energy. This heavy use of resources creates a steady stream of solid waste to be handled by waste disposal services. As the population grows, so does the burden on these services. One immediate way to reduce this burden is to modify habits which generate excess waste. Students will learn about using more sustainable practices in their daily lives in this activity.

Procedure:

1. The Friday before you plan to do the activity, tell the class that they will participate in an experiment concerning waste production during the following week. Explain that the waste students generate during lunch will be recorded for the entire week. Encourage students to bring or buy their usual lunch on Monday in order to gauge their conservation progress as their awareness of their consumption patterns grows throughout the week.

2. Each day of the following week, set up a weighing station in the cafeteria and require all your students to weigh any items that they plan on throwing away, including food wastes, packaging, bottles, etc. Record the weight of each student's trash, and later transfer the amounts to a chart in your classroom. This chart should also include the total weight of all trash generated by the class that day.

3. Sometime during the beginning of the week you might want to give students hints on how to reduce their waste. Suggestions should include: only buying as much food as they plan to eat, avoiding items with excess packaging, bringing reusable containers from home, and recycling glass, aluminum and plastics.

4. At the end of the week, have each student fill out the worksheet included with this activity. Ask students which conservation methods seemed to be most effective. Which were most convenient? Which do they think would be best to implement on a school level? On a community or city level? Nationally? Also, have students brainstorm about specific ways the practices in their cafeteria could be changed (e.g., see if the art department would like some of the containers, check whether recycling is done whenever feasible, compost the food waste or see if local farmers could feed it to animals).

Follow-up Activities:

1. With the data in front of them and some new ideas, students may feel challenged to try to reduce waste during another week of testing. They can be encouraged in their efforts by the story of one student who carried his brown paper bag home every day to use again the next. He put a mark on the bag for each trip he made. By the time the bag was too torn to use again, it carried his lunch to school 32 times.

2. Once students have learned conservation techniques for themselves, they may also wish to challenge another class to a competition to see who can average the least amount of waste. The competition could be expanded to different grade levels, or even different schools in the area. Local newspapers and magazines might be interested in featuring such a competition in their publication, especially with suggestions from students about ways for the community to decrease waste generation.

Concept:
Changing consumption patterns can help reduce the pile-up of garbage contributing to current waste disposal problems.

Objectives:
Students will be able to:
• Identify the parts of the products they use which become waste after the item is used and which of those parts are reusable.
• Develop a personal plan for reducing their resource consumption.
• Strategize with other students about ways to conserve resources on class, school, community, state and national levels.

Subjects:
Environmental science, biology, family life

Skills:
Brainstorming, collecting and recording data, applying knowledge

Method:
By weighing and recording their waste at lunch every day for a week, students learn how conservation efforts can impact the total amount of trash generated.

Materials:
A scale to weigh the garbage (you might want to pre-adjust it with the weight of one cafeteria tray and place the trash on the tray)
Copies of Student Worksheet

Waste A-Weigh

	Mon.	Tue.	Wed.	Thurs.	Fri.
Personal waste:	_____	_____	_____	_____	_____
Class waste (total):	_____	_____	_____	_____	_____
Class average (per person):	_____	_____	_____	_____	_____

Did you have more or less waste than the class average?

Did you and/or the class create more or less waste as the week went on?

    If less, how much less? (subtract the last day from the first to discover the amount saved)

You   _____

Class   _____

    What if your class could reduce garbage by 10% — how much garbage would be avoided? How much garbage would be avoided if your whole school conserved at this rate?

	CLASS	SCHOOL
In one day?	_____	_____
One month?	_____	_____
The school year?	_____	_____

Wildlife Endangerment

Answering the Call of the Wild

Long before *Homo sapiens* walked the Earth, the planet belonged to an enormous array of mammals, reptiles, insects, fish, birds and plants. From the tiniest organism, these species evolved over hundreds of millions of years into a rich collection of flora and fauna. But in just the past few decades, untold numbers of plant and animal species have disappeared forever from the Earth and many more are threatened with **extinction**.

Scientists have named 1.8 million species, but estimate that between 4 million and 40 million share our planet.[1] If extinction trends observed for vertebrate animals (the most commonly studied group of species) hold true for all organisms, extinction is a very real possibility for about one-quarter of all species.[2]

Extinction and **endangerment** occur for a variety of reasons. Some species are lost through natural occurrences. No one knows for sure why the dinosaurs became extinct 65 million years ago or what happened to many mammals 10,000 years ago. The natural or "background" rate of extinction is believed to be from one to three species a year. However, the current rate of extinction is about 1,000 per year.[3] Certain animals and plants may die out in our own time regardless of what we do. Extinction is a fact of life on Earth. However, premature extinction caused by human activities can and should be prevented.

The single biggest threat contributing to the premature extinction of the plants and animals is **habitat alteration**. Other causes of species endangerment include pollution, **overharvesting**, and introduction or **invasion of non-native species**.

Human Homewreckers

Growth in human population is a leading cause of habitat destruction. As human numbers increase, more land is used for agriculture and development, destroying crucial wildlife habitat. Natural habitats are destroyed as they are paved over, built on, polluted, lumbered and mined. Most ecologists agree that reducing the size of its natural habitat increases a species' risk of extinction. Timber clear-cutting, mining, farming and the conversion of open space into commercial and residential developments have squeezed many of our native plant and wildlife species into smaller and fragmented areas.

The destruction of a plant species is extremely serious, as it can harm an entire ecosystem. In the words of biologist Paul Ehrlich, "Every time we remove a plant species, we probably eliminate something on the order of ten animal species."

Although all habitats play a role in the biosphere, the tropical rainforests are especially precious. Of the 1.8 million recorded species, greater than 50 percent live in tropical rainforests. Considering that more than half of the tropical forests have already been destroyed, the enormity of the destruction, in terms of both number of acres and number of plant and animal species, is staggering. Species found only or predominantly in rainforests, including most primates, are especially vulnerable. One half of all primate species on the planet are threatened.[4]

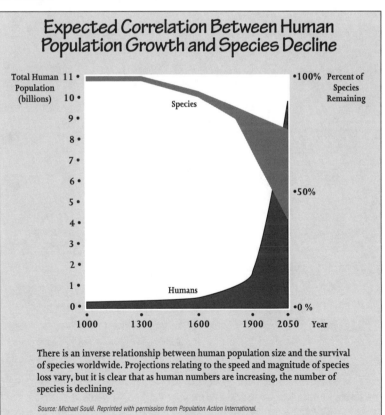

There is an inverse relationship between human population size and the survival of species worldwide. Projections relating to the speed and magnitude of species loss vary, but it is clear that as human numbers are increasing, the number of species is declining.

Source: Michael Soulé. Reprinted with permission from Population Action International.

Answering the Call of the Wild

Wetlands ecosystems in the United States represent another diverse but vulnerable habitat. Of the endangered or threatened species in the U.S., experts estimate that about 45 percent of the animal species and about 25 percent of the plant species use wetland habitat. The nation's wetland acreage shrank by one million acres between 1985 and 1995 as wetlands were drained for agriculture, industry, shopping malls, housing subdivisions and other development, or dredged for transportation or other purposes. The United States has already lost more than half of its original wetlands.[5]

The clash between humans and wildlife is evident in other parts of the United States as well. Consider Florida, where the population increases by more than 600 people every day, crowding out such native species as the West Indian manatee and Florida panther.[6] The dwindling manatee population falls victim to power boat propellers while grazing on sea beds. The nearly extinct panther has lost its home to subdivisions, citrus groves and other development. According to the U.S. Fish and Wildlife Service, there are only 30 to 50 Florida panthers left in the wild.

In addition to direct habitat destruction from expansion of agriculture and development, population pressures also contribute to habitat loss through climate change. Most

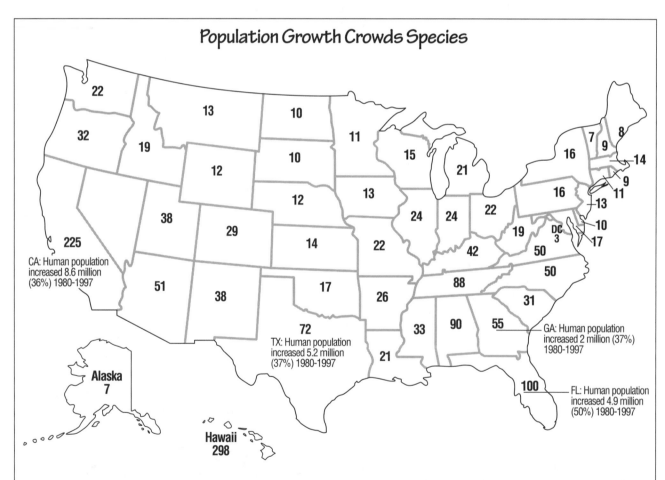

Population Growth Crowds Species

CA: Human population increased 8.6 million (36%) 1980-1997

TX: Human population increased 5.2 million (37%) 1980-1997

GA: Human population increased 2 million (37%) 1980-1997

FL: Human population increased 4.9 million (50%) 1980-1997

This map depicts the number of endangered species found in each state (May, 1998). The fastest growing states: California, Texas, Florida and Georgia, have more endangered or threatened species than nearly every other state.

Sources: U.S. Fish and Wildlife Service (www.fws.gov/r9endspp/listmap.html), and U.S. Census Bureau, Population Estimates Program, Demographic Estimates of Population Change.

Answering the Call of the Wild

climatologists now agree that human actions have a notable effect on the Earth's climate. Increases in concentrations of greenhouse gases in the atmosphere from the burning of fossil fuels like oil, coal and natural gas are driven in part by population growth, and are predicted to dramatically alter our future climate.

Species that are isolated to the coldest climates on mountain tops, as well as those who dwell on small islands may see their habitats disappear from increases in temperatures or rises in sea level. This habitat destruction will also put many more species in danger of extinction.

Presently, habitat destruction is the direct cause of decline for an estimated 75 percent of bird and mammal species in danger, 68 percent of all threatened reptile species and 60 percent of all threatened fish species.[7] Human technology, too, has adversely affected certain species. Dams on rivers disrupt spawning patterns of salmon who live in the ocean, and lay their eggs up river in fresh-water streams. In order to help young salmon downstream past dams and the lakes that lie behind them, biologists have, on some rivers resorted to removing the fish from the rivers, transporting them around the dams, then putting them back. In Florida, hatching sea turtles are fatally lured away from the ocean when they mistake the reflected city lights for the starlit sky over the water.

In 1973, the U.S. government attempted to protect threatened wildlife by enacting the Endangered Species Act. This legislation, along with related acts such as the Marine Mammal Protection Act of 1972, was designed to protect species that were deemed threatened or endangered in the United States. Although this legislation has been instrumental in saving some species, it has not been effective in keeping species from becoming endangered in the first place. Yet, ecologists have found that, just as it is easier to treat a symptom before it becomes a serious medical condition, it is easier to help threatened wildlife before they become critically endangered. The list of endangered species recognized under the U.S. Endangered Species Act grew from approximately 380 when the law was passed in 1973 to 1,134 at the end of 1997.[8] When written, the Endangered Species Act was designed to be periodically reviewed by Congress. During past reviews, or reauthorizations, Congress has made changes that strengthen the Act. There is always the potential, however, for future changes that would diminish its effectiveness. At the time of writing, many countries, including Canada, did not even have their own national law for protecting endangered species.

Polluting the Ark

Humans have another devastating influence on wildlife — pollution. Birds, mammals, fish, shellfish and their food sources are all vulnerable to human-generated toxins that are released into the environment. Shellfish, and other organisms, that dwell at the bottom of bodies of water, are at serious risk of contamination by bacteria and toxins, and of death from oxygen depletion.

The Chesapeake Bay is the nation's largest estuary. Steady population growth in the Chesapeake watershed has turned the bay into a catch basin that collects the refuse of innumerable pollution sources, including factories, farms and sewage treatment plants. Runoff from lawns, roads, parking lots and farmland carries pesticides, petroleum, and other toxins into the bay. These pollutants have reduced the Chesapeake's seafood catch to a shadow of 19th century levels. Catches of crabs, oysters and fish decline, while jellyfish populations increase, as do bacterial counts.

During certain times of the year pollution causes a **dead zone** in the Gulf of Mexico. The dead zone, about the size of the state of New Jersey, is an area of oxygen-depleted water where no fish can live. As the Mississippi River empties into the gulf, the agricultural and industrial pollution it carries creates an excess of nutrients in the environment. This excess causes algae to bloom, which uses up all the available oxygen, making the water uninhabitable to fish and other marine life.[9] Persistent toxic chemicals have proven deadly to aquatic ecosystems in North America's Great Lakes, where various species of fish now suffer from tumors, lesions and decreased reproductive capacities. Of the ten most highly valued

Answering the Call of the Wild

species of fish in Lake Ontario, seven have now almost totally vanished.[10]

Killing for Profit

In addition to habitat destruction and pollution, **over-exploitation** of wildlife poses a significant threat to many species. Over-exploitation occurs when a plant or animal is killed or taken out of the environment faster than they can replace their numbers.

Many of the world's most beloved animals, such as tigers, gorillas, rhinoceros and elephants, are victims of illegal over-exploitation, commonly known as poaching. The result of this **poaching** brings precious ivory and fur coats to the black market, medicinal preparations to Asia and elsewhere, and artifacts to collectors worldwide. The bones and teeth of tigers are highly valued as ingredients in traditional Asian medicines. While the tiger is also threatened by habitat destruction, poaching has accelerated so much in recent years that it is now considered the leading threat to tiger's survival, according to the World Wildlife Fund. The tiger population has dwindled from around 100,000 in 1900 to about 6,000 individuals today. Three of the eight species of tiger have become extinct since the 1940s. Many other species fall victim to the same fate as well: Over-hunting affects 31 percent of threatened reptiles.[11]

Not all over-exploitation happens illegally. Many species have been over-hunted or over-fished because they did not have adequate legal protection. As world population grows, pressure on these species will continue to increase. Marine species have been particularly hard-hit; two-thirds have declined because of over-harvesting. Cod, some sharks and sturgeons — the fish which supply high-quality caviar, have been particularly affected.[12]

Unwelcome Neighbors

Often species become endangered not because humans destroy their habitat, but because we change it, by introducing into an area species that weren't there before. Sometimes these new neighbors eat the native species; sometimes they just crowd the natives out. Either way, native species suffer.

Humans introduced the brown tree snake to the Pacific Island of Guam shortly after World War II. The snake, which feeds on small animals, including birds and their eggs, has no natural predators on the island, and so its population skyrocketed. One survey found densities of up to 12,000 snakes per square mile. The Guam rail is just one of the species devastated by the snakes. Now believed to be extinct in the wild, there were an estimated 80,000 of the birds as recently as 1968.[13]

The American chestnut was once one of the dominant trees of North America. Growing to nearly 100 feet, the wood was valuable for timber, and the trees produced abundant nuts that were important sources of food for people and wildlife alike. In 1904, scientists discovered a fungus growing on chestnuts in New York City. The fungus, which is fatal to American chestnuts, had been brought by humans to America, probably from Asia. It spread rapidly, 20 to 50 miles each year, killing virtually every tree it encountered. By 1950, the trees were essentially gone from our forests.[14]

Myriad other exotic pests exist, from Zebra mussels in the Great Lakes, to Mediterranean fruit flies in California. As our population increases, and our economies expand, more and more commerce and travel happens between different ecosystems. We are continu-

Answering the Call of the Wild

ally increasing the chance that a person will, purposefully or accidentally, release the next unwelcome neighbor.

Key to Our Survival

Although humans have endangered so many plant and animal species, we depend on these and other species for our very survival. The planet's **biodiversity** provides the world with crucial **ecosystem services** — pollination, pest control, cleansing of water supplies and soil creation—upon which all species depend.[15] The extermination of plant populations can change the climate locally and also have severe regional effects through disturbance of the water cycle.

Food, medicine and shelter are all derived from the abundant organic resources of the Earth. More than a quarter of the prescription drugs on the U.S. market are derived from plant species.[16] Some of these drugs are used to fight cancer, malaria and heart disease.

Additionally, loss of biodiversity deprives us of tools that might help in the struggle to feed ever-increasing numbers of people. For example, only a few of the more than quarter million known plant species have been investigated for their potential as crops. The world's growing human population depends on fewer than 20 crop plants for 90 percent of its food supply. Genetic information from wild plants may help this limited, and therefore vulnerable food supply withstand the effects of disease, insects or climactic change. In the early 1970s, genetic information from a wild Mexican corn species was used to protect U.S. corn crops from a devastating fungus. Many other opportunities for creating new foods and medicine exist and are awaiting discovery and development. However, the continued destruction of the rainforests over the next few decades promises to permanently remove virtually all possibility of benefiting from this resource.

Out of the vast array of species inhabiting the Earth, humanity uses only one-tenth of one percent. The potential for the other 99.9 percent is enormous and mostly unexplored. However, with every species that is driven to extinction, we lose some potential to cure disease, improve crop productivity and enhance our standard of living.

With the aid of public education, people of the United States and other countries need to realize the serious ramifications of these daily losses. Unlike many things in our lives today, once a species is gone, it can never be recreated.

Endnotes

[1] John Tuxill and Chris Bright. "Losing Strands in the Web of Life." *State of the World 1998*. Washington, DC, p. 42.

[2] Op. cit. note 1, p. 54-55.

[3] Op. cit. note 1, p. 41.

[4] Op. cit. note 1, p. 47.

[5] John H. Cushman. "Million Wetland Acres Lost in 1985-1995: Loss is One-Third of the Previous Decade, Despite New Protections." *New York Times*. September 18, 1997.

[6] The figure represents net migration (people moving in, minus people moving out) to Florida. Census Bureau Web page: www.census.gov/population/estimates/state/st9097t2r2.txt

[7] Op. cit. note 1.

[8] U.S. Fish and Wildlife Service web page: www.fws.gov

[9] Op. cit. note 1, p. 53.

[10] Environment Canada web page: www.ec.gc.ca

[11] Op. cit. note 1, p. 50.

[12] Ibid.

[13] American Association of Zoological Parks and Aquariums. Guam Rail fact sheet: http://aza.org/Programs/SSP/ssp.cfm?ssp=41

[14] North Carolina A&T State University School of Agriculture web site: http://moore.ncat.edu/news/jul96/chestnut.html

[15] Op. cit. note 1.

[16] Ibid.

Bye, Bye Birdie

Concept:
The rate of wildlife endangerment is increasing. Difficult decisions are required to determine how to prioritize our efforts to save endangered species.

Objectives:
Students will be able to:
• Develop criteria that ecologists, wildlife managers and public officials might use to make decisions about protecting endangered species.
• Conduct research on an endangered species through the Internet and other sources.
• Present their findings to the class, showing how their species measured up against the chosen decision criteria.

Subjects:
Biology, environmental science, language arts

Skills:
Critical thinking, cooperation, research, writing, evaluation, public speaking

Method:
Students determine which factors should be considered in deciding the fate of endangered species. They then conduct research to find out about an endangered species, and prepare a short presentation, justifying the preservation of the species.

Materials:
Research materials from the library and/or Internet

Introduction:

Humankind is now precipitating the extinction of large numbers of animals, birds, insects and plants. Estimates are that without human influence, one species in a million would go extinct each year. Because of human activities, over 1,000 species out of a million go extinct each year. We stand a good chance of losing 20% of all species by the year 2020.[1]

Scientists believe that many of the species being lost carry untold potential benefits for the health and economic stability of the planet. With limited funding available for conservation, many believe that humanity should make some tough choices and decide which species can and should be saved.

In the following activity, students will develop a method for making these tough choices on wildlife preservation and compare the relative "value" of different species.

Procedure:

1. Before beginning the activity, be sure that your class is familiar with the concept of biodiversity, the measure of variety of living things and their ecosystems. Emphasize that biological diversity provides us with products (including pharmaceuticals, foods, materials for building and clothing, etc), as well as crucial "ecosystem services," such as clean water, breathable air, natural climate control, and providing stability to the environment. While humans are drawn to plants and animals that appeal to our hearts or our sense of beauty, often the ones that are valuable to us are the species that are most unique, regardless of their size or appearance.

   Then, working individually or in pairs, have students determine which factors should be considered before a decision is made to save a species or let it become extinct. They should list each reason they think is important and write a one-paragraph defense of each.

2. Students will now apply the criteria they developed. Working individually, students should "adopt" one of the endangered species listed on the next page (make sure that each student "adopts" a different species). Give them time to research information about their species. The Web site of the U.S. Fish and Wildlife Service (www.fws.gov) contains extensive information about the ecology of most of these species.

   The students should prepare a short presentation which describes the species, states its importance, and gives reasons why it should be preserved. Students should also discuss threats to the species' survival. These might include habitat destruction, poaching or overhunting, disease, lack of adaptability to changes in climate or other ecological systems, increase in numbers of predators or competitors, etc. If they have difficulty finding information on lesser-known species, students may wish to bolster their research by looking into similar species.

3. Divide the class into groups of 6-8 students. Students in each group will present their findings on their "adopted" species to the group. As the presentations are made, students should rate each species using the criteria developed in the first part of the activity. Ask students if they would change the criteria they developed earlier after they researched their species and rated the others. Have students explain the changes they would make.

4. As the final part of the activity, students must decide which species they will "save" and why. Analysis should focus on the relative possibility of success, examine the value of the species and include less concrete factors such as the preservation or loss of beauty. In addition to the students' individual ratings, each group should try to reach consensus on which species should be "saved."

Follow-up Activity:

There are many endangered species of plants and animals throughout the United States. Students can contact the U.S. Fish and Wildlife Service (1849 C St, NW, Washington, DC 20240, www.fws.org) or your state fish and game agency to obtain a list of threatened or endangered species in your area. Contacting a nearby nature center or natural history muse-

Bye, Bye Birdie

um might also provide helpful information. Once students know which species are endangered in your area, they can research whether or not any efforts are being taken to protect the endangered animals or plants. Preservation projects could be initiated through your school, scouts, 4-H, nature clubs, or hunting and fishing clubs.

1. Wilson, E. O. (1992). The Diversity of Life. Cambridge, MA: Harvard.

2. An **indicator** species is one that shows the effects of habitat alteration before others. Miners used to bring canaries into coal mines because they acted as an indicator species. If the canary died, the miners knew the air was bad, and that they should vacate the mine.

3. By protecting an **umbrella** species, ecologists are able to protect many other species that share the ecosystem. This is usually because the umbrella species requires a large area of undisturbed habitat, which is also good for the other species that share the habitat.

4. A **keystone** species is one whose presence is necessary for other species to survive and thrive. Often, the keystone species provides some ecological service that no other species can provide, such as pollinating a certain type of plant.

Selected List Of Endangered Species

Species	Where found	Teacher's notes
Alabama cave shrimp	U.S.A.	Indicator[2] for water quality
American burying beetle	U.S.A.	Decomposer: helps remove decaying animals
Asian elephant	Southeast Asia	Important for domesticated use
Attwater's prairie chicken	Texas	Indicator for healthy coastal prairie, potential game animal
Black rhinoceros	Africa	Threatened by poachers, important for tourism industry
California condor	U.S.A.	Carrion eater: helps remove decaying animals
Cheetah	Africa	World's fastest land animal
Chinchilla	Bolivia	Valuable fur species
Chinook salmon	U.S.A.	Important food species for humans
Cracking pearly mussel	U.S.A.	Indicator species for clean water
Everglade kite	U.S.A.	Umbrella[3] species: eats snails, snails need healthy everglades
Giant panda	China	Umbrella species: undisturbed bamboo forest
Grizzly bear	U.S.A., Canada	Umbrella species: needs wilderness
Humpback whale	Oceania	Important for tourism industry
Indiana bat	U.S.A.	Eats mosquitos and other insects
Karner blue butterfly	U.S.A.	Umbrella species: endangered savanna/barrens ecosystem
Kirtland's warbler	U.S.A., Canada	Umbrella species: scrub pine habitat, valuable for tourism
Mexican long-nosed bat	U.S.A.	Keystone[4] species: important pollinator for cactus species
Mountain gorilla	Africa	One of Homo sapiens closest relatives
Mountain sweet pitcher plant	U.S.A.	Indicator species for healthy wetlands, valuable for collectors
Nene goose	Hawaii	State bird of Hawaii
Northern spotted owl	U.S.A., Canada	Umbrella species: old-growth forests
Peregrine falcon	U.S.A., Canada	Indicator species for pesticides in food chain
Piping plover	U.S.A., Canada	Requires undisturbed beaches for nesting
Przwalski's horse	China	Domesticated horses are descendants from this species
Red wolf	U.S.A.	Important predator
Scrub mint	U.S.A.	Potentially valuable for medicinal use
Snow leopard	Asia	Threatened by poachers
Utah prairie dog	U.S.A.	Keystone species: their towns offer habitat for other species
Vernal pool tadpole shrimp	U.S.A.	A living fossil: it has been around over 70 million years
West Indian manatee	U.S.A.	Helps keep seabeds from becoming overgrown
Whooping crane	U.S.A., Canada	Largest North American bird, important for tourism
Wood bison	Canada	Numerous historical uses for food, clothing, etc.

No Water Off a Duck's Back

Concept:
Human actions, such as oil spills, can cause devastating environmental effects for wildlife.

Objectives:
Students will be able to:
- Conduct scientific experimentation.
- Analyze data, and draw conclusions from the results of their research.
- Depict data graphically.
- Calculate impacted area of large oil spills based on a small-scale observed model.

Subjects:
Biology, environmental science

Skills:
Lab preparation, mathematic calculations, analyzing data, drawing, estimation, graphing, observation

Method:
Students conduct experiments to identify ways oil spills can affect wildlife adversely and describe possible negative consequences to wildlife, people and the environment from human-caused pollutants.

Materials:
Cooking oil
Several shallow containers
Eye dropper
Hand lens
Feathers (natural)
Liquid detergent (dishwashing liquid)
Hard-boiled eggs

Introduction:

The impacts of environmental pollution often are difficult to see. A major oil spill, however, provides dramatic evidence of potential impact to wildlife. Examples include damage to feathers, killing of embryos when oil seeps into eggs, suffocation of fish when gills are clogged, and death to marine and terrestrial animals who ingest food and water contaminated by oil.

People are involved in efforts to prevent oil spills and their consequences. They also are involved in efforts to "clean up" after such spills take place. Such actions are not always successful, and sometimes they have unfortunate consequences as well. For example, the process of using detergents to clean oil from the feathers of birds caught in spills may also damage the birds' feather structure and arrangement and thus the birds' waterproofing. Birds may also be more susceptible to disease during this time of stress and may be weakened to the extent that it is more difficult for them to secure necessary food and water. Obviously, food and water sources may also be affected in quality.

Oil spills are just one example of pollution that can have adverse short- and long-term effects on wildlife, people and the environment. Students will examine some of the possible consequences for wildlife of human-caused pollution.

Procedure:

Divide the class into groups of three or four. Each group needs a shallow pan partially filled with water. Instruct students to complete the following instructions:

1. Add a known amount of oil, one drop to one dropper-full, depending on the size of the container. Observe the interaction of oil and water. Measure the area covered by the oil. Using this information, have students estimate the area that might be affected by an oil spill involving:

   a) A tanker truck holding 8,000 gallons of oil

   b) A ship holding 300,000 gallons of oil

   c) A supertanker holding 83,000,000 gallons of oil

   Discuss and compare estimates with other groups. Graph estimates and compute average figures.

2. Put enough oil in a small container to submerge three hard-boiled eggs. Add the eggs. Put the eggs under a good light and watch closely. Remove one egg after five minutes and examine it — before, during and after pulling off the shell. Try to remove the excess oil from the outside before attempting to peel the egg. Remove the second egg after 15 minutes and the third egg after 30 minutes, repeating the procedure, examining each carefully. Discuss observations. What effect could oil have on the eggs of birds nesting near the water?

3. Examine a feather with a hand lens. Sketch what you see. Dip the feather in water for one or two minutes, and examine again with a hand lens. Sketch and compare to the original observations. Place the feather in oil for one or two minutes, and then examine with a hand lens, sketch and compare with other sketches. Then dip the feather in water with detergent in it, rinse in clean water and examine again. Discuss changes in the feather after exposure to oil and then to detergents. What effect could these changes have on normal bird activity?

4. Discuss other possible effects on birds from an oil spill. Discuss possible impacts on other wildlife species, on humans and on the environment. What trade-offs are involved? Do we have to choose between oil and birds, as well as other wildlife? What are some alternatives? What are other examples of human-caused pollutants that can have negative consequences for wildlife, people and the environment? What is being done or can be done about these as well?

Follow-up Activity:

An extension of the activity might include using a variety of oils (cooking oil, motor oil, crude oil) to compare effects on feathers and eggs. Food coloring can be added to clear oils to facilitate observation of effects. Other pollutants can be used to see what, if any, effects they have on eggs and feathers. Exercise caution, however; do not use any unusually dangerous substances.

Adapted by permission from Project WILD. The original activity appears in Project WILD: K-12 Activity Guide, 2nd Ed., *Council for Environmental Education*, 1992.

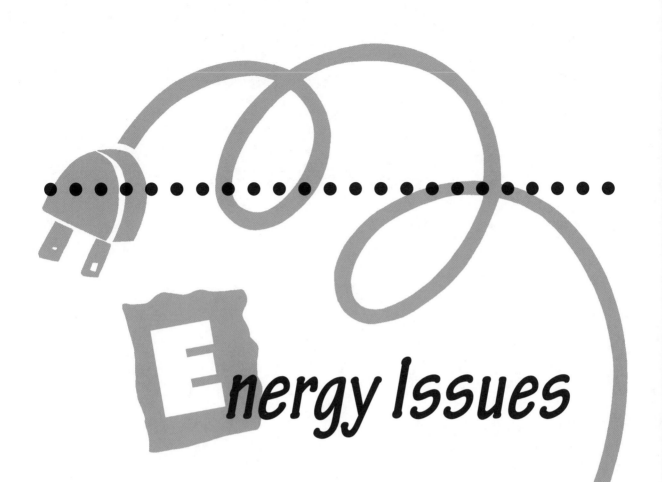

Energy Issues

Energy Futures

When it comes to oil, the world's people seem to have an unquenchable thirst. Wasteful habits coupled with population growth fuel the demand for increased energy production. The World Energy Conference projects that global energy consumption will rise 54 percent between 1990 and 2020.[1] Most of the increased energy production is likely to be supplied by coal, oil and natural gas. Finite resources and environmental concerns may necessitate changes in energy use over the next 50 years.

People in some countries consume much more energy than others. The average amount of energy used by each person in the world each year is equal to 1,439 kilograms of oil. However, the amount used by a person in the United States is 7,918 kilograms, and is 7,639 in Canada — well above the average. There are many countries where people use much less energy. The amount of energy used by one person in Asia is equivalent to only 738 kilograms of oil, and someone living in Africa uses only 299 kilograms — only 3.8% of the energy consumed by a North American.[2]

Fossil Foolish

Fossil fuels, such as oil, coal and natural gas, provide 86 percent of energy produced in the world each year.[3] **Oil** is the dominant source of energy, providing 40 percent, coal provides 25 percent, and natural gas provides 21 percent of all energy produced.[4] Such heavy reliance on fossil fuels fosters concerns on two grounds. First, although new reserves are discovered each year, the Earth's supply of these fuels is finite. Since we are using oil, coal and natural gas at much faster rates than the earth creates them, our reserves of these fuels will eventually run out.

Second, burning fossil fuels for energy is responsible for 85 percent of carbon dioxide emissions (the rest come from burning and logging of forests).[5] Most scientists now agree that rising concentrations of carbon dioxide (CO_2) and other greenhouse gases in the atmosphere is resulting in potentially dangerous changes in global climate. Predicted increases in fossil fuel use are expected to raise annual carbon emissions to 9.7 billion tons by 2015, an increase of 61 percent over 1996's 6 billion tons of emissions.[6]

Natural gas is the fastest growing fossil fuel. By 2015, it is expected to provide a greater portion of global energy than coal.[7] It is also the cleanest burning fossil fuel. It releases the least amount of carbon per unit of energy produced. Oil releases 1.38 times as much, and coal releases 1.79 times as much.

Of the three primary fossil fuels, **coal** is found in the largest supply on Earth. It is the most common source of energy consumed in India and China, and generates more electricity in the United States than any other source.[8] In addition to carbon emissions, coal combustion releases sulphur dioxide and nitrogen oxides which pollute the air and lead to acid rain. Other environmental concerns about coal include land degradation and water pollution from mining, and disposal of hazardous coal ash.[9]

In 1996, 64 million barrels of oil per day were produced in the world. Oil is expected to continue to be the dominant source of energy in the world for several decades. Experts predict that world oil consumption could reach as high as 105 million barrels per day by 2015.[10] The United States, at 17.7 million barrels per day in 1996, is the biggest oil consumer.[11]

Energy Futures

In 1996, the United States produced 6.5 million barrels of oil per day.[12] This level is enough to make it the world's second biggest oil producer, but it is 30 percent lower than peak production in the early 1970's.[13] Furthermore, in addition to all the oil it produces, the United States is still dependent on oil imports for 46 percent of its total energy consumption.[14] As of 1996, U.S. oil reserves were 34 percent lower than in 1977.[15]

1,100 billion barrels is a rough estimate of how much oil is left in reserves around the world, enough to last about another 40 years at current rates of consumption.[16] Two-thirds of known reserves are located in the Middle East; Saudi Arabia, the world's biggest oil producer, holds one quarter alone.[17]

Driving Up the Stakes

Two-thirds of the petroleum consumed in the United States is used for transportation.[18] In the United States, the car has become a prized possession. There is one car for every 1.3 people and close to four million miles of public roads.[19]

With the increase in population comes an increase in the number of vehicles on the road. Urban planners respond by building more roads and expanding the existing roads—a temporary solution for congestion. According to the Federal Highway Administration, congestion will likely increase by more than 400 percent over the next 20 years on the nation's freeways and by 200 percent on other roads. In addition, while fuel efficiency of cars doubled between 1974 and 1988, very little improvement has been made since then. Average fuel efficiency of new cars is even declining due to increased use of sport utility vehicles which get fewer miles to the gallon.[20] If the average U.S. car got just ten more miles per gallon we would save as many barrels of oil as the country imports from the Middle East.[21]

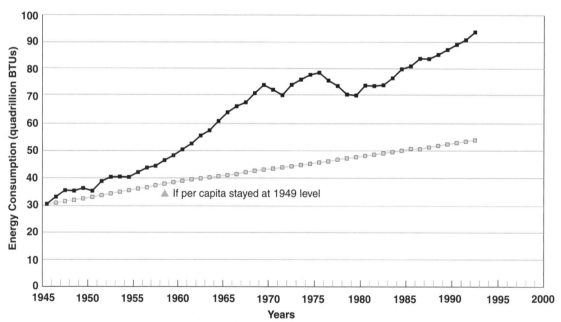

U.S. Energy Consumption

 If per capita stayed at 1949 level

The top line is the actual energy consumption of the United States, which is influenced by per capita use and the size of the population. The bottom line indicates the increase in energy consumption only as a result of population growth, as it does not include growth in **per capita consumption** since 1949. Therefore, the difference between the top and bottom lines indicates the increase in energy consumption per capita, up from 204 million BTUs in 1949 to 354 million BTUs in 1996.

Source: Annual Energy Review 1996. Washington, DC: Energy Information Agency, U.S. Department of Energy, 1997.

Energy Futures

American transportation habits differ greatly from those in other industrialized countries. In the 50 largest U.S. metro areas, 73 percent of people commute to work alone by car, 12.9 percent carpool and only 6.5 percent use public transportation, while 7.6 walk or bicycle.[22] In European cities, about 40 percent commute by car, 37 percent use public transit, and the rest walk or bicycle. Only 15 percent of the population in industrialized Asian cities, such as Tokyo, drive to work by car. Such habits illustrate why the United States, with less than five percent of the world's population, consumes about a quarter of the energy produced in the world each year.[23]

Often, people commute by car because they do not have any other convenient way. More and more, however, urban planners in the United States are looking at how to design communities where residents wouldn't need to drive in order to get to work, school, stores, etc.

Worldwide, the transportation sector creates 21 percent of all energy-related greenhouse gas emissions.[24] Personal automobiles make up the vast majority of this sector. Emissions from transportation are expected to double by 2020 as population and economic growth in developing countries like South Korea, the Philippines, Thailand, India and China spark rapid increases in car ownership.[25]

More for Less

One important way to reduce the use of fossil fuels is to improve the energy efficiency, not only of our cars, but also of our household appliances, lights, and heating and cooling systems, among other things. Substantial improvements could be made just with the technology already available. For example, lighting uses about 20 percent of U.S. electricity. If everyone used energy-efficient flourescent light bulbs, we could save the amount of energy produced by 120 power plants.[26]

Super windows, insulated with six sheets of glass, can actually absorb heat in the winter rather than letting it escape, dramatically reducing the amount of energy necessary to heat a building. Similarly, windows have been designed for warm climates that let in light but only 20 percent of the heat of normal windows. Some of these technologies are actually cheaper to install that more conventional ones, and those that are not pay for themselves in a couple of years with the amount of energy costs they save.[27]

Energy Alternatives

Although fossil fuels are the predominant energy sources in the industrialized world, they are not the only game in town. Research has been continuing since the early 1970's to develop and improve alternative sources of energy. Environmental concerns and finite resources require that we switch to cleaner, more efficient energy alternatives. Both **nuclear power** and **renewable energy sources** have been examined as possibilities to replace fossil fuels. Nuclear power presently provides 6.4 percent of the world's energy. Renewable sources, which consist almost entirely of **hydroelectric** (water) power provided 7.2 percent.[28] However, both of these energy sources has significant shortcomings. Neither is expected to increase as fast as fossil fuels in the short term, and will produce a smaller portion of energy in the immediate future.[29]

Nukes or No Nukes

In the years following World War II, the nuclear knowledge that led to the production of atomic weapons was redeployed for peaceful energy purposes. Nuclear fission emerged as a usable source of energy, but not without risks. Dangers such as radiation poisoning, meltdown risks and unsafe disposal of nuclear wastes pose threats to the future of nuclear energy.

After 50 years of significant technological effort to support nuclear development, nuclear energy has become widely used. Approximately 30 countries produce energy from nuclear generators, accounting for 17 percent of all electricity generated globally.[30]

Although nuclear energy is now used throughout industrialized countries, its future is still suspect. Several nuclear power plant failures have brought to the public eye the potential risks of this energy source. Controversy has developed concerning the elimination of the hazardous waste as well as the safety and loca-

Energy Futures

tion of the reactor sites. Extensive research is being done to address the safety of nuclear power. But it is not clear that any of these problems can be resolved in time to make nuclear fission a major option for the foreseeable future. In fact, while nuclear power increased rapidly from 1970 to 1990, since 1990, it has begun to level off, and is predicted to decline in the future.[31]

Earth, Wind and Solar Fire

Many believe that clean, renewable fuels—solar, wind, hydroelectric and geothermal—should play a significant role in meeting future energy needs. Renewable resources are mostly still in the primitive stages of development, but they offer the world potentially large primary energy sources, sustainable and available to every nation in one form or another.

Renewable energy supplies already fill almost ten percent of U.S. energy needs.[32] Hydroelectric power makes up the vast majority of this energy. Many renewable energy sources have several comparable advantages. For example, although they are not free from environmental consequences, they do not have nearly the environmental impact of synthetic fuels.

Of all renewable sources, **solar energy** is likely to be the cornerstone of a future sustainable energy system. Sunshine is available in great quantity and is more widely distributed than any other source. A few decades from now, societies may use the sun to heat most of their water, and new buildings may take advantage of natural heating and cooling to cut energy use by more than 80 percent. **Wind power** also has great potential to provide electricity in most countries. Electricity is generated by propeller-driven mechanical turbines perched on strategically located towers.

Hydroelectric power supplies 20 percent of the world's electricity[33] and two-thirds of Canada's electrical needs.[34] Although there is still growth potential for this energy resource, environmental constraints may limit development. Shortcomings, such as flooding, siltation, human displacement and wildlife endangerment surround the building of dams and reservoirs for the harnessing of hydroelectric power.

Energy Futures

Geothermal energy, the latent heat from the Earth's core, can provide electricity when there is no sun or wind. After hydroelectric power, geothermal energy is the next most common renewable source. Although geothermal resources are localized, they can provide energy to a number of areas along fault lines.

Currently, renewable energy sources are quite expensive, but if national governments and private companies make a substantial and sustained commitment to further research and development, costs should fall, and the potential of these renewable sources can be realized.

Planning for Our Energy Future

The amount of energy consumed has increased over the years with growth in the global economy and world population. Over the last half century, the population has doubled, the world economy has increased five times, and the amount of energy consumed has tripled.[35] We face difficult energy and economic choices in the years ahead. It is apparent that the supply of fossil fuels will not be sufficient to keep up with increased consumption, spurred on by population and economic growth. In addition, continued expansion of fossil fuel use poses dire threats to the biosphere.

There is no time to waste in planning for a sustainable energy future, one that will ensure economic security as well as ecological preservation. Efforts on the international, federal, state, and individual level could produce solutions to the energy dilemma while at the same time making positive steps toward taking care of the planet. Individuals can alleviate the ill effects of fossil fuel combustion by conserving energy whenever possible. As a nation, we must commit ourselves to the research, development and implementation of cleaner, more efficient energy alternatives. But ensuring the safety of our planet will require global collaboration on sustainable energy policies, as well as reducing population growth.

Endnotes

[1] *World Resources 96-97*. Washington, DC: Oxford University Press, 1996. p. 280.

[2] *Energy Statistics Yearbook 1995*. New York: United Nations, 1997. Population-weighted per capita energy consumption statistic for North America (the United States and Canada is 7890 kg of oil equivalent per person).

[3] *Annual Energy Review, 1996*. Washington, DC: Energy Information Agency, U.S. Department of Energy, 1997.

[4] Ibid.

[5] *The International Energy Outlook 1997*. Washington, DC: Energy Information Agency, U.S. Department of Energy, 1997.

[6] Ibid.

[7] Ibid.

[8] Coal data: op. cit. note 1, p. 276. United States electricity data: op. cit. note 3.

[9] Op. cit. note 1, p. 279.

[10] Op. cit. note 5.

[11] Op. cit. note 3.

[12] Ibid.

[13] Christopher Flavin. "Fossil Fuel Use Surges to New High." *Vital Signs 1997*. Washington, DC: W.W. Norton and Co., 1997. p. 46.

[14] Op. cit. note 3, Chapter 5: Petroleum. Figures from 1996.

[15] *U.S. Crude Oil, Natural Gas, and Gas Liquids Reserves, 1996 Annual Report*. Washington DC: Energy Information Agency, U.S. Department of Energy, 1997.

[16] Oil reserves estimate: *Oil and Gas Journal* cited in op. cit. note 15. Estimate of years reserves will last: op. cit. note 1, p. 275.

[17] Op. cit. note 13.

[18] Op. cit. note 3. Table 1.3 shows total petroleum consumed. Table 2.1 shows petroleum consumed by the transportation sector.

[19] U.S. Department of Transportation, Bureau of Transportation Statistics webpage: www.bts.gov.

[20] Christopher Flavin and Seth Dunn. "Responding to the Threat of Climate Change," *State of the World 1998*. Washington, DC: Worldwatch Institute, 1998. p. 120.

[21] L. Hunter Lovins and Amory B. Lovins. "How Not to Parachute More Cats." Snowmass, CO: Rocky Mountain Institute, p. 5.

[22] U.S. Census Bureau Webpage: www.census.gov/population/socdemo/journey/msa50.txt. Data from 1990 census.

[23] Op. cit. notes 2 and 3.

[24] Op. cit. note 20.

[25] Emissions projection: Op. cit. note 20. Car ownership projection: op. cit. note 5.

[26] Op. cit. note 21, p. 6.

[27] Amory B. Lovins and L. Hunter Lovins. "The Negawatt Revolution: Abating Global Warming for Fun and Profit." Snowmass, CO: Rocky Mountain Institute, 1994. p. 2.

[28] Op. cit. note 3.

[29] Op. cit. note 5.

[30] Op. cit. notes 2 and 3.

[31] Op. cit. notes 5 and 13.

[32] Op. cit. note 3.

[33] Ibid.

[34] Environment Canada website (www.ec.gc.ca/water/).

[35] Op. cit. note 1, pp. 277-278.

Are People the Problem?

Concept:
In order to determine whether a region is "over-populated," students must consider consumption levels of resources and energy in addition to numbers of people.

Objectives:
Students will be able to:
• List ways we depend on energy.
• Rank countries in terms of population size and energy consumption.
• Draw correlations between population growth and energy consumption trends.

Subjects:
Social studies, math, environmental science

Skills:
Collecting and recording data, analyzing and interpreting data, estimation, mathematical calculations, graphing

Method:
Through data calculations and discussion questions, students will examine the relationship between population and energy consumption.

Materials:
Copies of Student Worksheets 1 and 2 for each student

Introduction:

When studying population pressures, it is important to consider consumption levels and their environmental impacts. In this activity, students inquire into the relationships between numbers of people and energy consumption. After this examination, students are asked to consider the statement: *The United States is the most overpopulated country in the world today*.

Procedure:

1. Hand out Student Worksheet 1 to the students. Before beginning the activity, have students suggest some of the ways we use energy in this country. What aspects of our lives depend on energy being available? Have students list them.

2. Have students complete Student Worksheet 1 and the first half of Student Worksheet 2 either individually, in pairs, or as an entire class. Tell students to leave the third column in Student Worksheet 1 blank for now.

3. Discuss some of the students' answers to the questions in Student Worksheet 2. Tell the class they will test these answers by calculating the per capita energy consumption of the world.

4. Have students follow the directions on the second half of Student Worksheet 2. Then, have a general discussion or have students write their responses to this statement: *The United States is the most overpopulated country in the world today*.

Follow-up Activity:

After determining the extent of energy consumption in the United States and the increase in energy consumption worldwide, students should now examine the environmental impacts of increased energy use worldwide. Lead a discussion on the detrimental effects of increased fossil fuel use. How can less developed countries get ahead if they do not implement the energy consumption habits of industrialized countries?

Adapted with permission from University of Denver Center for Teaching International Relations. The original activity appears in Teaching About Population Issues, by George Otero, Jr. and Richard Schweissing, Center for Teaching International Relations, University of Denver, CO, 1977.

Suggested Answers to Student Worksheet 1

Energy Consumption	Population	Per Capita Energy Use (kg)
Europe/Central Asia, 33.6%	East Asia/Pacific, 33.9%	North America, 7,823
North America, 28.6%	South Asia, 22.0%	Europe/Central Asia, 3,097
East Asia/Pacific, 22.2%	Europe/Central Asia, 15.4%	Middle East/ N.Africa, 1,374
Latin America/Caribbean, 5.7%	Sub-Saharan Africa, 10.1%	Latin America/Caribbean, 960
Middle East/N.Africa, 4.8%	Latin America/Caribbean, 8.4%	East Asia/Pacific, 934
South Asia, 3.4%	North America, 5.2%	Sub-Saharan Africa, 237
Sub-Saharan Africa, 1.7%	Middle East/ N.Africa, 4.9%	South Asia, 222

Suggested Answers to Student Worksheet 2

1. a) 29% b) 3%

2. Answers may vary, but remember: a decrease in the *population* might help decrease energy consumption, but a decrease in the *growth rate* would not, unless it decreases to a negative rate.

3. Answers may vary. However, a decrease in population growth does not *automatically* create an increase in energy consumption.

4. Some of the many possible answers include: increase in air pollution, increased climate change, more ozone layer depletion, shortage of fuels and more political conflicts.

5. The data suggest that factors such as energy consumption should also be considered when discussing the problem of overpopulation.

Are People the Problem?

Do countries with the smallest population size have the smallest population problem?

Energy has been a vital prerequisite for development in technology, science, medicine, etc. It is an important factor in the world today. By looking at its relationship to population size, we can shed some light on the above questions.

Look at these figures for the seven basic world areas.

Area	Energy Used[1] (metric tons of oil equivalent)	Energy Use[2] Percent of World Total	Population	Population Percent of World Total
Europe/Central Asia	2,658,274,000	33.6%	858,314,040	15.4%
East Asia/Pacific	1,762,310,000	22.2%	1,887,116,379	33.9%
South Asia	271,293,000	3.4%	1,222,040,541	22.0%
Middle East/N. Africa	376,793,000	3.4%	1,222,040,541	4.9%
Sub-Saharan Africa	133,471,000	1.7%	563,168,776	10.1%
Latin America/Caribbean	451,011,000	5.7%	469,803,125	8.4%
North America	2,267,710,000	28.6%	289,894,647	5.2%
World Total	**7,920,862,000**	**100%**	**5,564,533,468**	**100%**

What do the data tell us? List the world areas in decreasing order of energy consumption and then population size. Indicate the percentage after each. Leave the category "Per Capita Energy Consumption" blank for now.

highest	Energy Consumption	Population Energy use	Per Capita
1.	%	%	
2.	%	%	
3.	%	%	
4.	%	%	
5.	%	%	
6.	%	%	
7.	%	%	
lowest			

1 Data: World Development Report 1997. *The World Bank, New York: Oxford University Press, 1997.*
2 Data: Population Reference Bureau, 1997 World Population Data Sheet.

Are People the Problem?

Part 1:

1. 5.2% of the world's population consumes _____ % of the world's energy while ...

    22% of the world's population consumes_____ % of the world's energy.
    What might account for this?

2. In your opinion, would a decrease in the North American population growth rate decrease national energy consumption?

3. In your opinion, would a decrease in the population growth of South Asia automatically increase energy consumption in South Asia?

4. If all world areas eventually reach an energy consumption level comparable to that of North America, what problems might result?

5. How does the information presented here suggest that the problem of overpopulation involves more than a simple increase in numbers?

Part 2:

1. Now, turn back to Student Worksheet 1 and calculate the energy use per person and again list the areas in descending order. *(Note: You should convert your answers to kilograms; 1 metric ton = 1,000 kilograms).*

2. Do you still feel the same about your answer to the first question on Student Worksheet 1?

3. Considering what you have studied, again respond to this statement: *The United States is the most overpopulated country in the world today.*

Getting Around

Introduction:

North Americans have a long-standing love affair with their cars. There are more cars per person in the United States than in any other country. As the population increases, so do the number of cars on the road, and hence the congestion and pollution. Motor vehicles are major contributors to air pollution, ozone depletion, climate change, acid rain and the loss of scenic beauty as roads and parking lots pave over the American landscape. Using less or cleaner burning fuel would reduce this pollution. After the oil embargo of 1973, Americans sought smaller, more fuel efficient vehicles, but now with low gas prices, sport utility vehicles (SUVs) and minivans are becoming more popular. These larger vehicles emit more pollution than cars because the 1975 policy mandating higher fuel efficiency was more lenient on these automobiles. With the international pressures to reduce greenhouse gas emissions, our transportation habits are the source of debate. Some current options follow:

- Increase fuel efficiency of SUVs and minivans.
- Develop alternative fuels for internal combustion, like ethanol and methanol.
- Provide electric or hybrid electric/internal combustion vehicles.
- Expand public transportation systems in metropolitan areas.

Procedure:

1. In order to assess transportation habits and viewpoints in their local area, students will develop a survey to conduct in the community. As a class, have students devise the survey questions (see examples on next page). The students might want to question people about their desire for some of the alternative transportation options.

2. While developing the survey students should consider how best to compile the data. Have students word the questions in a manner which is easy to evaluate. This might be with yes/no questions, multiple choice, other styles, or a combination of styles (see sample questions on next page). Also, have students determine whether they wish to do a demographic breakdown of their data. If so, they should add spaces for survey takers to check off factors such as their age and gender.

3. Once the content of the survey is determined, a representative from the class should type it up. Then copies should be made so that each student has at least ten surveys to administer.

4. Conducting the survey may be done in a variety of ways. Since students wish to get a diverse sample from the community at large, it may be easiest for them to go to a busy area, such as a shopping mall or outside of a grocery store or subway station. Students can either seek permission to set up a table or they can walk around with a clipboard and ask questions of interested passers-by. Another option would be to go door-to-door in their neighborhoods if they have parental and school approval. Respondents should be assured that their answers will be kept completely anonymous. Also, please remind students that the purpose of this activity is to collect data and not to make judgments upon any individual's responses.

5. Each student should be responsible for tallying his/her own results. These results can then be compiled by one or two students in the class.

6. What do these results say about transportation habits in your community? Have students draw basic conclusions from the survey results. Consider having these results published in the school and/or local community newspaper.

Follow-up Activity:

Students can formulate recommendations for managing the community's transportation problems. They can explore the advantages and disadvantages of implementing various options, such as creating or widening roads, building a mass transit system, encouraging carpooling, limiting growth, etc. This activity need not end in the classroom. Students can voice their ideas at city council meetings or through letters to the editor of the area newspaper.

Concept:
Transportation habits in the U.S. and Canada contribute greatly to each nation's dependency on fossil fuels. These habits need to be evaluated as we seek solutions to growing transportation problems.

Objectives:
Students will be able to:
- Create and conduct a transportation survey.
- Analyze the collected data and publicize the result.
- Suggest ways of managing transportation in their local area.

Subjects:
Environmental science, language arts, social studies, family life

Skills:
Developing and administering a survey, tabulating and interpreting data, evaluation

Method:
Students conduct a community survey to determine local transportation habits.

Materials:
Copies of Sample Questions and Survey Tips

Getting Around

Yes/No Survey

All questions have only **yes** or **no** answers. You might want a few comment-type questions.

1. Do you drive a vehicle?
2. Would you characterize traffic in your area as congested?
3. Are you aware of a place where you could get ethanol?
4. If an electric car suited your needs in all areas except had a slightly higher cost and was limited to commuting use only, would you buy it?
5. Did you know about electric cars being available on the market?
6. Do you use your car to commute to school or work?
7. Do you carpool? (If so, how many people are in your carpool?)
8. Do you think the area needs more roads and highways?
9. Do you feel that your area's public transit system is adequate for your needs?

Multiple Choice Survey

The choices should be labeled (a, b, c, etc.), or there should be places for people to mark their choices.

1. What size vehicle do you drive, if you own one?
   motorcycle
   minivan
   compact car
   van
   sport utility vehicle

2. How often do you check the air in your tires?
   once a week
   once a month
   once a year
   never

3. When buying a vehicle what features are most important?
   gas mileage
   color
   style/appearance
   roominess/comfort
   engine size
   other

4. How would you characterize traffic in your area?
   very few cars on the road
   few cars on the road
   moderate traffic
   congested
   very congested

5. What type of gas do you use?
   unleaded
   premium unleaded
   ethanol
   methanol
   diesel
   other

6. How many miles do you put on your car each week?
   0-100
   101-300
   301-600
   601-1100
   1101+

7. How many cars are owned by your household? (Circle)
   0   1   2   3
   4   5   6

8. Do you drive the speed limit?
   always under
   sometimes under
   at speed limit
   sometimes over
   always over

9. What types of alternative transportation do you use? (Circle all that apply)
   None
   bike
   bus
   subway
   light rail
   carpool
   walk

10. How often do you use alternative transportation?
   never
   rarely sometimes
   mostly/often
   always

An Energizing Policy

Introduction:

In comparison with other industrialized countries, America is lagging in its efforts to reduce emissions. Although North America comprises only five percent of the world's population, it consumes 29 percent of the world's energy. In the mid-1980s, oil prices dropped sharply, discouraging investment in U.S. oil exploration, conservation and development of alternative energy sources and energy-efficient technologies. Consequently, greenhouse gases have continued to increase, up 8.8% between 1990 and 1996. Therefore, goals set in 1992 at the UN Conference on Environment and Development (UNCED) no longer seem attainable. With a better understanding of the economic and political approaches to reduce emissions, the participants at the 1997 Framework Convention on Climate Change (COP3) Kyoto Conference began new international discussions and strategies for reducing greenhouse gas emissions.

Procedure:

1. Distribute copies of the *Student Worksheet*.

2. A list of resources where students might wish to start their research has been provided. Be sure to encourage them to go beyond this list. If students request literature from organizations, advise them to write or call at least one month before the paper is due.

3. Allow students creativity with this project, and encourage them to think of both the international and domestic positions surrounding energy issues. To attain a greater understanding of the complexity of energy issues, students should elaborate on the many viewpoints surrounding their topic.

4. When grading the research papers, look for demonstrated research, clarity of thought, persuasive argumentation and critical thinking skills.

Follow-up Activity:

As a class, have the students put together a comprehensive proposal for the United States' or Canada's energy policy and send it to the lawmakers. To prepare for this activity, divide the students into groups, based on the focus of their papers. In these groups, students will work together to create their portion of the energy policy proposal for the country. Each group will decide what position it is taking and provide detail of how to accomplish this position. These proposals may include several recommendations, but it is important to be as specific as possible. For instance, if recommending increased energy conservation measures, be precise about what form these measures would take and how they should be implemented. For each recommendation, give a full explanation as to why this plan would be best for the country. Informing students of this follow-up activity up front may be useful in minimizing the need for further research during this stage. Once each group has written its proposal, compile the group papers into the comprehensive energy policy proposal. Each group's section can be a separate chapter in the proposal. Finally, the class should work together to develop an introduction and conclusion to the comprehensive proposal, and then it could be sent to the lawmakers.

Office of the President
The White House
1600 Pennsylvania Ave., NW
Washington, DC 20500
email: president@whitehouse.gov

Representative _____
The U.S. House of Representatives
Washington, DC 20515
Who's mine? www.house.gov

Senator_____
The U.S. Senate
Washington, DC 20510
Who's mine? www.senate.gov

House of Commons
Parliament Buildings
Ottawa, Ontario K1A 0A6
Who's mine? www.parl.gc.ca

Concept:

Develop energy policies to meet a country's energy needs while reducing greenhouse gas emissions.

Objectives:

Students will be able to:
• Research a specific energy issue.
• Determine economic and environmental costs and benefits of current energy types and consumption levels, along with possible alternatives.
• Formulate a proposal for energy use.

Subjects:

Language arts, environmental science, social studies, economics, civics/government

Skills:

Critical thinking, research, writing, decision making, persuasion

Method:

Students research a topic related to energy use and policy in the United States or Canada and formulate a position, weighing costs and benefits.

Materials

Copies of Student Worksheet
Research materials from various energy associations (see attached list), public interest groups and library resources

An Energizing Policy

North America is the largest consumer of energy per capita, and our primary source of energy in the United States is coal, a nonrenewable resource. Is our country on the right track? Are there other options? Should we lower our energy use and if so, how?

Your assignment is to identify the best course of action for the United States (or Canada) on any of the topics below. Describe the different options within your topic and address both the positive and negative aspects of these options. You should explore environmental and economic costs and benefits. Then, formulate a position as to what you think is best for the United States (or Canada) and why. A list of resources has been provided to help you start your research. Whatever course of action you choose, be sure to back it up with the data you uncover in your research.

Possible Energy Topics:

1. Weigh the pros and cons of our current sources of fuel for vehicles, along with some other options that are not in wide use. For example: gasoline vs. ethanol, or catalatic converter vehicles vs. electric cars, hydrogen or solar powered cars, etc.

2. Propose the degree to which we should rely on domestic vs. imported oil by looking at the current trends and future options.

3. Discuss the benefits and drawbacks of nonrenewable vs. renewable energy resources.

4. Transportation systems currently focus on highways for vehicles. Compare this to funding and developing alternative and mass transit systems.

5. Look into oil exploration and report on the possibilities of new sources like the Arctic National Wildlife Refuge. Are there others? What are the pluses and minuses of oil drilling in these areas?

6. Analyze the trends in household and business energy use. Compare the energy-efficient technologies for these consumers to each other and to less efficient technologies.

7. Report on the possible methods for reducing consumption of gasoline: increasing taxes vs. mandating fuel efficiency.

8. Look at the current level of funding for research and development of alternative energy sources and propose what it should be. (Higher or Lower?)

9. Research how oil exploration and/or vehicle manufacturers are subsidized and hypothesize about how this affects their productivity vs. subsidizing alternative fuel development.

An Energizing Policy

GOVERNMENT AGENCIES:

U.S. Department of Energy
PA-40
1000 Independence Avenue, SW
Washington, DC 20585
202/586-5575
www.doe.gov/

National Alternative Fuels Hotline
PO Box 12316
Arlington, VA 22209
800/423-1DOE
www.afdc.nrel.gov/misc/sources.html
Nation Clean Cities Hotline
800/224-8437

Natural Resources Canada
Public Inquiries; Main Floor
580 Booth Street
Ottawa, Ontario Canada
K1A 0E4
613/995-0947
www.nrcan.gc.ca; www.es.nrcan.gc.ca/

Environment Canada/ The Green Lane
www.ec.gc.ca/
www.ed.gc.ca/climate

INDUSTRY ORGANIZATIONS:

American Gas Association
1515 Wilson Boulevard
Arlington, VA 22209
703/841-8400
www.aga.com

American Petroleum Institute
1220 L Street, NW
Washington, DC 20036
202/682-8000
www.api.org

Electric Power Research Institute
1019 19th Street, NW, #1000
Washington, DC 20036
202/872-9222
650/855-2000 (CA Headquarters)
www.epri.com

Interstate Natural Gas Association of
America
10 G Street, NE, Suite 700
Washington, DC 20006
202/626-3200
www.ingaa.org

National Bio-Energy Industries
Association
122 C Street, NW, 4th Floor
Washington, DC 20001
202/383-2540

National Hydrogen Association
1800 M Street, NW, Suite 300
Washington, DC 20036
202/223-5547
www.ttcorp.com/nha

Nuclear Energy Institute
1776 I Street, NW, Suite 400
Washington, DC 20006
202/739-8000
www.nei.org

Renewable Fuels Association
1 Massachusetts Avenue, NW, Suite 820
Washington, DC 20001
202/289-3835

Solar Energy Industries Association
122 C Street, NW 4th Floor
Washington, DC 20001
202/383-2600
www.seia.org

PUBLIC INTEREST GROUPS:

Consumer Energy Council of America
Research Foundation
2000 L Street, NW, #802
Washington, DC 20036
202/659-0404
www.cecarf.org

Public Citizen
1600 20th Street, NW
Washington, DC 20009
202/588-1000
www.citizen.org/

Union of Concerned Scientists
1616 P Street, NW, Suite 310
Washington, DC 20036
202/332-0900
www.ucsusa.org

World Resources Institute
1709 New York Avenue, NW, Suite 700
Washington, DC 20006
202/638-6300
www.wri.org/wri/

Energy Council of Canada
30 Colonnade Rd., Suite #400
Ottawa, Ontario K2E 7J6
613/952-6469
www.energy.ca/

Rich and Poor.................

The Rising Tide of Poverty

We live in an economically divided world. One-fifth of the world's population enjoys relative wealth, while the other four-fifths have barely the means of survival. As the wealthy industrialized countries speak of economic progress, the ranks of the poor in less developed countries continue to grow. This disparity of wealth and the spread of poverty threaten the future quality of life for all of Earth's inhabitants.

For the majority of the world's people, poverty is far more than an economic condition. Poverty's effects extend into all aspects of a person's life, such as susceptibility to disease, limited access to most types of services and information, subordination to higher social and economic classes, and complete insecurity in the face of changing circumstances.

The number of people living in slums and shantytowns is rapidly increasing. A growing number lack access to clean water and sanitation and hence fall victim to the diseases that arise from this absence. There is noticeable progress in some places, but on the whole, poverty continues and the numbers of people living in poverty multiply. About one-third of people living in developing countries, or 1.3 billion people still struggle to provide for their basic needs on one dollar a day.[1]

Who Are the Poor?

Most of the world's more than one billion poor live in Africa, Asia and Latin America. The poor are overwhelmingly illiterate, and therefore lack access to information and ideas that could help them escape poverty. Three-quarters of the poor live in rural areas and are dependent on agriculture for their main source of income.[2] With most of the land owned by a wealthy few, the majority of the world's population is landless. Population growth divides family **subsistence farms** into smaller and smaller plots, until they no longer provide subsistence. Then, typically, poor people are forced to work as dispossessed laborers for others, unable to achieve economic prosperity.

Poverty is not fairly distributed among people. Women, children, the elderly and ethnic minorities are inevitably hardest hit. Women are disadvantaged by the fact that they frequently cannot own land or get access to credit, and have less access to education and good employment opportunities. For children, chronic hunger can harm their health and mental development and stunt their growth. Worldwide, 160 million children are malnourished, and 110 million children are out of school.[3] Lacking sufficient nourishment and clean water, one in ten of these youngsters dies before her or his fifth birthday.[4]

What A Difference!

Great disparities in living standards exist between the world's rich and poor. In 1996, the world had 358 billionaires. Their income and assets totaled more than the combined annual incomes of countries where 45 percent of world population lives.[5] Wealthy nations have almost tripled their per capita income since mid-century, but that figure in the poorest countries has remained basically constant. Developing countries make up only $5 trillion of the $23 trillion of the global **Gross Domestic Product** (GDP) every year, despite the fact that they are home to 80 percent of the world's people.[6] Furthermore, a full 60 to 70 percent of people in most countries earn less than their nation's average income.

Island of Wealth in a Sea of Poverty

Source: Ann Ninan, Terra Viva's cartoonist in Cairo, On the Road from Rio to Beijing. ICPD Sept. 1994.

The Rising Tide of Poverty

In recent years, the term "developing country" has become a misnomer: many countries are not so much developing as they are losing their fights to eradicate poverty. Only 15 countries have seen rapidly rising incomes since 1980. In 70 countries, average incomes are lower than they were in 1980.[7] Though industrialized countries experienced an economic resurgence, other regions of the world did not share in this prosperity. Less developed countries in Africa and Asia endured economic decline, accompanied by rapid population growth, famine and ecological deterioration.

No Place Like Home

Although most of the world's poor are residents of less developed countries, due to unequal distribution of wealth, people in even the world's richest countries can fall victim to vicious cycles of poverty. In the United States, for example, the richest one percent of the people own 36 percent of the nation's wealth.[8] Throughout the developed world, in places like Canada, the United States, Australia and countries in Europe, a total of 100 million people live below the poverty line, and an estimated five million people are homeless.[9]

The housing situation in less developed countries is also bleak. Low-income housing is almost non-existent in most developing-world cities. Generally, those on low incomes either rent rooms, live on the streets or construct shacks in **shantytowns**, illegal settlements of cardboard shacks surrounding cities. Thirty to 60 percent of all people in developing countries live in shantytowns.[10] Without indoor plumbing, shantytown dwellers use open latrines which produce airborne poisons and contaminate the water supply. The location of shantytowns, often near garbage dumps and hazardous waste sites, further endangers their residents. Disease and death are everyday occurrences for millions of urban poor.

The appearance of these shantytowns is usually due to the migration of people from the countryside, where jobs in largely agriculture-based economies are scarce, to the city in hopes of finding work and building a better life. It is estimated that over one million people each week relocate to urban areas in the developing world.[11]

Impoverish the Earth

Continued poverty places much of the world's people on a collision course with environmental disaster. Most of the world's countries depend on the export of agricultural products for their livelihood. But agricultural expansion can often cause ecological stress. Wealthy landowners, cultivating more and more acres for commercial crops, continue to push subsistence farmers onto poor land. Farmers, pushed onto marginal land by population growth and inequitable land distribution, attempt to increase their cropland by cutting forests and cultivating land on steep slopes. Both of these practices increase the incidence of soil erosion, resulting in droughts and floods.

Such natural disasters have occurred in recent years with droughts in Africa, India and Latin American, and floods throughout Asia,

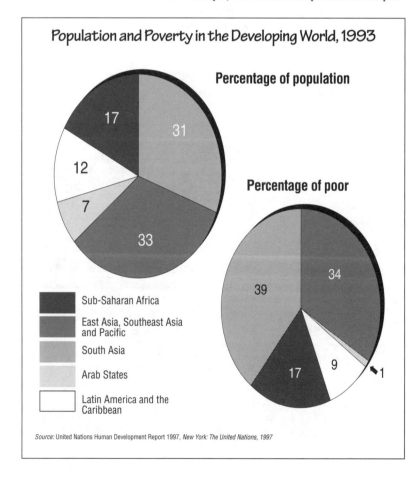

Population and Poverty in the Developing World, 1993

Percentage of population

17, 31, 12, 7, 33

Percentage of poor

39, 34, 17, 9, 1

- Sub-Saharan Africa
- East Asia, Southeast Asia and Pacific
- South Asia
- Arab States
- Latin America and the Caribbean

Source: United Nations Human Development Report 1997, *New York: The United Nations, 1997*

The Rising Tide of Poverty

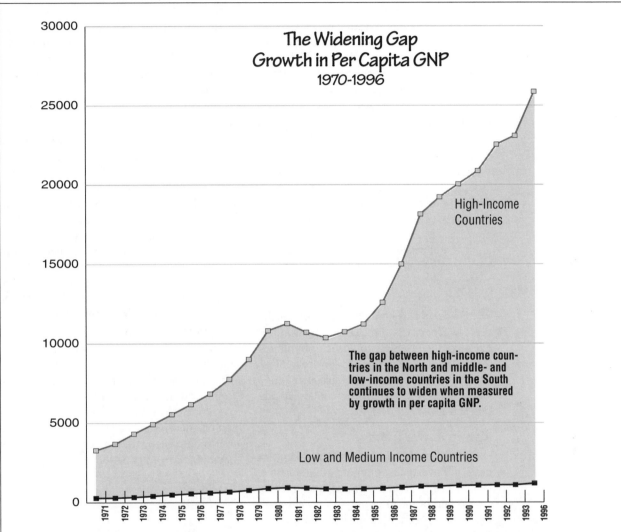

The Widening Gap
Growth in Per Capita GNP
1970-1996

High-Income Countries

The gap between high-income countries in the North and middle- and low-income countries in the South continues to widen when measured by growth in per capita GNP.

Low and Medium Income Countries

Why does the gap in per capita GNP continue to widen? The economies of high-income nations have grown steadily over the past 25 years but the population growth rates have slowed or stabilized. And while many middle-income countries have recently had strong economic growth, they have also had high population growth rates, so there are more people sharing the same economic pie. In many of the poorest countries, the economies are barely keeping up with, or are falling behind, a high population growth rate.

Source: World Development Indicators 1998, World Tables 1995, World Tables 1993, all published by The World Bank.

parts of Africa and the Andean region of Latin America. The poor, living on vulnerable hillsides and along unprotected shores, are overwhelmingly the victims of these disasters.

Population and Poverty

How are population growth and poverty related? Scholars agree that poverty frequently contributes to rapid population growth. Low wages, poor education and high infant death rates are all symptoms of poverty, and they are also associated with high fertility rates which cause rapid population growth. Educating women and girls, and making good employment opportunities available to women are two of the most effective ways of decreasing both poverty and fertility rates.

The Rising Tide of Poverty

Does population growth contribute to poverty? On the household level, larger family size means that parents are able to invest less in the health and education of each child. These children then have less potential and skills they could use to obtain a good-paying job.

On the national level, in the short run, rapid population growth always means a decrease in per capita income, as limited resources are spread over more people. Over the long run, the situation gets a little more complicated. Some economists argue that a growing number of available workers and consumers may accelerate economic growth, or even be necessary for economic growth. They argue that if people invest enough in the country's economy, it will grow fast enough, and create jobs fast enough, to absorb the growing numbers of people.

However, it is important to point out that very few economies in the developing world are growing fast enough to absorb population growth at the rate of three to four percent per year. The result is greater unemployment, more landlessness, further environmental degradation and poverty.

Reversing the Trend

Although the challenges to breaking the cycle of poverty are monumental, failure to launch an assault on poverty will guarantee the destruction of much of our shared biosphere. Progress has been made since the 1960's: child death rates have been cut in half, malnutrition has been reduced by a third, the percent of children out of school has decreased from one-half to one-quarter, and life expectancies are increasing.[12] In addition, the **poverty gap,** or the amount of money that would be needed to bring every one in a developing country up to the poverty line, would be only three percent of those developing countries' annual incomes. And only one percent is necessary to draw everyone out of extreme poverty.[13]

Studies on every continent show that as **literacy rates** rise, especially those of women, so do income levels, nutrition levels and child survival rates. Population growth slows as child survival and infant mortality rates improve and

parents no longer need to have more children than they desire so they can be sure enough survive to adulthood. As school enrollment for children and women's participation in the paid workforce increases, children become more expensive and less vital to a family's economic survival, and the number of children a couple desires usually falls.

The World Bank advocates a two-branched approach to eradicating poverty. First, a country needs to make investments in basic social services to provide its people with primary health care and education. The slower the rate of population growth, the easier it becomes to effectively provide these services. And second, the country needs to promote an economic development pattern that makes efficient use of the available labor. Following this plan, people in developing countries will be prepared and able to become productive members of society and will have the employment opportunities to do so.

However, international reforms are equally as important, since poor countries often have heavy debts to other countries and to big banks, which sometimes causes them to sacrifice their natural resources in order to pay off the debts. Clearly, eradicating poverty will require cooperation and humanitarian planning from every nation.

Endnotes

[1] *United Nations Human Development Report, 1997.*

[2] Ibid.

[3] Ibid.

[4] *United Nations Human Development Report, 1996.* New York: United Nations Development Programme. p. 26.

[5] Op. cit. note 4, p. 2.

[6] Ibid.

[7] Op. cit. note 4, p. 1.

[8] Op. cit. note 4, p. 17.

[9] Op. cit. note 4, p. 5.

[10] Op. cit. note 4, p. 24.

[11] Op. cit. note 4, p. 25.

[12] Op. cit. note 1.

[13] *World Development Report, 1990.* Washington, DC: The World Bank. p. 28.

The Lion's Share

Introduction:

The relationships between income, consumption, family size and total population are complex. The following activities help students to examine the relationship between popultion and economic growth by examining the per capita gross domestic product (GDP) in countries around the world. Students will also examine how family size and income in North America are related to the amount of money each of us spends for food, shelter, transportation and the many services and products that make our lives more comfortable.

Procedure:

Distribute copies of the Student Worksheet. After students have a chance to work through the questions, go over answers in class. The follow-up activity is best assigned for homework.

Note: Gross Domestic Product (GDP) is defined on Part 2 of the *Student Worksheet*. Students may be more familiar with the term GNP (Gross National Product), so you may want to explain to students that it is virtually the same thing. The only difference is that GDP measures economic activity within a country's borders, while GNP also includes a country's economic activity occurring in other countries. Both figures provide a good insight into the economic "might" of a country.

Suggested Answers for Student Worksheet:

Part 1:

a) *housing and utilities; yes; the low-income family*

b) *$3,708 on food per year; $7,596 on housing and utilities per year*

c) *$5,754 per person; $927 per person for food*

d) *$3,836 per person; $618 per person for food*

Part 2:

a) The United States has the highest GDP; Kenya has the lowest. The countries should be ranked as follows:

1. United States
2. France
3. China
4. Canada
5. Russian Federation
6. India
7. Mexico
8. Indonesia
9. Saudi Arabia
10. Chile
11. Kenya

b) See the listing below for per capita GDP. Note to students that the figures do not mean that each person receives this amount, since GDP involves more than wages paid and wealth is distributed unequally. However, GDP does tend to indicate the relative availability of goods and services in a particular country.

Concept:

Just as family size and income determine lifestyle, a country's population size directly relates to its per capita Gross Domestic Product (GDP).

Objectives:

Students will be able to:
• Demonstrate how family size and income are related to the amount of money spent on necessities, goods and services.
• Explain the relationship between a country's population size and its per capita GDP.
• Calculate their possible living expenses in the future, based on their goals and expectations.

Subjects:

Social studies, math, economics, family life

Skills:

Analyzing data, math calculations, research, preparing a budget

Method:

Students analyze a series of data tables related to income, population, relative wealth, consumption patterns and family size. In the last part of this exercise, students analyze their own potential earning and spending patterns based on research and the data provided.

Materials:

Copies of Student Worksheet

Country	Per Capita GDP 1995 (in U.S. dollars)	Ranking
United States	$26,423	2
China	581	9
India	349	10
Saudi Arabia	6,605	4
Kenya	341	11
Russian Federation	2,326	7
France	26,439	1
Chile	4,739	5
Indonesia	1,025	8
Mexico	2,724	6
Canada	19,221	3

The Lion's Share

c) See listing on previous page for ranking; China moved down the most, followed by India, while Saudi Arabia and Chile both moved up 5 places in the ranking. The change in ranking indicates that straight GDP figures do not necessarily indicate how wealthy the average person in the country is likely to be. The countries which moved down had large GDP's, but had to divide it among a very large number of people. The reverse is true for the countries that moved up in the ranking.

Part 3:

a) India had a 88 percent increase; the United States had a 143 percent increase.

b) India's per capita GDP was $250 in 1980 and increased to $349 in 1995 (39 percent increase); U.S. per capita GDP was $11,891 in 1980 and increased to $25,055 in 1995 (111 percent increase). These figures show that when a population growth is also considered, increases in GDP for the whole country can be misleading. Also, the disparity between India and the United States becomes more pronounced.

c) When a country's population is growing at a faster rate than the GDP, a substantial increase in GDP will not mean more money for most individuals in that country.

Follow-up Activity:

As these activities indicate, population growth and economic growth do not necessarily go hand in hand. Also, students should realize that population and economic growth rates are influenced by local and global factors.

Have students bring in an article or articles about current economic, political, or social events in a particular country. The article can be about a specific event (such a flood or civil war), or about a general economic or social trend (for example, increased trade to South Africa or later marriage and childbirth among Indonesian women).

Have students look up the current GDP (or GNP) and population of the country featured in the article and determine the per capita GDP as they did in Part II of the activity. Students could then examine the article in light of the per capita GDP and write a report predicting whether the reported event or trend will affect future population and economic growth in the country, and what those effects might be.

For a longer project, students could collect articles over a period of time, or conduct more in-depth research on a country before writing their reports.

The Lion's Share

This activity is divided into four parts. In the first part, you will see how a middle-income and low-income family in the United States spend their salaries. You will then calculate how much money is available for each family member if family size increases. In the second part, you will work with a chart showing the Gross Domestic Product for several countries. From this chart, you will calculate the individual and family "share" of the GDP for each country. In the third part, you will examine one example of how GDP and population size relate to each other. Finally, you will plan a hypothetical budget for yourself.

Part 1:

Look at the Monthly Budget chart below and compare how these two families spend their money. Answer the following questions:

a. What item takes the largest percentage of the family income in the low-income family? Is the same true for the middle-income family? Which family spends a larger percentage of its income on food?

b. The chart show figures for one month. How much does a low-income family spend on food in a year? On housing?

c. What is the average amount of money available to each low-income family member in a year? How much does each member have for food in a year? (Assume that the money and food are divided equally among all family members even though children may actually consume less than adults.)

d. If the family grew by two more children and the income remained the same, what would be the average amount of money available for each family member in a year? How much would each member have for food?

Monthly Budget for a Family of 4 (in 1995 dollars)[1]					
Low-Income*			Middle-Income**		
	% Income	**Amount**		**% Income**	**Amount**
Food	16	$309		13	$455
Housing and Utilities[2]	33	$633		29	$1,031
Transportation[3]	18	$335		18	$637
Clothing	5	$102		4	$164
Health Care	7	$134		4	$159
Taxes, Pension, and Social Security	6	$116		17	$620
Other[4]	15	$289		15	$548
Total	**100%**	**$1,918**[5]		**100%**	**$3,614**

Source: U.S. Bureau of Labor Statistics, Consumer Expenditure Survey Data, 1995, Table 1 (order #2710).

*Based on annual household income before taxes of $16,114
** Based on annual household income before taxes of $44,753
[1] Figures are for families of all sizes within income group. Expenses will vary depending on actual family size.
[2] Includes shelter, fuel, utilities and public services, household operations, furnishings and housekeeping supplies.
[3] Includes vehicle purchases, gasoline and motor oil, other vehicle expenses and public transportation.
[4] Includes life insurance, entertainment, personal care, reading, education, tobacco and smoking supplies, alcoholic beverages, cash contributions and miscellaneous expenditures.
[5] Where expenditures exceed income, the difference is made up by personal debt, private assistance, and/or programs and services subsidized by federal, state and local government agencies.

The Lion's Share

Part 2:

Review the chart below. GDP stands for Gross Domestic Product, which is a measure of a country's goods and services (i.e., the wealth of the country).

a) Which country has the highest GDP? The lowest? Rank the countries by putting a number next to their GDPs (1=highest, 11=lowest).

b) Using the population figures on the chart, calculate the per capita GDP (i.e. each person's "share" of the GDP) for each country. Does this mean that each person in these countries receives the amount you calculated?

c) Now rank the countries according to the per capita GDP. Which countries moved the most on the scale? What does their change in ranking indicate?

GDP and Population of Selected Countries, 1995		
Country	**Gross Domestic Product (in U.S. currency)**	**Population**
United States	$6,952,020,000,000	263,100,000
China	697,647,000	1,200,200,000
India	324,082,000,00	926,400,000
Saudi Arabia	125,501,000,000	19,000,000
Kenya	9,095,000,00	26,700,000
Russian Federation	344,711,000,000	148,200,000
France	1,536,089,000,000	58,100,000
Chile	67,297,000,000	14,200,000
Indonesia	198,079,000,000	193,300,000
Mexico	250,038,000,000	91,800,000
Canada	586,928,000,000	29,600,000

Source: The World Bank; World Development Report 1997, Tables 1 and 12.

The Lion's Share

Part 3:

Look at the chart below, which contrasts India's GDP and population with the U.S. GDP and population.

a) Notice that the GDP has increased for both countries. What was the percentage of increase for each country from 1980 to 1995?

b) Calculate the per capita GDP by dividing the population into the GDP for both countries for each year.

c) Using this information, explain why a substantial increase in a country's GDP does not necessarily mean more money for most individuals living in that country.

INDIA

Year	GDP	Population
1980	172,321,000,000	688,994,000
1995	324,082,000,000	929,400,000

UNITED STATES

Year	GDP	Population
1980	2,708,150,000,000	227,757,000
1995	6,592,020,000,000	263,100,000

Source: *The World Bank*, World Development Report 1997, Tables 1 and 12.

Part 4:

The first chart you analyzed shows how two typical American households spend their money. Imagine that you are setting up your own household and are preparing your budget. Will you be married? Having children? Going to college? Sharing an apartment with friends?

After you decide on your hypothetical situation, look in the classified ads of your newspaper to see how much monthly rent you would have to pay for your house or apartment. Use the grocery ads to calculate your food bill for a month. Check your household's present utility bills to estimate the costs you may anticipate. Look at car ads and estimate monthly car payments, insurance, and gasoline, or calculate monthly bus or subway fare. Then add a figure for miscellaneous expenses such as medical bills, clothing, taxes, entertainment, etc. What is your monthly total?

As a last step, turn again to the newspaper and look in the employment section. Do any of the jobs for which you might be qualified provide enough money to meet your monthly bills?

As you do the above activity, divide expenditures into either necessities or luxuries. If your income were to be reduced, what items would you forego? Are they mostly items you listed as luxuries? Do you think people in countries with low GDP's spend the same percentage of their income for luxury items that you do?

Living on $500 a Year

Concept:

To understand the distribution of wealth in the world today and the need for economic development, students must first gain an understanding of the nature of poverty.

Objectives:

Students will be able to:
- Evaluate the effectiveness of the reading as a tool for change.
- Compare change in per capita GNP in the U.S. and Sub-Saharan Africa over a 20-year period.
- Examine their owns needs and wants and prioritize them in a critical light.
- Identify the most pressing problems facing poor countries and brainstorm solutions to those problems at the international, national, community, and individual level.

Subjects:

Social studies, economics, language arts, family life

Skills:

Critical thinking, evaluation, decision making, brainstorming, cooperation, problem solving

Methods:

Students read and discuss a short passage on living on $500 a year and then evaluate their own needs and wants in a short activity. Finally, students divide into teams where they role-play different groups and organizations and brainstorm on ways to close the gap between rich and poor nations.

Materials:

Copies of Student Reading
Copies of Student Worksheet
Situation Cards

Introduction:

The following exercises helps students imagine the life of a poor family in a "less developed" country. Through reading, discussion and activities, students will come to understand what "less developed" means for the three billion people for whom it is not a statistic but an experience of daily life. The activities focus on identifying basic needs and on ways we can work to lessen the gap between the developed and the developing countries.

Part 1: Reading and Discussion

Copy the suggested reading and distribute it to the class. Give all the students a chance to read through the article. Make sure to leave plenty of time for discussion so that the message does not seem overwhelmingly bleak and hopeless for the students.

Discussion Questions:

Evaluating the Article as a Tool for Change

1. How did this article make you feel? Why do you think you felt that way?

   Students may answer that they felt sad, angry, helpless, upset, or that they didn't want to think about it or don't believe the information is true.

2. Can you think of other situations where you felt the same way?

   Some answers might include: When I see a homeless person, when my friends are in trouble, when I hear about environmental problems, when something goes wrong and I don't know what to do.

3. What were some intangible things that weren't taken away from the family in the reading?

   Students might need some help getting started on this question. Answers might include: family, love, religion, culture, a sense of community. The teacher can discuss with students how poverty puts severe psychological as well as physical stress on a family, but that factors such as a strong sense of community, culture and family can make life more bearable.

4. Why weren't these more positive things mentioned in the article?

   Because the article focuses on material well-being.

5. What was the author's purpose in writing this article? Why do you think the author decided to make this article so grim?

   Answers might include: the author wants to shock the reader, the author wants the reader to feel angry and guilty, the author wants to make the reader understand the seriousness and importance of the problem.

6. Do you think that the author made the right choice by making the article depressing? What might he have done differently to communicate his message effectively?

   Teachers may want to ask this question at this point of the discussion and again at the end of the activities to see if there is a difference in student response. Teachers may also want to have students list alternative ideas and use those ideas a basis for follow-up activities in persuasive writing.

Evaluating the Information

1. The information in the article has been updated to use 1996 figures. What would you guess that the GNP per capita for the United States and a Sub-Saharan African country were 20 years before in 1976?

   The teacher should then draw the chart below on the board and fill in the line for 1996 using the data from the article. The teacher should then ask the students to guess what the per capita GNP per-capita for the United States and Sub-Saharan Africa was in 1976. Note: Student answers will vary widely. Once the students have made a variety of guesses, write the correct information in the boxes.

2. Where has there been a larger change?

   The United States. The GNP per capita in the United States has more than tripled, while the GNP per capita in Sub-Saharan Africa has grown, but not yet doubled.

3. Why do you think that is the case?

   While the world's economy as a whole has grown dramatically over the years, the growth has not benefited all nations equally. The United States has a strong, established economy and a relatively slow rate of population growth. On the other hand, most

Living on $500 a Year

	Per-capita GNP United States	Per-capita GNP Sub-Saharan Africa
1976	$8,180	$340
1996	$28,020	$510
% Change	243% increase	50% increase

1976 data source: World Tables, 1988-89 Edition, *The World Bank*
1996 data source: 1998 World Data Sheet, *Population Reference Bureau*

nations in Sub-Saharan Africa have weaker economies with high rates of population growth, meaning that while their economies have grown, they have grown more slowly, and the growth has to be divided by a larger pool of people.

4. Are you surprised by this information? Did you expect there to be more change or less?

5. What else might have increased besides income levels?

Cost of living. Inflation. Both have increased substantially in the United States.

Note: the 1976 dollar figures are not adjusted for inflation. When the 1976 figures are expressed in 1995 dollars, the difference in growth rates are even more dramatic — per capita GNP for the United States in 1976 is $8,510, for Sub-Saharan Africa the 1976 GNP per capita is $460 (World Tables 1995, The World Bank).

6. In what other ways has life in the United States changed since 1976?

Answers will range, some answers might include: widespread use of computers, information technology, more home conveniences like microwaves and VCRs, more women in the workplace, civil rights movement.

7. Based on the information in the chart, would you say that the scenario in the article you read is still relevant for much of the world's population?

Yes, the scenario is still true for many of the world's people. Things have improved for some people in some places, but many people still live in extreme poverty and with continued population growth and environmental problems the situation will probably continue.

8. What are some things (both positive and negative) that people do to escape or alleviate poverty?

Answers might include: seek more education; turn to crime or drugs; migrate to another city; state, or country; work in a high risk job or illegal job (prostitution, smuggling); borrow money (often at high interest rates); or sell belongings.

9. How would eliminating poverty help to solve problems in both the United States and in the world?

Part 2: Needs vs. Wants

In North America, we live a culture that emphasizes abundance. Students are constantly bombarded with messages that tell them to want and seek more material satisfaction. In such an environment, it can be difficult to appreciate what they already have, much less understand what it means to live with less. In this activity, students clarify the difference between needs and wants, reevaluate their consumption patterns, and determine what they would be willing to sacrifice to accommodate others.

Procedure:

1. Instruct students to draw a line lengthwise down the middle of a sheet of paper. Students can work individually or in small groups.

2. On the left side they will list the basic needs of every human being; water, food, clothing, shelter, etc.

3. On the right, they will list the things they need or want for their own lifestyles: color-TV, stereo, video game system, car, fast food, movies, hot water, etc. Next to each item, they should name some of the resources or

Living on $500 a Year

products needed to produce, use, and maintain these things: oil (for plastic and fuel), electricity, iron, aluminum, pesticides, grain, water, etc. Give the students enough time to write between ten and fifteen items.

Notes: The teacher may want to go through some of the examples of products we use regularly, and the resources they are made of or use to operate, to get students started. Students can use the article as a guide, but should be encouraged to list from their own lives as well.

4. Tell them to select three items on the right that they would be willing to give up so that people who currently lack the basic necessities (listed on the left) can survive. Have them cross those items off their lists.

5. Tell the students to select an additional three items. Have them cross those items off their lists.

6. Continue to have students cross out items until they only have a few left.

Discussion Questions:

1. Which were the first items to go on your list? What did you elect to keep? Why?

2. Do you think that most North Americans would be willing to lower their consumption level to help others in developing countries? Why or why not?

3. Are there any alternatives to giving up those items on your list? What are they?
   Sharing, using less of everything, recycling, finding more efficient/less wasteful ways to make or run products.

4. How do you think that giving up these items on your list would affect your happiness? What makes you the happiest? What do you most enjoy doing?
   Make a list on the board — be sure to include items like friends, family, playing sports, reading, singing, playing in a band, etc.

Basic Necessities	My Needs or Wants
food	stereo (oil — for plastic, water, electricity, steel)
water	TV (metal, oil — for plastic, electricity, glass)
shelter	fast food hamburger (grain, pesticide, oil, fertilizer, wood, metal, beef)
clothing	hot water (water, oil or gas, copper, lead, iron)

Living on $500 a Year

Part 3: What Can We Do?

In this activity, students will work in groups to brainstorm on how to eliminate poverty and close the gap between rich and poor countries. Each group will approach the problem from a different point of view as determined by a *Situation Card*.

Procedure:

Divide students into six groups. Give each group a *Situation Card* and a copy of the *Student Worksheet*. Tell the students that they must work together and their work will be graded as a group. After all the groups have had a chance to work, have each group prepare a short presentation for the class. Discuss the similarities and the differences between the groups' ideas and approaches. Were there any basic agreements? Any fundamental differences?

Note: This activity can be a short, one class period assignment, or it can be expanded to a longer activity where the students do research and prepare a display and a rehearsed presentation. See the Suggested Resources for Further Research *at the back of the book for information on research sources.*

Living on $500 a Year

In order to understand the long road ahead for less developed countries, we must make a radical adjustment of our picture of the world. It is not easy to make this mental jump. But let us attempt it by imagining how a typical American family, living in a small suburban house with an income of $28,000 (the U.S. per capita GNP), could be transformed into an equally typical family of the less developed world. We will use Africa as a model, where the majority of the countries have a per capita GNP under $500. (Note: *GNP* refers to the Gross National Product, which is a way of measuring the economic value of a country's goods and services. *Per capita* means that the figure shows a relative measure of the population's wealth; i.e., each person's "share").

We begin by shutting off the electricity and removing everything that uses it — lamps, appliances, radio, television.

Next we shut off the heat and air conditioning.

We take out the beds, chairs, rugs, and curtains. We are left with only a few old blankets, a kitchen table and a wooden chair. Along with the dressers go the clothes. Each family member may keep in his "wardrobe" his oldest suit or dress, a shirt or blouse. We will permit a pair of shoes to the head of the family, but none for the wife or children.

Next we shut off running water. If the family is lucky, there we will be a latrine and pump down the road to share with the community.

We move to the kitchen. The appliances have already been taken out, so turn to the cupboards. A box of matches, a small bag of flour, some sugar and salt may stay. A few moldy potatoes, already in the garbage can, must be rescued, for they will provide much of tonight's meal. We will leave a handful of onions, and a dish of dried beans. All the rest we take away, the fresh vegetables, the canned goods, the meat, the milk.

Now that the house is stripped, we take it away. The family moves to the tool shed. It is crowded, at least they have shelter.

Although the family is in a smaller space, their numbers have increased. Instead of being an average North American two-child family, they now have six children (the average in most of Africa). All other houses in the neighborhood have also been replaced with small structures, jammed together, full of people.

Communication must go next. No more newspapers, magazines, books — not that they are missed since we must also take away the family's literacy. Instead, we will allow one radio in the shantytown.

Next, government services must go. No more postal carrier, no more fire fighter. There is a school, but it is three miles away and consists of two classrooms. They are not overcrowded since only half the children in the neighborhood, mainly boys, go to school.

There are no hospitals or doctors nearby. The nearest clinic is ten miles away and is tended by a midwife. It can be reached by bicycle, provided that the family has a bicycle, which is unlikely. Or one can go by bus — there is usually room on top, if not inside.

Finally, money. We will allow our family a cash hoard of $10. Meanwhile they must earn their keep. Since the children are not likely to be in school long, most of them will work beside their parents all day. As peasant cultivators with three acres to tend they may raise the equivalent of $200 to $500 worth of crops a year. If they are tenant farmers, which is more than likely, a third or so of the crop will go to the landlord, and probably another 10 percent to the local moneylender.

But there will be enough to eat, or almost. The average human body needs a daily input of 2,000 calories just to replenish the energy consumed by its living cells, and people in Sub-Saharan Africa average 2,095 calories. Like any insufficiently fueled machinery, their bodies run down sooner; the life expectancy in Africa is 53 years old.

This is life as lived by hundreds of millions of people. Of course it is just an impression — it is missing the many strong smells and sounds of streets overflowing with humanity. It is also missing the sense of familiarity these people have with their situation; what may seem shocking to us is softened for those who have never known anything else. But the impression provides the general idea of life in the Less Developed Countries, adding a picture of reality to the statistics by which underdevelopment is ordinarily measured. When we are told that half the world's population enjoys a standard of living "less than $500 a year," this is what that figure means.

Updated and adapted by permission from Harper and Row Publishers, Inc. The original passage appears in The Great Ascent, *by Robert Heilbroner (Harper and Row Publishers, Inc., 1963) pp. 33-37.*

Living on $500 a Year

Situation Card: Your Class

Your class has decided that as a senior project, that you will all work together to make others aware of the extreme poverty in many parts of the world, and take some sort of action to help the poor in other countries. At first this task seems overwhelming, so your group has been elected to come up with a class plan. Using the worksheet as a guide, discuss ways a small group of students can raise awareness and take action to combat this problem. Be as creative as you can and don't forget to help students make the connection between their own behavior and what happens overseas. Remember that the more low-cost and free activities that you can think of, the more you will be able to do.

Situation Card: Village Leaders

Your group is made up of the respected leaders of a small, impoverished African village. Life has been very hard for your village in the last few years, and your group has been chosen by the community to try and alleviate some of the poverty and improve the situation. If you come up with a plan to improve life for the people in your village, you can expect to receive a very small amount of money (about $500) from the local government and an international relief organization. Only one of your group is literate, so please select that person to write down all of your ideas. Please use the worksheet and your first-hand knowledge of the local situation to formulate a plan to improve the lives of the people in the village. Remember, you won't be able to do everything, so focus on those things that will make the most difference.

Situation Card: USAID Country Team

Your group works for the U.S. government in the *United States Agency for International Development* (USAID) in a South Asian country where the majority of the people live in conditions like those described in the article. Your mission is to work with the government and people of that country to make the lives of the people better, but you only have a limited budget, and Congress may cut your resources once again. Using the worksheet to get started, determine the best way to accomplish your mission given your limited resources. What are the greatest needs? What do you concentrate on first? What is the most efficient way to help those people who are the most in need? Remember, you won't be able to do everything — decide as a group on what is most important.

Living on $500 a Year

Situation Card: Local Community Group

You are members of a small community group in North America and you have become concerned about the extreme poverty in many parts of the world, and would like to organize and take action to help others in your community understand the problem and to help the needy in some of the world's poorest countries. At first this task seems overwhelming, so your group has decided to write an action plan. Using the worksheet as a guide, discuss ways a small group of citizens can raise awareness and can take action to combat this problem. Be as creative as you can and don't forget to help others make the connection between their own behavior and what happens overseas. Remember that the more low-cost and free activities that you can think of, the more you will be able to do, as your budget is extremely limited.

Situation Card: Special Working Group of the United Nations

The Secretary General of the United Nations has declared that eliminating poverty is the most important goal of the UN. Your group is a special team brought together to decide the best way to improve the lives of the world's most poor, and to close the gap between rich and poor countries. Since this is such a large project, the secretary has asked you to identify the top four problems contributing to the problem of poverty and the inequity between nations, and to suggest ways of solving those problems. Using the worksheet as a starting point, identify the four most serious problems and come up with a plan for addressing one of these problems. Remember, you can think big, but that ultimately your plan should make a real difference in people's lives.

Situation Card: Government Advisors in a Developing Country

You are advisors to the newly-elected prime minister in an impoverished developing nation. Your party campaigned on the promise to eliminate poverty and to improve the lives of the people. Now that you have been elected, the prime minister has asked your group to come up with an action plan to relieve the worst of your country's problems. You are committed to helping your people and eager to get started, but your budget is extremely limited and probably won't increase much in the next few years. Using the worksheet as a guide, determine the best way to accomplish your mission given your limited resources. What are the greatest needs? What do you concentrate on first? What is the most efficient way to help those people who are the most in need? Remember, you won't be able to do everything — decide as a group on what is most important and then go from there.

Living on $500 a Year

What Can We Do?

Group Situation:

Names of People in the Group:

Note: This worksheet is a tool to get you started. Feel free to record your group's goals, ideas and action plan on other pieces of paper as needed.

1. Based on the scenario outlined in your situation card, identify the most important and pressing problems facing your group and write goals or priority statements for your group to work towards accomplishing.

   Examples of Goals and Priority Statements:

   Raise $500 dollars for housing construction in an African village.
   Adequate nutrition for every person in our country.
   Clean drinking water for everyone in our town.
   Health services for all the poor families in the country.
   Every child in the world will complete school through grade six.

2. After you have written down four or five goals, pick one goal that your group will work on first.

3. What are some simple short-term things that could be done to help you meet your goal?

4. What are some long-term things that could be done to help you meet your goals?

5. Using the back of this sheet or another sheet of paper, create an action plan and with a time-line for reaching your goal.

Population and Economics

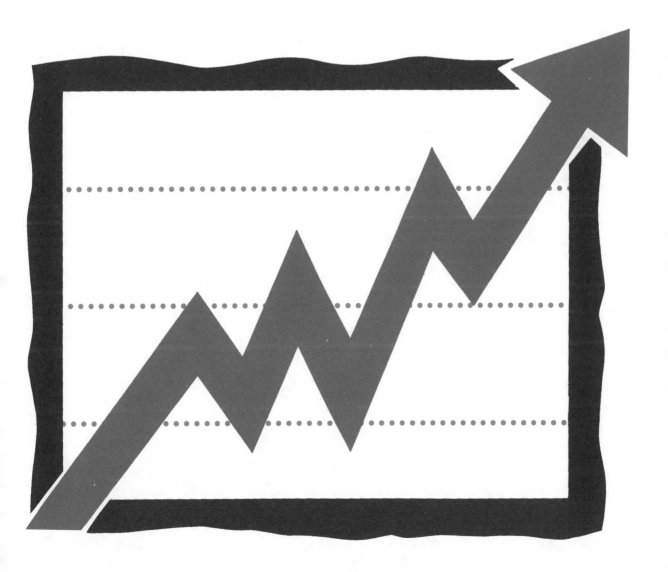

Economic Growing Pains

It is a commonly held belief that economic growth always improves the health of nations and the well-being of the people living in them. In the United States, the promise of continued economic growth has been a constant theme in advertising campaigns, selling everything from automobiles to political candidates. Now, in this age of global interdependence and environmental awareness, we may be "outgrowing" these long-held economic principles.

Much of our economic growth is dependent upon using the finite resources of the Earth, from the plants and animals we harvest, to the oil and ore we mine. But if rapid growth of human populations and per capita resource consumption continues we may reach a point where the Earth can no longer sustain its inhabitants. Warning signs of the Earth's limitations are already apparent in the deterioration of our life-support systems: shrinking forests, expanding deserts, eroding croplands, thinning ozone layer, accumulation of greenhouse gases, increasing wildlife extinction and biological damage from air pollution and acid rain.

Many people have resisted environmental regulations to reduce pollution, and protect wetlands, biodiversity and scarce resources because they fear that these efforts hamper economic growth, and thus human well-being. At times trade-offs between environmental protection and the economy are easy to see. Take logging in the Pacific Northwest, for example. Protection of old-growth forests seems to come at the expense of loggers' jobs. In other cases, clean air and clean water regulations can increase the costs of producing goods, and company owners may lower wages or lay off workers in order to maintain profits.

Nonetheless, Robert Repetto, Senior Economist of the World Resources Institute, argues that "much of the alleged burden that environmental protection measures impose on the economy is illusory."[1] He and others have concluded that we perceive conflict between economic and environmental interests only because we have flawed measures of economic progress.

The most common measure of economic growth and also of a nation's general welfare is the **Gross Domestic Product (GDP)**, which is defined as the total value of all the goods and services bought and sold in a given year. However, GDP measures have several shortcomings. First, they make no distinction between "good" spending and "bad" spending. For example, pollution increases this measure of economic growth not once, but twice — first with the sale of products from factories that produce the pollution, and second when money is spent to clean up the pollution. In other words, according to GDP measures, pollution is good for the economy. Furthermore, GDP measures do not count things which have no monetary value, such as community and volunteer work and use of our natural resources. The figures do not account for the economic services nature provides people by conserving soil, cleaning air and water, providing habitat for wildlife and supporting recreational activities. GDP measures ignore resource depletion and count sales of resources only as income. For example, the only economic value placed on a forest is for its harvested timber.[2]

OZONE SHIELD

GLOBAL CLIMATE

OLD-GROWTH FOREST

AIR QUALITY

HABITAT

NATURAL SCENERY

SPECIES DIVERSITY

TOPSOIL

WATER QUALITY

AQUIFERS

The Other Infrastructure

THINK OF IT AS AN INVESTMENT. —

Economic Growing Pains

Ecological Economics

Because traditional economic thought tends to ignore the role of the environment in the economy, a growing number of economists are calling for new ways of thinking about the economy and of measuring economic progress. Robert Costanza and Lisa Wainger of the International Society for Ecological Economics recommend that environmental interests be incorporated into economic planning, since a healthy economy can only exist in symbiosis with a healthy ecology. They point out that "the most obvious danger of excluding nature from economics is that nature is the economy's life-support system, and that by ignoring it, we may inadvertently damage it beyond repair."

All economists agree that the environment serves as a **source** and a **sink** for the economy.[3] That is, the economy draws resources and energy from the biosphere (source) and then gives them back in the forms of byproducts and waste (sink). Where ecological and traditional economists differ is in their beliefs in the ultimate ability of the Earth to keep providing these services with ever-increasing levels of production and consumption.

Source: Reprinted with permision of Harley Schwadron.

Herman Daly, Senior Research Scholar in the School of Public Affairs at the University of Maryland and founder of the International Society of Ecological Economics, argues that economists traditionally have taken the environment for granted because when traditional economic theories were first developed, the ability of the biosphere to provide resources and absorb wastes was considered infinite relative to the demands of the economy.[4] However, through population growth and increased consumption levels, the scale of the economy has now grown to the point that the sources and sinks are becoming scarce relative to the demands of the economy.

In Daly's view, using economics to explain the human condition today without recognizing the role of the environment in the economy is "as if biology tried to understand animals only in terms of their circulatory system, with no recognition of their digestive tract."[5] On the other hand, Daly' critics point out that improvements in technology — making our cars, appliances and power plants more efficient — compensate somewhat for the impact of economic growth on the environment. They can allow us to produce and consume more without taking quite as much from sources or putting quite as much into sinks

A Sustainable Economy

Ecological and traditional economists have very different ideas on how natural resources, which they call "natural capital," must be treated if we are to maintain a "sustainable economy." By a sustainable economy, we mean an economy that meets the needs of people today without threatening its ability to meet the needs of future generations. *Traditional economics* says that if you use natural resources and convert them to man-made things like cars or buildings, the world will be just as well off, or better off, than it was before. The new things, or "physical capital," created replace the value of the natural capital that was lost. An economy is sustainable as long as it does not deplete the total amount of capital. It does not matter what form the capital is in.

On the other hand, the *ecological economics* argues that because our natural capital is scarce, it

Economic Growing Pains

needs to be treated as a special case. Man-made products, or physical capital, cannot fully replace the loss of our natural capital. Natural resources provide a number of crucial services, such as protection from ultra-violet rays and purification of water. The ecological economists claim that benefits gained from new roads or malls cannot match or outweigh the costs of pollution and resource depletion. Therefore, in order to have a sustainable economy, natural capital must remain intact. This does not mean that you cannot use any natural resources, only that they must not be used faster than they are replaced.

Clearly, these two types of economists would make very different recommendations on what use of natural resources is best for the economy and for the well-being of future generations. Consider the example of the loggers and the old-growth forests. According to traditional economists, rapidly logging old-growth forests can be economically desirable because the trees, or natural capital, that are cut down are transformed into furniture, new homes or paper. The total amount of capital remains the same; it just takes a different form.

However, according to ecological economics, rapidly logging the old-growth forests is *not* economically desirable if the forest is depleted faster than it is replaced because the value of the new homes cannot fully replace the natural benefits and services lost when the forest is cut down. From this analysis, we see that if the role of the environment in the economy is recognized, protecting environment does not conflict with economic progress. In fact, because the economy is dependent on the environment, if an investment is not good for the environment then it cannot be good for the economy either.

New Alternatives

Many organizations are now working on developing new ways of measuring economic growth which incorporate the environment's role in the economy. One group, Redefining Progress, has created an alternative to GDP measures called the **Genuine Progress Indicator** (GPI). The depletion of natural resources such as wetlands, farmlands non-

renewable minerals (including oil) and the costs of pollution all lower the GPI. GPI measures also account for the use of chemicals which deplete the ozone or cause other long-term environmental damage.[6]

Both the United Nations and the World Bank are in the process of developing new economic indicators. The United Nations Statistical Division has devised a measure called the Environmentally Adjusted Domestic Product (EADP). EADP measures count depletion of natural resources as a loss in capital which is subtracted from the overall growth. When this measure was applied to Mexico, the country's economic growth was 13 percent

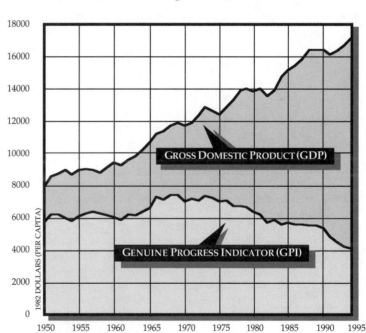

Gross Production vs. Genuine Progress 1950-1995

GROSS DOMESTIC PRODUCT (GDP)

GENUINE PROGRESS INDICATOR (GPI)

1982 DOLLARS (PER CAPITA)

"When social and environmental costs are taken into account, the overall health of the economy shows a steady decline since the 1970s," according to Redefining Progress, a nonpartisan, public policy institute. Redefining Progress developed the Genuine Progress Indicator (GPI) to account for more than 20 indicators of economic well-being missing from the traditional Gross Domestic Product (GDP), such as natural resource depletion, volunteer work and income distribution.

Source: Reprinted with permission, © 1995, Redefining Progress.

Economic Growing Pains

lower than initially measured by GDP measures, due to damaging ecological practices. The United Nations argues that these new measures allow economic growth to be "evaluated in new and more realistic terms."[7]

Making new decisions about how economies should work using these new measures of evaluation may push us towards what Herman Daly calls the "steady-state economy."[8] Unlike our present economy, the steady-state economy is characterized by a constant population of humans and a constant amount of available goods. This economy focuses on producing a quantity and quality of goods that will provide for a decent standard of living for both present and future generations. In the interest of conserving resources and preserving our environment, Daly also argues that the rate of input and output should be reduced to the lowest feasible levels. This ensures that the economy will never outgrow the ability of the Earth to perform its roles of sink and source. The availability of natural resources can be sustained if we live off the dividends, rather than using up our natural capital. Limiting our use of fossil fuels, for example, will, in turn, limit the amount the Earth will have to absorb from the production of gases contributing to air pollution, acid rain and global climate change. In this scenario, the Earth's ecosystems could be maintained indefinitely and more people could enjoy a better quality of life.

Some communities have started to recognize that environmental and economic interests go hand and hand, and are recreating their cities in line with this idea. The citizens of Chattanooga, Tennessee, for example have made a commitment to becoming an "environmental city." By re-focusing its economy, Chattanooga has expanded business investment and jobs at the same time as improving its air and water quality. One example of an environmentally friendly business located there is the manufacturer of zero-emission buses. Chattanooga continues to target other environmental businesses to expand or relocate there, and they are building an environmental conference center. All of these efforts have effectively revitalized the city after decades of economic depression.

Growing Together

Achieving a sustainable economy will require an international commitment to slowing population growth worldwide and reducing consumption levels of finite resources, especially in industrialized countries. Even if resources are used efficiently, consumption of water, energy and forest products will continue to rise if human numbers increase.

"Despite what leading economic indicators may imply," write Sandra Postel and Christopher Flavin of the Worldwatch Institute, "no economy can be called successful if its prosperity comes at the expense of future generations and if the ranks of the poor continue to grow." These new economic indicators will help the economy develop in a way that results in the ends we all value: improved quality of life, and protection of the health of our Earth and its inhabitants.

Endnotes

[1] Robert Repetto, et al. "Has Environmental Regulation Really Reduced Productivity Growth? We Need Unbiased Measures." *Publications Brief*, October 1996. World Resources Institute, Washington, D.C.

[2] For further information, please see Clifford Cobb, et al. "If the Economy Is Up, Why Is America Down?" *The Atlantic Monthly*, October 1995; Chapter 2: "Growth as a Means to Human Development," *Human Development Report* 1996, The United Nations; and the work of Redefining Progress, San Francisco, CA.

[3] Holly Stallworth, "The Economics of Sustainability," OSEC Issue Brief # 5. Office of Sustainable Economics and Communities, U.S. Environmental Protection Agency. www.epa.gov/oppeinet/oppe/osec/osecbak/index.htm.

[4] Herman Daly. 1996. *Beyond Growth: The Economics of Sustainable Development*. Boston: Beacon Press. p. 34.

[5] Herman Daly, 1988 quoted in op. cit. Note 3.

[6] Factsheet: "What's Wrong with the GDP as a Measure of Progress." Redefining Progress, San Francisco, CA.

[7] *The Human Development Report 1996*, The United Nations, Box 2.10. Original source: Bartelmus, Peter. "Environmental Accounting: a Framework for Assessment of Policy Integration." Paper presented at International Monetary Fund seminar on Macroeconomics and the Environment, Washington, D.C., 10-11 May, 1995.

[8] Op. cit. note 4, p. 31.

Population Growth—It All Adds Up

Introduction:

Many industries and most communities are built with the assumption that there will be ever-increasing populations — or, that growth is vital to survival. The purpose of this activity is to identify the ways industry encourages population growth and to examine the ultimate utility of such motivation. Students will reexamine the values expressed by the cliches, "Growth is good" and "More is better."

Procedure:

1. Ask the students to collect ads which reflect in some way the concept of "growth." This may be an ad announcing the growth of a company into some new region or product. It may be an ad that encourages growth by the product or service it is selling. It may be a promotional ad encouraging movement into an area by industry. It could be an ad which directly or indirectly promotes child-bearing and/or large families. Ads for new housing developments, shopping centers or vacation spots could also be clipped. If students have difficulty in locating enough print ads for this assignment, they can also write a brief synopsis of television or radio ads, or even describe billboards and bus ads.

2. Arrange the ads or descriptions of ads on the wall around the room so the group can see them. Allow the group 5-10 minutes to wander about the room to become familiar with the ads.

3. Begin discussion with the general question, "How do ads encourage growth?" Some responses may be:

   a) Appeals to better quality of living (housing ads)

   b) Appeals with tax incentives (chamber of commerce ads for industry)

   c) Appeals to the right location (access to resources, markets, etc.)

4. Once the kinds of appeals have been identified, the focus should shift to the general question: "Does the product or service really improve the quality of life?" A variety of more specific questions should be used to get at this question:

   a) How does the product or service limit the quality of life? (Look at the negative side.) For example, a new subdivision of quality homes may appear to be an improvement on the surface, but consideration should be given to such things as the additional demands on resources.

   b) What other factors must also be considered? An ad to invite industry into an area also implies needs for community planning, support services, etc.

   c) What, specifically, is being improved? Often, this becomes a difficult answer to ferret out of a glamour ad.

5. A final question to be raised in this discussion should be, "Could the same results be achieved without the growth that is being advocated?" Answers to this question will require some creative thinking on the part of individuals in the group. The solutions they are now looking for have not been extensively explored. However, the whole growth scheme must be assessed carefully in a world that is becoming acutely aware of its finite resources and continued population growth rates.

Follow-up Activities:

1. Economic and population growth often come into conflict with environmental quality and aesthetic beauty. Many communities throughout the U.S. have proposed moratoriums on growth to preserve an area's livability. Arrange for students to attend a local city council meeting, chamber of commerce meeting, or local planning commission meeting to observe discussions on growth in their local areas and draft a report of their findings.

2. In recent years, numerous ads have appeared promoting products or services which claim to help the environment. These products include anything from water conservation devices to unbleached toilet paper and all-natural cosmetics. Have students collect ads promoting "ecologically sound" products and services. They should examine these ads critically to determine if, in fact, these items aid environmental preservation.

Adapted by permission from University of Denver Center for Teaching International Relations. The original activity appears in Teaching About Population Issues, *by George Otero, Jr. and Richard Schweissing, Center for Teaching International Relations, University of Denver, CO, 1977.*

Concept:
In a world with finite resources and a growing population, we must re-evaluate our perceptions of "growth."

Objectives:
Students will be able to:
• Identify ads which reflect the desire for growth.
• Examine the ads and discuss how they encourage growth, whether they improve quality of life and whether the same results could be achieved without growth.
• Collect and critically examine ads for products claiming to be "ecologically sound."

Subjects:
Economics, social studies, environmental science, family life

Skills:
Collecting, analyzing data, critical thinking, research, discussion

Method:
Students collect and analyze print ads which promote growth and discuss whether an increased quality of life can be achieved without growth

Materials:
A wide variety of magazines and newspapers (including business and real estate sections of newspapers)

Changing Values

Concept:
Changes in the global economy and environment often affect the values held by individuals and the larger society.

Objectives:
Students will be able to:
• Examine values that have traditionally been held in North America and determine whether they have changed in recent years.
• State currently held values related to growth in our society.
• Participate in a class discussion or debate about what values are commonly held today.

Subjects:
Economics, social studies, family life

Skills:
Critical thinking, values clarification

Method:
Students examine principles of growth that have been traditionally held in North America and determine whether they have changed in recent years.

Materials:
Copies of Student Worksheet

Introduction:

A **value** is a principle or belief that is regarded as being desirable by an individual or a group of individuals. There is often an emotional attachment to values. People and their societies have certain values because they serve various desires and/or needs. But the situations of people's lives change with time and so often do their values. The values of past generations do not always meet our present needs.

Certain junctures in the course of world history have brought about a change in values. For example, as people become more concerned about the environment, they may rethink their habits and beliefs. Long-held economic values may also change as nations become more interdependent.

Procedure:

Listed on the *Student Worksheet* are some of the principles and beliefs that have been widely held by Americans in the past. Some of these values are still held; others have been replaced by new values. If the value listed is still widely held in the community, students should state "no change." If the value listed has changed or is changing, they should state the

new value that has replaced it or is replacing it. Students should also state briefly what they believe is the cause of the change. (Note: A diversity of opinion should be tolerated)

Discussion:

1. Of the ten values listed, how many have changed? How many do you think have changed for the better? For the worse?

2. Are there any that have not changed that you would like to see changed?

3. Are there any economic, social or environmental values which you hold that are different from those of your parents? Your grandparents?

Follow-up Activity:

Divide the room in half. For each value stated, have those students who believe the value is still held stand on one side of the room, and have those who believe the value has changed or is changing stand on the other side. Students can now debate and defend their positions.

Adapted by permission from Kendall/Hunt Publishing Company. The original activity, "The Olden Days," appears in Global Science: Energy, Resources, Environment Laboratory Manual. *Copyright 1981, 1984, 1991, 1996 by Kendall/Hunt Publishing Company.*

Changing Values

A *value* is a principle or belief that is regarded as being desirable by an individual or a group of individuals. There is often an emotional attachment to values. People and their societies have certain values because they serve various desires and/or needs. But the situations of people's lives change with time and so often do their values. The values of past generations do not always meet our present needs.

Listed below are some of the principles and beliefs that have been widely held by Americans in the past. Some of these values are still held; others have been replaced by new values. If the value listed is still widely held in the community, state "no change." If the value listed has changed or is changing, state the new value that has replaced it or is replacing it. Then state briefly what you believe is the cause of the change.

1. It is important that we have economic growth.

2. People ought to have large families.

3. Be productive.

4. Everyone has the right to have as many children as they want.

5. Everyone has the right to own a car.

6. Americans have a right to the resources of the world.

7. Material wealth is a measure of your worth as an individual.

8. There is no problem that science and technology can't solve.

9. The bigger the better.

10. All useful land should be available for development.

The World's Women

Women: The Critical Link

Student Reading

"Women hold up half the sky,"
reads an old Chinese saying. Indeed, women have traditionally been the world's farmers, childbearers and caretakers of young and old — the backbone of families and societies. Despite their vast contributions to humanity, women continue to suffer from gender discrimination in much of the world. Being born female in most of the developing world means a lifetime as a second-class citizen, denied most of the opportunities available to males in the areas of health, education, employment and legal rights. This second-class citizenship is detrimental first and foremost to the well-being of women themselves; however, it is also a major contributor to sustained rapid rates of population growth in the world.

The delegates at the 1994 United Nations International Conference on Population and Development (ICPD) concluded that "Eliminating social, cultural, political and economic discrimination against women is a prerequisite of... achieving balance between population and available resources and sustainable patterns of consumption and production."[1] Why does improving the status of women have an impact on population growth and environmental degradation? As we shall see, many of the social, cultural and economic conditions which keep women dependent on men are the same conditions which encourage high fertility.

If parents have limited resources to invest on their children, and they know that there is little opportunity for their daughter in the paid work force, they will not make her health or education a priority. As this girl grows up, the only source of security for her will be to marry and have children at an early age. When women lack the skills or opportunity to earn wages to support themselves, they will be economically dependent on their husbands. As they grow older, if they have no savings and the government does not provide any form of social security, they must depend on their male children to take care of them.

On the other hand, breaking down the barriers which deny women access to health and family planning services, education, employment, land and credit both increase women's autonomy and encourage lower fertility rates.[23] Across continents, when women have more control over their lives, when they are less dependent on children and their role as a mother for support and security, they choose to have smaller families and to start them later. Throughout this reading we shall see how discrimination against women in health services and nutrition, education and work all lead to higher fertility and population growth, and how equal access to these resources encourages lower fertility and better conservation of resources.

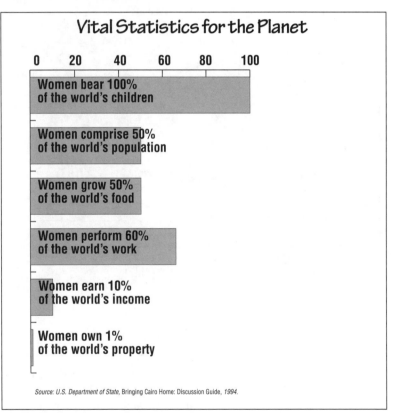

Source: U.S. Department of State, Bringing Cairo Home: Discussion Guide, 1994.

Healthy Bodies, Healthy Lives
Nutrition

The need for women to have male sons to provide for them in their old age, combined with high infant mortality rates, creates a strong driving force for women to have many children, in hopes that they will have at least one or two boys who will live to maturity. This preference for sons disadvantages girl children from a very

Women: The Critical Link

early age. Frequently they are not fed as well as their brothers, and they receive less medical attention. A study in Bangladesh showed that even under five years old, boys received 16 percent more food than girls.[4] In India, girls are more likely to suffer acute **malnutrition**, but forty times less likely to be taken to a doctor.[5]

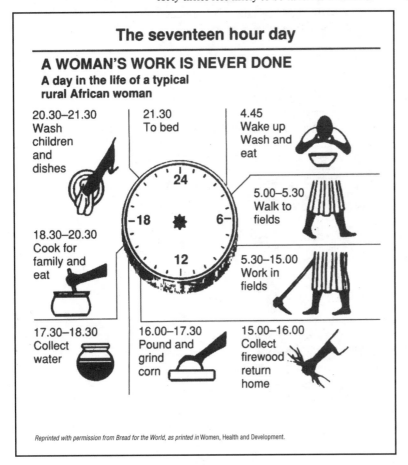

The seventeen hour day

A WOMAN'S WORK IS NEVER DONE
A day in the life of a typical rural African woman

20.30–21.30 Wash children and dishes

21.30 To bed

4.45 Wake up Wash and eat

5.00–5.30 Walk to fields

18.30–20.30 Cook for family and eat

5.30–15.00 Work in fields

17.30–18.30 Collect water

16.00–17.30 Pound and grind corn

15.00–16.00 Collect firewood return home

Reprinted with permission from Bread for the World, as printed in Women, Health and Development.

Women are frequently malnourished even during pregnancy. Anywhere from 20 to 45 percent of women of childbearing age in the developing world do not eat the recommended 2250 calories each day under normal circumstances, let alone the extra 285 calories needed during each day of pregnancy.[6] Sixty percent of pregnant women in developing countries suffer from nutritional anemia, characterized by a low red blood cell count.[7] Malnutrition during pregnancy causes infants to be born prematurely and with low birth weight, thus leading to high **infant mortality rates.**

Young Motherhood

Marriage and first childbirth at a young age is both detrimental to women and a cause of population growth. Demographically, young marriage and early childbirth lead to higher fertility, but they also can have serious consequences for both a young woman's health and her options in life. Nonetheless, in Africa, 50 percent of women are married by age 18. Forty percent of women in southern Asia and 30 percent of women in Latin America are also married by their eighteenth birthday.[8] Compared to 10 percent in developed regions, 40 percent of women in developing regions have given birth before the age of 20.[9] Pregnancy and childbirth are much more dangerous for girls who have not yet fully developed, especially if their growth is stunted from malnutrition.

Teen mothers are more likely to be anemic, less likely to seek **pre-natal care**, more likely to have complicated labor, and more likely to have a premature and **low birth weight** infant. Mothers aged 15 to 19 are twice as likely to die in childbirth as mothers who are between the ages of 20 and 25, and the children of these younger women are also twice as likely to die.[10] Early pregnancy affects other aspects of young women's lives as well. It is the leading cause of women dropping out of school in Africa and Latin America. It hurts the chances women have to improve their lives, health, educational attainment, employment and decision making power in their families and communities.[11]

Maternal mortality, or death due to childbirth or pregnancy-related causes, is the leading cause of death among women of reproductive age in developing countries. Worldwide, it claims the lives of half a million women each year, but the vast majority of these births occur in the developing world. The average number of maternal deaths per 100,000 births in the fifty countries that make up Sub-Saharan Africa is 980, compared to only eight in the United States and four in Canada![12] Many maternal mortalities could be prevented easily and cheaply. It is estimated that about half could be avoided by preventing unwanted pregnancies.[13]

Women: The Critical Link

An **unwanted pregnancy** can be a pregnancy that a woman does not want at all because she desires no more children, or a pregnancy that comes at the wrong time — closely following another pregnancy or when the mother is very young or very old. Limiting a woman's total number of pregnancies, and increasing the space between pregnancies through use of family planning reduces a woman's risk of **hemorrhaging** (excessive bleeding) when she gives birth.[14] Responsible for one quarter of all maternal deaths, hemorrhage is the most common cause of maternal mortality. Another 13 percent of maternal deaths results from unsafe abortions of unwanted pregnancies.[15] Prevent unwanted and mistimed pregnancies, and you prevent most of the 228,000 maternal deaths due to hemorrhage and unsafe abortion each year.

According to Nafis Sadik, Executive Director of the United Nations Fund for Population Activities (UNFPA), family planning represents "the freedom from which flow all other freedoms."[16] Access to family planning information and services not only allows couples to plan the number and timing of their children, but it reduces infant mortality and improves the health of both women and children by allowing a woman to conceive at only the times when she is healthiest and ready to have a child.

About 55 percent of couples worldwide use some method of **family planning**, a five-fold increase since the 1960's.[17] Total **fertility rates** have dropped from between five and seven children per woman to around three or four children. However, 350 million couples still lack access to a full range of contraceptive options and services. An estimated 120 million more women would use **contraception** if information and services were available to them.[18]

Access to barrier methods of contraception such as condoms is important not only for preventing unwanted pregnancies, but also in preventing the spread of sexually transmitted diseases such as AIDS. In 1994, women represented about 40 percent of all AIDS cases worldwide. However, women are contracting the virus at a faster rate than men, and by the year 2000, women are expected to comprise half of all the AIDS cases.[19]

Education Opens Doors

Discrimination against girls in education is another condition that hurts women and leads to population growth. Although advances have been made over the past decades, enrollment of girls in primary and secondary schools is still far below that of boys in many countries. Presently, 65 percent of girls and 78 percent of boys are enrolled in primary school in developing countries. Thirty-seven percent of girls and 48 percent of boys are enrolled in secondary school.[20] Educating girls is one of the most effective ways of giving them a degree of self-sufficiency, providing them with the skills to obtain a good job and enhancing their decision-making power in their families and communities.

Because it increases women's self-sufficiency, education decreases their dependency on having many children for security and status. The years of education a woman has is one of the best predictors of how many children she will have and how healthy they will be. Repeatedly, studies have shown that educated women marry later, want fewer children, are more likely to use effective methods of contraception, and have greater means to improve their economic livelihood.[21]

In Africa, where **illiteracy** among adult women is still around 50 percent, the average number of births per woman is over five. In Latin America and the Caribbean and eastern and south-eastern Asia, where illiteracy rates for women have fallen to around twenty percent, the number of births per woman is under four.[22]

Women's Work

Women are disadvantaged in all forms of work. They are responsible for a larger share of unpaid work, and they are discriminated against in both informal and formal sector employment. Women frequently work more hours per week than men. In Indonesia, women work 78 hours per week while men work 61, and in Uganda women work 50 hours a week to men's 23 hours, more than twice as much.[23] However, globally women only make up 35 percent of the paid labor force.[24]

Women who are denied employment opportunities that give them status and eco-

Women: The Critical Link

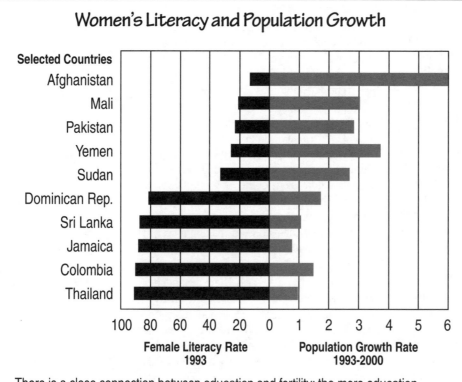

Women's Literacy and Population Growth

Selected Countries

Country	
Afghanistan	
Mali	
Pakistan	
Yemen	
Sudan	
Dominican Rep.	
Sri Lanka	
Jamaica	
Colombia	
Thailand	

100 80 60 40 20 0   1   2   3   4   5   6

**Female Literacy Rate
1993**   **Population Growth Rate
1993-2000**

There is a close connection between education and fertility: the more education
women have, the more likely they are to have small families.

Source: UNDP Human Development Report, 1996. New York: The United Nations, 1996.

nomic security have no choice other than to marry and begin having children at an early age. On the other hand, when women have equal access to paid employment, they tend to have smaller families and start them later. This trend both opens up new opportunities for women and slows population growth and environmental degradation.

Invisible Work

Women are responsible for performing the vast majority of unpaid household work. In the developing world, this work includes childcare, collecting water and gathering fuelwood for cooking and heating, and for growing, processing and cooking the food for the family. Women grow 60 to 80 percent of the food grown in Africa.[25] This work ties women to the land, and they are frequently the ones most affected by environmental degradation. Desertification and resource depletion increase the amount of time women

must spend collecting firewood and water.

When wood is scarce, women must burn cow manure as fuel instead of saving it for use as fertilizer for their crops. According to a U.N. Population Fund report, every ton of fertilizer burned can cost as much as 110 pounds of grain lost from the next harvest. Ironically, environmental degradation and pollution give women incentives to have more children to help them farm and collect wood and water. Higher fertility increases the rate of population growth, which is often one of the leading causes of the resource scarcity to begin with.

Another form of women's work includes work in the **informal economy**. This sector of the economy is comprised of people providing goods and services, usually out of their homes. In several countries, women represent over 40 percent of people active in the informal sector, and in Honduras, Jamaica and Zambia, they make up a large majority.[26] Where women comprise a larger percentage of the informal labor force than men, it is because of lack of opportunities or other obstacles to wage employment.[27]

Women frequently face obstacles to success in the informal sector as well. They usually lack access to credit — small loans which they can use to start up small businesses to generate more income for their families. Studies have shown that when given access to low-interest credit, women repay their loans and increase their income and assets, which they use to improve the education, health and nutrition of their families.[28]

Visible Work

Women who work in the formal sector marry an average 2.4 years later than women

Women: The Critical Link

who do not.[29] And when a woman must leave her job and sacrifice possible earnings in order to deliver or care for a young child, women's paid employment discourages couples from having large families. However, several barriers still block women's equal opportunity in the paid work force such as the inability to get maternity leave or affordable child care. Furthermore, even where women comprise a sizable percent of the paid labor force, they usually hold jobs of lower status and make lower wages than men.

The average women's wage is less than 60 percent of the average man's wage.[30] Throughout much of the world, women's paid labor is concentrated in "pink collar" professions ,including teaching, cleaning, nursing, waiting tables and working in textile mills.[31] Despite gains in both women's participation in the paid labor force and advancements within it, women still hold only 14 percent of all managerial and administrative jobs, and they make up less than 5 percent of the world's heads of state, major corporations and international organizations.[32]

Giving women equal access to nutrition, health services, education, land, employment and credit is a critical step in promoting their human rights. Women who have been well nourished, well educated and who have access to a wage-earning job have a choice about what to do with their lives. They do not have to be dependent on a husband or having male children for their security. As women become more equal partners in their marriages, family size declines. When skills and opportunities are combined with access to reproductive health and family planning services, women and their partners are able to have only the number of children they wish to have when they wish to have them, fertility rates fall and population growth and resource depletion slows.

Endnotes

[1] Programme of Action adopted at the International Conference on Population and Development, Cairo, 5-13 September 1994. p. 14.

[2] Nafis Sadik. "Investing in Women: The Focus of the '90's." *Beyond the Numbers: A Reader on Population, Consumption, and the Environment*. Ed. Laurie Ann Mazur. Washington, DC: Island Press, 1994. p. 210.

[3] Ruth Dixon-Mueller. "Women's Rights and Reproductive Choice: Rethinking the Connections." *Beyond the Numbers: A Reader on Population, Consumption, and the Environment*. Ed. Laurie Ann Mazur. Washington, DC: Island Press, 1994. p. 240.

[4] Op. cit. note 2, p. 212.

[5] Ibid.

[6] Op. cit. note 2, p. 213.

[7] Adrienne Germain and Jane Ordway. "Population Policy and Women's Health: Balancing the Scales. "*Beyond the Numbers: A Reader on Population, Consumption, and the Environment*. Ed. Laurie Ann Mazur. Washington, DC: Island Press, 1994. p. 137.

[8] Op. cit. note 2, p. 211.

[9] The World's Women: Trends and Statistics. New York: The United Nations, 1995. p. 69.

[10] Op. cit. note 2, p. 215.

[11] Op. cit. note 9, p. 15.

[12] 1997 World Population Datasheet (wall chart). Washington, DC: Population Reference Bureau, 1997.

[13] Op. cit. note 2, p. 216.

[14] Ibid.

[15] A. Tinker and M. Koblinsky. "Making Motherhood Safe," World Bank Discussion Paper no. 202. Washington, DC: World Bank, 1993. p. 3.

[16] Op. cit. note 2, p. 209.

[17] Op. cit. note 1, p. 32.

[18] Ibid.

[19] Op. cit. note 9, p. 72.

[20] Op. cit. note 2, p. 220.

[21] Op. cit. note 9, p. xx; Op. cit. note 2, p. 221.

[22] Op. cit. note 9, p. 92.

[23] Op. cit. note 2, p. 225.

[24] Op. cit. note 2, p. 222.

[25] Op. cit. note 2, p. 224.

[26] Op. cit. note 9, p. xxii.

[27] Op. cit. note 9, p. 116.

[28] Op. cit. note 9, p. 118.

[29] Op. cit. note 2, p. 222.

[30] Op. cit. note 9, p. 127.

[31] Op. cit. note 2, p. 223; Op. cit. note 9, p. xx.

[32] *Gender Equity*. Washington, DC: Centre for Development and Population Activities, 1996, p. 8.

A Woman's Place

Concept:
The status of women in regions throughout the world influences fertility rates and therefore the rate of population growth.

Objectives:
Students will be able to:
- Analyze and describe the status of women in a sub-Saharan African nation using examples from the student reading.
- Express their values as they respond to the reading.
- Simulate the size and make-up of their own families using statistical probability and cultural and personal preferences.
- Research the status of women in different countries.
- Present research findings to the class.

Subjects:
Social studies, family life, language arts

Skills:
Cooperation, observation, public speaking, research, calculating averages and probability, critical thinking, analyzing data

Method:s
After reading and discussing a passage based on a typical woman's life in sub-Saharan Africa, students will simulate planning a family as a North American couple and a couple from a developing nation. Students then work in cooperative learning groups to create a brief oral report on the status of women in different countries based on individual research.

Materials:
2 Copies of Student Reading and Student Worksheet

One penny for each member of the class

Introduction:

In every country and culture, women play vital roles in society, but often the only role that they are recognized for is their reproductive one. Women around the world have made great progress in improving their lives and the lives of their families, but they still face many inequities in political representation, economic well-being, health and human rights. These inequities do not only affect individuals but entire societies, as there is an increasing amount of evidence that improving the status of women is key to improving the health and well-being of families and stabilizing fertility rates around the world. In this activity, students explore the complex relationship between women's status, development and fertility.

Procedure:

Part 1: Fatima's Story

1. Give each student a copy of the student reading *Fatima's Story* and a copy of the Student Worksheet. Explain to the students that *Fatima's Story* is the story of a woman who lives in sub-Saharan Africa but her situation is typical to that of women in many countries in Africa, Asia and Latin America.

2. After the students have had a chance to read *Fatima's Story*, divide the class into small groups of four to six students and have them answer the discussion questions on the worksheet as a group.

3. Once the students have had a chance to discuss and answer the questions, go over the answers as a class. Be sure to save time to discuss the final question "What would you do if you were Fatima?"

   Alternative: Have each group do a role-play of what Fatima and Jalal Din might do in this situation. The main characters would be Fatima, Jalal Din, and Jalal Din's mother; other students could play the roles of Zarin or Aziz, the local teacher, the local family planning worker, a relative, a concerned neighbor, or the narrator.

Based on the activity, "The Value of a Son, The Value of a Daughter", appears in Choose a Future! Issues and Options for Adolescent Girls, *The Centre for Development and Population Activities, 1996.*

Part 2: It's a Toss-up!

Many students want to have a certain number of boys or girls when they have children, but what happens if they don't get what they want right away? This exercise simulates the kinds of situations people face in planning their families.

1. Have each student take out a piece of paper and write down the number of children they would like to have, including the number of boys and the number of girls that they want.

2. Give each student a penny and explain that *heads* is a girl and *tails* is a boy. Ask the students to imagine that they are now part of a couple and want to start a family. Have them flip the coin to determine the sex of their first child. After recording on their sheets if the first child is a boy or a girl, the student must decide whether to flip again (have another child) or stop. Continue this process until all students feel their families are complete. Determine the average number of children per couple (remember you will have to double the number of people in the class as each student is assumed to have a mate).

3. Next, tell the students that you are going to repeat the exercise but this time they must imagine that they live in a culture similar to that of Fatima's where having sons is very important. Ask each student to decide whether they want two, three, or four sons, and how many daughters they would like as well. Repeat the steps above. Tell the students to continue to flip the coin (have more children) until they have the number of sons and daughters they want, or until they feel they don't want any more children. Determine the average number of children per couple as above and compare the two numbers.

Discussion Questions:

1. Were you able to "have" the number of children you originally said you wanted in the first scenario? In the second? How about the number of sons and the number of daughters you wanted? Why?

2. What factors, besides income, determine how many children people have?

A Woman's Place

Possible answers might include cultural and religious traditions and values, family traditions, career choices, lifestyle and use of family planning.

3. Why might a boy child or a girl child be preferred in a North American family? How might this preference vary from one culture to another?

   Parents may feel that they could better "relate" to a boy or a girl based on their own experiences. There are also stereotypes that might determine preference, such as that "girls are better behaved than boys." In many developing countries, parents depend on sons to help support them in their old age, while girls often marry early and live with their husbands' families.

4. What difference does it make to a society's population whether there is a tradition of large family sizes or a tradition of small families?

   In a society where most people have many children, the population grows quickly and the society must provide more goods and services for more people.

5. How do your personal family-size decisions affect other people in the society? How do they affect the natural environment?

   One person's decisions may not seem very significant in a large society. However, each person's decisions multiplied by everyone in the society add up to a lot. This is the same principle as voting in a national election. Think about what would happen if everyone make s the same choice as you do.

Adapted with permission from Carolynn S. Howell, Palm Bay High School, Melbourne, FL.

Part 3: Researching a Women's Place

1. Divide the class into groups of four students. You can assign students to groups ahead of time, or have students select their own groups.

2. Each group will be assigned one of the following countries to research (if the class has fewer than 36 students, eliminate countries from the list):

Pakistan	Nigeria
Brazil	Poland
Saudi Arabia	Jamaica
Australia	India
China	

3. Each student will have a specific area to study related to the status of typical women in his or her group's assigned country. Each student will research one of four categories:

   - **education of women** (includes literacy rate, average years of schooling)
   - **employment of women** (includes employment rate, types of employment, average wages, employment in the home)
   - **health of women** (includes life expectancy, vulnerability to disease, nutrition, fertility)
   - **legal and political status of women** (includes women's rights, laws relating to women's status, representation in government)

   For instance, if a group is assigned to research Pakistan, each group member will focus on one of the above four categories related to women's status in Pakistan. For each category, students should determine how women's opportunities compare to those of men.

   Reference materials such as world almanacs and encyclopedias may be helpful, but students should seek out any other resources in their school, local library, and on the world wide web that will provide them with some facts and figures. See the end of this book for ideas on further resources.

   Allow two or three days for students to accumulate information on their particular categories. Then students should meet in their groups and share information on their findings. Together, group members will create a brief oral presentation on the status of women in their assigned country. The presentation may include visual aids, such as a poster or a skit, and may be presented by a group representative or all four group members.

4. After all groups have presented their findings, lead a discussion on the similarities and differences in the reports. In which countries is women's status closest to that of men? In which countries do women have the lowest status? How is the fertility rate in each region related to the status of women? How is the status of women related to population growth? To environmental quality?

A Woman's Place

Fatima is a mother with five children — the son, Aziz, and four daughters.

Her husband, Jalal Din, is a reliable man and a good father. He and Fatima are farmers and they work hard together in the fields.

They all live together with Jalal Din's mother, who is a widow. She is a good woman, but she is always critical and nags at Fatima. In fact, she talks from early morning until she goes to bed. "When are you going to light the fire? It is broad daylight already!" And, "Wives should obey their husbands." Sometimes she criticizes Fatima for work not done, sometimes for spending too much money. And she always complains that Fatima has produced only one son and burdened her dear Jalal Din with one daughter after another!

Fatima has learned to live with her mother-in-law and to keep her mouth closed. In this way, she is a very dutiful wife and daughter-in-law. But she did do something in secret last month — well, it was a secret between her and Jalal Din — which they didn't tell Jalal Din's mother. Fatima started practicing family planning. The big reason she made this decision was that she wasn't feeling very well. As you know, having 5 children in 9 years can make a woman feel unwell. She has a backache and she is tired most of the time. But she has so much work to do — finding firewood, carrying water, preparing food, washing the family's clothes, working in the fields — when can she rest?

But there was another reason Fatima started using family planning. It was because of her eldest daughter, Zarin. She is the first child — and a lovely little girl, a joy to everyone. Zarin goes to school along with Aziz. Every afternoon she brings her exercise book home and proudly reads to her mother what she has written. She is so happy in school! But Fatima knows that if she has another baby, Zarin must leave school to care for the new baby while Fatima works in the fields. There is simply no other way all the work can be managed. In a way, Zarin knows this too — because she has seen this happen to her little friends. Almost all of them no longer go to school, but instead care for younger brothers and sisters.

Today there is a terrible scene in the house when the family gathers to eat. The old woman is wailing and pulling her hair. They family is alarmed and gather around her where she sits on the floor. Between sobs, she finally tells them. At the village well this morning, she talked with an old friend who told her someone had seen Fatima at the family planning clinic.

"You are very bad!" she shouts at Fatima. "And you will pay! You will pay for such wickedness. Now you will have no more sons. And who will care for you in your old age? Aziz is a good boy, but he is only one. A family needs many sons. Think of our name. Who will help Jalal Din in the fields? Who will take care of me, if God forbid, something happens to Jalal Din?"

Jalal Din sits next to his mother and comforts her. And he looks at Fatima as if he doesn't know what to do. Zarin is also looking at Fatima. She knows what this is all about — at least she knows what it will mean to her. There are tears in her eyes.

Fatima really has a problem. What would you do if you were Fatima?

A Woman's Place

1. What are Fatima's problems? What are her concerns?

2. What are some of the things that Fatima must do everyday for her family?

3. If Fatima was married when she was 16, about how old is she now? What if she was married at 23?
   (Remember, she has had 5 children in 9 years.)

4. What are the concerns of Fatima's mother-in-law? Why is it important for her to have grandsons? Is she concerned about the effect on her granddaughters of another baby in the family? What does this say about how she values her granddaughters?

5. What are some reasons sons are more highly valued than daughters in Fatima's culture?

6. How do Fatima and Jalal Din's views differ from those of his mother? Is there a generation gap?

7. Why did Fatima and Jalal Din decide to start practicing family planning? Do you think it was a wise decision?

8. How might it benefit Fatima and her family if she has no more children?

9. How might it benefit Fatima and her family if she had another son?

10. What will happen to Zarin if her parents have more children? How might it affect her future?

11. What should Fatima do about her mother-in-law and her wish to have more grandsons? How could her husband help?

12. What would you do if you were Fatima?

Based on the activity, "The Value of a Son, The Value of a Daughter", appears in Choose a Future! Issues and Options for Adolescent Girls, The Centre for Development and Population Activities, 1996.
Reading, "Fatima's Story" adapted from Working With Villagers, American Home Economics Association, 1977.

Gender Quest

Concept:
The issue of gender equality is not restricted to the developing world. Even in North America, there are observable differences between men's and women's roles in society.

Objectives:
Students will be able to:
• Explore their own perception of gender roles.
• Conduct research and gather evidence on the status of women in North America.
• Analyze their research on gender and draw conclusions based on that research.
• Report their findings to the class.

Subjects:
Social studies, family life, language arts

Skills:
Cooperation, observation, analyzing data, research, public speaking

Methods:
Students participate in a short role play and written exercise on gender roles and then examine materials to illustrate views of men and women throughout American history.

Then students have a chance to examine their own culture by acting as anthropologists from the Planet Gen-Der. Students work in teams to gather and examine evidence on the status of women in North America using sources such as television, magazines, song lyrics and news stories, and report their finding to the rest of the class.

Materials:
Historical materials (see Part 2 for suggestions)
Student Worksheet

Introduction:
Sometimes it is hard to see our own culture in an objective light. Acting as anthropologists from a distant world, students will examine North American culture to determine the status of women in North America. A few warm-up activities help to get students thinking about gender roles in our society, past and present.

Part 1: Warm-Up Activities

1. Ask each student to demonstrate a stance or a posture which depicts how men and women are perceived in society. Have the male students demonstrate men, and the female students demonstrate women. (If it is a same sex group, have them demonstrate one sex and then the other). While the students are holding the stance, go around and ask the students why they chose that stance, and what the stance or posture reflects about society's views of men and women.

   Note: Be sure to tell the students that the stance they choose does not have to reflect their personal views, but instead a view held by society as a whole.

2. Have students sit down and pull out a sheet of paper. Have the girls complete statement (a) and the boys complete statement (b). Tell the students not to put their names on the statements. After the students have had a chance to complete the statements, collect the statements and share some of them with the class.

   a) Because I am a woman,

      I must _____

      If I were a man I could _____

   b) Because I am a man,

      I must _____

      If I were a woman I could _____.

Discussion Questions:

1. Do you agree with all the statements or disagree with some of them?

2. Did you have trouble filling out the statement? Why or why not?

3. Imagine your parents or grandparents when they were your age. Would they have filled out the statement differently? What has changed? What has stayed the same?

4. Imagine you are a teenager in a developing country. Would you have filled out your statement differently? Why or why not?

Based on the activity, "Understanding Gender", appears in the Gender and Development: The CEDPA Training Manual Series, The Centre for Development and Population Activities, 1996.

Part 2: A Visit from the Planet Gen-Der

1. Begin by asking the students where our perceptions of men and women come from. Answers might include: observing others, from our parents and grandparents, stories we hear, from books, magazines, television, movies, music, etc.

2. Bring in a variety of materials to show students views of men and women at various points of American history. Show students materials from a variety of time periods and in a variety of formats. Discuss with students whether these materials reflect the reality of women's and men's lives or whether they are idealizations or stereotypes of how men and women behave. Ask students how they feel about the materials when they view them from a modern perspective. Are some of the materials silly? Offensive? Strange? Surprising? How does the message change over the years?

   Some suggested sources for materials: passages from novels and historical records, old song lyrics, old print ads from magazines and newspapers (you can usually copy them from the library), old educational films (check your school district archive), old television advertisements (some libraries carry compilation tapes of old ads), taped reruns from old television shows (some cable channels run old shows), scenes from old movies, etc.

3. Divide the class into groups of four to six people and give each group a copy of the worksheet. Go over the worksheet with the students. Give each group two or three days to collect their data. After the data are collected, each group should examine the material and information gathered and write a report or prepare a presentation summarizing their findings.

Gender Quest

You will assume the role of an anthropologist from the Planet Gen-Der, located in a faraway galaxy. As on Earth, there are two genders on your planet. The two genders enjoy total equality with regard to status and responsibility. They have achieved equal levels of education, employment in all professions and governing positions, and both genders share the raising of children and domestic responsibilities equally.

Your team of anthropologists has been dispatched to North America on the planet Earth for intensive field study. Your assignment is to study gender issues and relations in North American culture and determine whether the genders share an equal place in society as they do on Gen-Der. You will appear as human so as to go undetected by earthlings. Remember clues are everywhere — keep a notebook to record your observations and look for subtle messages as well as obvious ones.

For your mission you will have to collect the following materials and make the following observations to determine whether the two genders on earth have achieved total equality as they have on your planet:

1. Each member of your group should find a popular song related to your research and write out the lyrics. If possible, bring in a tape of the song to share with your group.

2. Each member of your group should collect four or five advertisements from magazines or newspapers pertaining to your topic.

3. Each member of your group should bring in two or three relevant articles from magazines or newspapers.

4. Have each person cut out or photocopy a comic strip related to your topic.

5. If one of your group members has access to a VCR, have that person tape five or six relevant TV advertisements. If you can, tape two or three scenes from popular TV shows and movies as well. If you have access to them, you can also tape several music videos. If no one has access to a VCR, then have each member of your group summarize an advertisement and a scene from a television show or movie in writing to share with your group.

6. Each member of the group should write a description of a public advertisement from a sporting event, a billboard or an advertisement on the side of a bus.

7. As a group, record the daily routines and rituals of a typical human female and typical human male (you can use group members, friends or family members for your models.)

8. Observe the behavior of the earthlings around you for more clues. Sit in the lunch room, on the bus, or in another public place and observe the people around you.

After several days of collecting your data, sit down with your group and examine your collected materials and observations. What conclusions can you draw about the relative equality between the genders? As a group, draft a report of your team's findings on whether the two genders enjoy total equality in North America as they do on your planet. Present evidence to support your conclusions. After completing your report, prepare a short presentation to present your group's findings to the interplanetary commission (the rest of the class).

Finding Solutions

Eco-Ethics

Introduction:

This activity is designed to give students the opportunity to examine their own values and beliefs as they relate to the environment, population and social issues. It is not the intent of this activity to prescribe "right" and "wrong" answers for the students. In some cases, students may perceive what would be the most ethical solution to a given problem, while admitting that they realistically might not choose that option. For each Dilemma Card, the action choices are preceded by "would you" rather than "should you." This will encourage students to offer what they probably would do in each given situation. It might be useful to compare students' reactions to each dilemma both before and after going through the student readings and lessons.

Procedure:

1. Copy and cut up the dilemma cards. Other dilemmas could be written that are more specific to problems in your area. Students could also be involved in the process of creating the Dilemma Cards with each student responsible for writing one dilemma. Dilemmas can be left entirely open-ended with no options suggested for consideration.

2. Divide the class into groups of four, and give each group a stack of Dilemma Cards. Place them face down at the center of the group.

3. The first student draws a card from the top of the stack. The student studies the situation, decides what he or she would do, and formulates his or her reasons.

4. When the student is ready — typically in less than two minutes — the student reads the situation and the options aloud to the rest of the group. The student gives the decision he or she has chosen, and briefly describes the reasoning involved. In turn, each of the other members of the group is invited to comment on the dilemma, and what he or she would do in the situation. The discussion of each dilemma by the members of the group should take about five minutes. The person whose dilemma is being discussed should have the opportunity to ask questions of the other members of the group, and to offer clarification about his or her decision. The discussion gives the students experience in having ideas examined by peers, and is intended to remind the students of the need to take personal responsibility for decision-making. It is not necessary and may not be desirable for the students to reach consensus; there are legitimately diverse views of the most appropriate and responsible actions to take in many situations. The purpose is to provide students with an opportunity to examine, express, clarify and take responsibility for their own reasoning.

5. The card is then returned to the bottom of the stack and the next student selects a card from the top of the stack. Continue this process until each student has had the opportunity to express his or her decision and rationale about a dilemma.

Follow-up Activity:

Have each student choose a dilemma and write a short paragraph on the positive and negative effects of all the options listed for that dilemma. They should indicate what additional information, if any, is needed in order to make a responsible and informed decision. Students should identify what seems, in their judgment, to be the most responsible decision — and explain their reasoning.

Adapted by permission from Project WILD. The original activity, "Ethi-Reasoning," appears in Project WILD's K-12 Activity Guide, Council for Environmental Education, copyright 1983, 1985, 1987, 1992.

Concept:
Lessons on population, environment and the global society should have their applications in daily personal decision making.

Objectives:
Students will be able to:
• Take positions on dilemmas.
• Formulate and present reasons for their positions.
• Discuss the dilemmas and positions in groups.

Subjects:
Environmental science, social studies

Skills:
Decision making, critical thinking, discussion, writing

Method:
While considering various dilemmas, students examine their own values and beliefs related to environmental issues, and evaluate possible actions they might take that have impacts on the environment.

Materials:
Copies of Dilemma Cards

Eco-Ethics

Dilemma Card

You are president of a large corporation. You are very interested in pollution control and have had a task force assigned to study the pollution your plant is creating. The task force reports that you are barely within the legal requirements. The plant is polluting the community's air and water. To add the necessary equipment to reduce pollution would cost so much that you would have to lay off 50 employees. Would you:

- add the equipment and fire the employees?
- not add the equipment?
- wait a few years to see if the costs of the equipment will drop?
- hire an engineering firm to provide further recommendations?
- other? (specify)

Dilemma Card

You love children and would like to have a large family. You are aware, however, of the world's population is expected to double in the coming century. Would you:

- plan to have a large family anyway?
- decide not to have children?
- limit yourself to one or two children?
- other? (specify)

Dilemma Card

You are finally able to build the home your family has dreamed about. After reviewing the plans for your home, you realize that you cannot include all of the features you had planned for, due to rising construction costs. If you can only choose to include one of the following features, would you choose:

- solar heating?
- recreation room with fireplace?
- hot tub and sauna?
- greenhouse?
- other? (specify)

Dilemma Card

You are having a picnic with your family at the beach and you see another family leaving to go home, without having picked up its own trash. It is clear the other family is going to leave litter all around. Would you:

- move quickly and ask them to pick up the trash before they leave?
- wait for them to leave and pick up the trash for them?
- do nothing?
- other? (specify)

Eco-Ethics

Dilemma Card

You are an influential member of the community. On your way home from work, you are stopped by a police officer and cited for having excessive auto emissions. Would you:

- use your influence to have the ticket invalidated?
- sell the car to some unsuspecting person?
- work to change the law?
- get your car fixed and pay the ticket?
- other? (specify)

Dilemma Card

A friend asks you a question about sex and how to prevent pregnancy. Although you don't know the answer for sure, you know enough to guess. What would you do and why? Would you:

- make up an answer based on the facts you know?
- try to help find the answer in a health book or in the library?
- suggest your friend talk to his/her parents or a teacher?
- admit to your friend that you do not know for sure?
- suggest talking to a sibling?
- other? (specify)

Dilemma Card

You have a job at a restaurant and notice that each day prepared meals are left over and are discarded. You feel this is a waste of good food, especially since many people in your city are without adequate food. Would you:

- suggest to management that leftover food be donated to a local homeless shelter?
- suggest to management that less food be prepared each day?
- do nothing?
- other? (specify)

Dilemma Card

There is an undeveloped green space in your town where you and your friends sometimes go for peace and quiet. It's home to some local wildlife and a small creek. The town officials are thinking about selling the land to a developer who wants to build a shopping mall. The mall would provide some jobs for area high school students. The mall also might be a place for you and your friends to hang out. What would you do and why? Would you:

- support the mall project at the expense of your green area?
- oppose the mall project all together?
- go to a city planning meeting to see if developers would consider another site?
- do nothing and let the adults decide?
- other? (specify)

Eco-Ethics

Dilemma Card

Your friend has just given you a lovely ivory necklace that she purchased on a trip to Africa. You are aware that African elephants are being slaughtered for their ivory tusks and are now an endangered species. Would you:

- accept the necklace and wear it often?
- accept the necklace but keep it in a drawer?
- explain to your friend why you do not wish to accept her gift?
- other? (specify)

Dilemma Card

Your parents make you mow and water your lawn. The area hasn't had much rainfall for some time and area officials are recommending that everyone conserve water. However, your neighborhood has strict rules about keeping each yard in order. Without regular watering your lawn will turn brown. What would you do and why? Would you:

- ignore the conservation warning and continue watering your lawn to keep it looking nice?
- sacrifice the beauty of your lawn by watering less often?
- plant different things in your yard that do not require so much care?
- other? (specify)

Dilemma Card

Your cafeteria at school has attempted to prepare food items that are popular with students (hamburgers, hot dogs, pepperoni pizza, fried chicken, etc.). While you and your friends enjoy these foods, you know that most of these items are high on the food chain, requiring intensive amounts of water and energy to produce. You are also aware that much of the grain produced in this country is used to feed livestock, while much of the world suffers from hunger and malnutrition. Would you:

- meet with school administrators to suggest having more meatless lunches served each week?
- bring your own lunch and not worry about the cafeteria menu?
- eat whatever is served?
- other? (specify)

Dilemma Card

The school you attend is not in walking distance of your home. You could catch the bus on the corner or drive in with a friend. The car would get you to school faster and without waiting outside. But the bus uses less gas per passenger. Would you:

- take the bus?
- get a ride in the car?
- carpool with other kids nearby?
- ride your bicycle?
- other? (specify)

Think Globally, Act Locally

Introduction:

Although some global issues may seem insurmountable, there are usually actions we can take as individuals on the local level that, collectively, will alleviate these problems and educate others. Sometimes there are varying degrees of involvement that are easy or very difficult to accomplish. Often, we have to weigh the potential effectiveness of possible actions to determine the best way to proceed. In this activity, students will consider various actions and potential outcomes to respond to many of the issues addressed in the previous activities.

Procedure:

1. For each global and local challenge listed in the attached chart: have students, either individually or in groups, add as many ideas as they can think of to the personal actions/potential solutions list. You might want to compile all ideas onto one class list.

2. Next have the students assess which aspects of the global and local problem are addressed by each idea. For example, recycling car oil will help the water pollution problem and lessen health problems caused by poor quality drinking water; thus students should write "A,1" in the Problems Addressed section on the chart.

3. The next two columns can be filled in together. Students should first evaluate the degree of personal commitment each idea would involve, rating the ideas: **E**asy, **A**verage, or **D**ifficult. Then students should evaluate the degree of effectiveness for each idea: **U**nlikely, **S**omewhat likely, **V**ery likely.

Discussion Questions:

1. Review the list of global problems related to overpopulation. Should any of the categories be changed? Any additions to or subtractions from the list? Ask students to arrange the list in order of importance or priority to them.

2. Also review the local problems list. Do any modifications seem appropriate for this list? Note similarities and differences between the global problems and local manifestations.

3. Some of the personal actions from the solutions list will positively affect more than one problem. For example, using the car less

affects air pollution, global warming and energy conservation. Have students note which ideas help more than one problem and draw arrows on their chart to the other global and local challenges affected.

4. Also, some actions may help solve one problem while contributing to another. An example of this is switching from disposable diapers to cloth. Using cloth diapers helps the waste disposal problem, since less mass will be sent to landfills; it also requires large amount of hot water to clean the diapers, thus contributing to the energy and water pollution problems. Have students circle the ideas which have such a dual effect and write the problem(s) negatively affected next to it.

5. Finally, discuss the intangible benefits of doing what you can to solve a problem. Is it possible to feel better by taking an action that by itself will not solve the problem than by doing nothing at all? Why or why not?

Follow-up Activity:

Ask students to look at their completed charts and determine whether there are any potential "actions" that they have done in the past, are doing currently or might want to do as a result of evaluating the effectiveness of personal activities to address certain global and local problems. Are there any actions best taken by a group of people, such as a school ecology club or civic organization?

Adapted with permission from the Office of Environmental Education, Washington State. The original activity, appears in Energy, Food, and You, *published by the Office of Environmental Education, Washington State (Seattle, WA).*

Concept:
To avoid becoming overwhelmed by global problems, we should concentrate on the local level, focusing on meaningful actions individuals can take to participate in global problem-solving.

Objectives:
Students will be able to:
• List personal actions which could help alleviate many of the global challenges discussed throughout the curriculum.
• Assess proposal actions on their potential effectiveness and convenience.

Subjects:
Environmental science, social studies, family life, civics/government

Skills:
Brainstorming, evaluation, critical thinking

Method:
Students come up with ways they, as individuals, can help meet the challenges to environmental quality and human well-being posed by global population pressures. They then think critically about the potential effectiveness of these proposed actions.

Materials:
Copies of Student Worksheets

Think Globally, Act Locally

Global Challenges Related to Population Pressures	Local Challenges Related to Population Pressures	Personal Actions/ Potential Solutions	Problems Addressed	Level of Commitment: Easy, Average, Difficult	Degree of Effectiveness: Unlikely, Somewhat likely, Very Likely
Rapid Population Growth A Too many people drain Earth's finite resources. B. Certain consumption patterns cause increased damage to resources and the environment.	1. Inadequate food, shelter education, and health services 2. Most local environmental and social problems worsen with too many people.	• Write a letter to the editor about the problems of unchecked population growth. • Limit the number of children you have to two or fewer.			
Climate Change A. Global warming/climate change B. Certain consumption patterns cause increased damage to resources and the environment.	1. Water shortages 2. Crop damage 3. Disruption of marine food chain (fewer fish to eat) 4. Increase in skin cancer	• Plant trees and shrubs in your yard. • Request that the local government set up a collection and recycling system for appliances containing CFC's.			
Diminishing Air Quality A. Airborne poisons B. Acid rain	1. Health problems from smog 2. Death of forests and wildlife 3. Decrease in crop production	• Check your car for smog control devices (and use unleaded gas). • Don't spray bugs; stomp them or take them outside.			
Water Issues A. Water pollution B. Acid rain	1. Health problems from poor quality drinking water 2. Crops, wildlife and people suffer from water shortages	• Take short showers instead of baths. • Make sure your used car oil is properly recycled, not poured into the sewage system.			
Deforestation A. Loss of oxygen producers B. Acid Rain	1. Disappearing native forests 2. Threatened extinction of several species 3. Hotter cities/homes	• Use fewer wood products. • Contact your local forestry service about helping replant logged areas.			
Land Use/Hunger A. Topsoil depletion due to misuse of land B. Hunger problems	1. Loss of jobs and food produced due to overused and wasted cropland 2. More hungry people 3. Illnesses related to lack of nutrients	• Organize a local food drive. • Eat lower on the food chain.			

Think Globally, Act Locally

Global Challenges Related to Population Pressures	Local Challenges Related to Population Pressures	Personal Actions/ Potential Solutions	Problems Addressed	Level of Commitment: Easy, Average, **Difficult**	Degree of Effectiveness: **Unlikely,** Somewhat likely, **Very Likely**
A. Population growth creates more waste B. Careless consumption patterns cause more waste	1. Overfull landfills (often improperly contained and sealed) 2. Toxins from incinerators 3. Smell from large compost plants	• Begin a local recycling program. • Buy products with minimal packaging.			
Loss of Biodiversity A. Nonrenewable resources becoming scarce B. Fossil fuel dependence creates environmental problems	1. Possible medical cures lost 2. Wildlife gene pool decreased 3. Beauty lost	• When hiking or camping, try not to alter the natural habitat in any way. • Join a wildlife protection society and start a local chapter.			
Energy A. Nonrenewable resources becoming scarce B. Fossil fuel dependence creates environmental problems	1. Air/water pollution cause health risks 2. Oil spills cause environmental damage 3. Political unrest due to competing for limited resources 4. Traffic jams due to auto dependence	• Install a solar hot water heater in your home. • Organize a car pool system for local commuters.			
Poverty/Homelessness A. Additional numbers needing food/shelter can make economic growth difficult, perpetuating the poverty cycle. B. Wealth is unevenly distributed	1. Inadequate food and shelter for many 2. Health and literacy levels are low	• Organize a food and clothing drive for a local charity. • Volunteer to tutor at a local homeless shelter.			
Status of Women A. Women have many children when they are most valued for bearing sons. B. Without education, women often do not know how to obtain and use family planning methods.	1. Women have families which are too large to support 2. Women miss opportunities to be anything other than caretakers	• Write letters of encouragement to local women who are positive role models. • Inform your legislators that you support measures to help raise the status of women both domestically and internationally.			

A Nonbearing Account

Concept:
Creative approaches are often necessary in creating awareness in and finding solutions to complex problems such as population pressures.

Objectives:
Students will be able to:
• Critically analyze a proposal for combating population growth.
• Develop their own "modest proposal" to address population concerns.

Subjects:
Language arts, social studies

Skills:
Critical thinking, discussion, creative thinking, writing

Method:
Students critically examine a proposal for combating population growth and then devise their own "modest proposal" to address this issue.

Materials:
Copies of Student Reading

Introduction:

In 1729, Jonathan Swift wrote the now classic article, "A Modest Proposal," a grotesque satire on the twin Irish problems of overpopulation and food shortage during that time. Not to be taken seriously as a plan for solving these problems, Swift's satire was meant to create awareness and get people talking about these social issues.

In the following article, "A Nonbearing Account," Professor Noel Perrin outlines his plan for lowering fertility rates in an effort to curb population growth. He describes why the program is necessary, how it should be implemented, and the anticipated costs and benefits. While not nearly as outlandish (or inhumane) as Swift's proposal, Perrin's article was probably written more as a tool for discussion than as a plan likely to be adopted by the federal government. Even so, many readers may find Perrin's ideas compelling and creative.

Procedure:

Distribute copies of "A Nonbearing Account." After students have a chance to read the article, lead a discussion using the following questions.

Discussion Questions:

1. What do you think of Perrin's idea to pay females of childbearing age not to have children?

2. Do you think his idea would work in the United States, significantly decreasing fertility rates? Would many women decide against childbearing entirely? Why or why not?

3. What segments of the U.S. population might look favorably on Perrin's proposal? What segments of the population might regard Perrin's proposal with scorn? Explain.

4. Perrin compares the financial costs of his plan to current costs of the U.S. welfare system. Do you think implementation of his plan would significantly reduce federal assistance to the indigent?

5. What do you feel is Perrin's attitude toward the status of women in the United States? In developing countries?

6. Do you think Perrin's plan would be possible to implement? Is it realistic?

7. Perrin notes that there is a precedent for governments paying women to have children. What sort of precedents might he have in mind? Can you think of any ways the U.S. government encourages childbearing? (Note: Perrin is most likely referring to tax incentives to have children.)

8. Do you think Perrin wrote this article to seriously win support for his plan or just to heighten awareness of population pressures by offering a "modest proposal"?

Follow-up Activity:

Have students draft their own "modest proposal" for slowing (or stopping) population growth nationally or globally, working either individually or in pairs. The proposal should clearly outline the necessity of the plan, logistics, costs and benefits. Students should be as persuasive as possible in their writing assignment.

A Nonbearing Account*

by Noel Perrin

Sometime in 1987 world population hit 5 billion. Sometime a little before 2000 it will hit 6 billion. Sometime around 2010 . . . Obviously growth like this can't continue indefinitely. We'll run out of parking space for all the cars. We'll run out of flight paths for all the airplanes. We'll eventually run out of essentials like food. A country like Nepal has already run out of firewood.

But how do you stop the relentless increase of humanity, currently proceeding at the rate of almost 2 million a week? Well, the interesting idea I've heard is to do it with money. More specifically, bank accounts. One for every women in the world. Forget the rest of the world for a minute: here is how the plan would work in the United States. Every girl, when she reached puberty, would notify her local population center. (These sunny offices had better be staffed entirely by women — well-paid ones, too.) At that moment a financial clock would start ticking.

If the girl went the next year without having a baby, she would get a government check for $500, placed in the bank account the center now opened for her. She could take it all out and spend it on angora sweaters, if she wanted. She could leave it in as the beginning of a fund for college. Whatever she liked. The next year, if she still hadn't had a baby, the government would increase the sum by a hundred, so that her second check would be for $600. The year after, $700. A young woman reaching the age of 20, and still not having had a child, would receive a check for around $1,200. No fortune, but worth having. Available without any discrimination of any kind. A Miss du Pont, an ordinary kid in Topeka, an intending nun, a teenage prostitute, all would get their checks.

Suppose the young woman *wants* a child, though. There's nothing to stop her, except a little financial self-interest. If at 21 she proceeded to have a baby, fine. Let's have a baby shower. The government payment, however, would abruptly drop to zero. But then, if she did not have another baby the next year, back would come a check for $500. If she went two years, she'd get $600, and so on up the modest pay ladder. A pleasant little extra income for the sex that has historically been underpaid.

Great bargain: What would all this cost? In the case of women who never do have children, plenty. Start at 13 with a check for $500 and by the time you reached menopause at 53, the check would be $4,500. To that point, you would have received a total of almost $100,000. A lot of money. But still a bargain. A great bargain. The same hundred thousand is about half the cost of bringing up one abandoned child in New York City. It's less than a fifth the cost of bringing up one psychologically disturbed child in a group home in the District of Columbia. The total cost the first year would be about a billion dollars in payments to girls, maybe 2 or 3 billion to set up the centers. The total cost the fifth year would be around $10 billion. The cost wouldn't level off for about 40 years — and when it did, it would still be under what we now pay as welfare. And most of the money would flow back out immediately to stores or get turned over somewhat later to happy bursars at colleges.

A Nonbearing Account

Do I possibly exaggerate when I say that when the plan was in full operation, and every woman in the country between puberty and menopause receiving her check, the cost would still be less than that of the current welfare system? I don't think I do. Try looking in the *Statistical Abstract of the United States*. The current figure is $770 billion a year — $298 billion in state and local money, $472 billion from the federal government. That table covers many things, including VA hospitals. So turn to a more modest table, the one called "Cash and Noncash Benefits for Persons With Limited Incomes." Here the total is $114 billion, all federal money.

Such a plan would be much harder to implement in, say, India, where most people don't have bank accounts and where the government would be hard pressed to find the funds. But it wouldn't be impossible. Such payment could be the first-ever democratic foreign aid — putting money directly in the hands of women, rather than in the pockets of businessmen and bureaucrats. Furthermore, India has already found ways to pay men to have vasectomies.

Of course there are problems with such a plan. Men will object to all this money going to women, money being power. There are bound to be accusations of racism, even though the offer would be voluntary, universal and totally color blind. There being no precedent (though there's plenty of precedent for the opposite case: governments paying women to have children), it would be hard to get started. The more stolid type of politician will call the plan impossible, utopian, dreamy, absurd.

But consider the alternatives. One, of course, is to go on exactly as we are — adding a billion people every few years until there is no more tropical forest, no more oxygen-carbon dioxide balance, no more space, and our world collapses in disaster. Another is nuclear war. A third (the likeliest, I expect) is mandatory birth control, starting one country at a time, with all the repression that implies. The repression is already there in China. And with the rigid immigration restrictions imposed by those countries that have started early against those that start late. Maybe even with population wars. How much more graceful to do it all with checks.

Noel Perrin is professor of English at Dartmouth College. He has written for The New Yorker and New York magazine.

* Reprinted with permission from Noel Perrin. The original article appears in Newsweek, April 2, 1990.

In Search of Sustainable Life

Introduction:

Planning for a quality future requires defining what "quality" means to people. We all want to live in a community that not only contains all the resources we need to survive, but is also safe, clean and provides adequate services. Such a community is possible as long as we take responsibility for the overall **quality of life** affecting ourselves, family, friends, and future generations. How can we tell if our quality of life has improved or deteriorated? The historically-used GNP and GDP indicators (Gross National Product and Gross Domestic Product) tell only the story of economic activity, omitting many of the social and environmental factors that contribute to quality of life. Factors such as safety, water quality and natural beauty should also be considered.

The purpose of this activity is to let the students explore those factors — factors that address the concept of **sustainability**. According to the World Commission on Environment and Development, a sustainable community is *"one which meets the needs of the present without compromising the ability of future generations to meet their needs."* Students will exchange ideas and develop their own community's Quality of Life Index.

Procedure:

1. To begin the exercise, have students share their responses to: "The one thing I would like to add or eliminate from my life to make me happy would be..." and "The one thing I would like to add or eliminate from my community to benefit most residents would be..." After students have thought personally and heard what their peers value, ask how the concepts of **quality of life** and **sustainability** relate to their responses.

2. Break the students up into small groups to brainstorm factors that they think contribute to a community's lasting quality of life. In Part 1, students may have thought of specific things to add to the community, but now they will be thinking in broader terms about the factors that comprise a healthy community over a long period of time, such as protected and adequate supply of drinking water and availability of good jobs.

3. After students have brainstormed for several minutes, ask each group to select and rank the seven most important factors for a community's quality of life.

4. An indicator is used to *measure* changes in a factor, e.g., a change in GNP indicates that our economy is growing or shrinking). In this step, students will develop indicators for each of the group's seven factors. For instance, to measure crime (a *factor*), you can use the crime rate statistics from the police department as an indicator. Open space (another *factor*) can be indicated by the amount of public park land or forest. Remind students of the importance of factor measurability when making an index.

5. Have each group present its indicators. Conduct a class vote to determine the top ten indicators of a community's health and sustainability.

Discussion Questions:

1. Do you think each of its indicators should carry the same weight?

2. What criteria will you use to weigh the indicators?

3. Would grouping these categories enhance the class index? (See "Index" for suggestions)

Follow-up Activities:

1. Select one of the factors for students to research in their own community. They should find out how to measure the factor (in order to make it an indicator), what role the indicator plays in their own community and research whether the indicators show improvement or decline in recent years. Students can draw up and send proposals addressing any of the indicators to local leaders and government officials. They might also want to send the list of ten indicators they developed as a class, so that city officials can determine what students care about in their community.

Example: If students select "crime" as one of the indicators, they could call the local police department to get statistics on the crime rate and how it is measured. They could also ask how this rate compares to that of neighbor-

Concept:
Planning for a quality future requires defining what "quality" means to all of us.

Objectives:
Students will be able to:
• Develop a *Quality of Life Index*.
• Express visions of a desirable community.
• Brainstorm important factors for a community's quality of life.
• Define the term *sustainable community*.

Subjects:
Social studies, economics, government/civics

Skills:
Brainstorming, problem-solving, decision-making, writing, researching data

Method:
Through a class brainstorming and a cooperative learning activity, students develop an index of what they consider to be the ten most important indicators of a healthy community.

In Search of Sustainable Life

ing communities. Has the crime rate gone up or down in recent years? Why might this be the case? Is crime a problem in and around schools? What are some proposals for making their area safer?

2. If your social studies curriculum includes the study of different areas of the world, have students compare the quality of life in their community to one that has been studied in class in a different country. How are they similar and dissimilar? Have students write a one-page paper comparing the two communities.

Generations Apart

Introduction:

Communities with recent new growth have probably undergone significant changes over the past decades. Those areas experiencing economic declines may also have undergone serious change in recent years. Good resources to document these changes are a community's senior citizens. In this activity students interview older residents to compare today's environment to its past.

Procedure:

1. It is useful to precede this activity with Activity 33: In Search of Sustainable Life.
2. Tell the students that they will be conducting interviews with older community residents. Ask them what questions they think will elicit the most relevant responses to the indicators decided upon in the Class Index from Activity 33: In Search of Sustainable Life. Students should, however, feel free to ask about other aspects of historical life in their communities. Keep a list on the board of their responses. Put together a sample questionnaire using both the students' and your own suggestions (See Sample Questionnaire).
3. Provide the students with a list of different options for interviewees (senior center residents, grandparents, nursing home residents, elderly community members). Many students will be first-generation residents so doing a bit of networking with nursing homes and/or retirement communities may be a good idea before sending students out.
4. Working in pairs or individually, students should spend about a week conducting their interview and constructing a written/oral report for class presentation.
Note: Try to make the exercise as "place specific" as possible. Much of the lesson's significance lies in communicating the uniqueness of each area and fostering a new appreciation for community. For example, a rural area on the East Coast will have a much different history than a core city in the Southwest.

The Interview:

1. Encourage the students to retell some of the stories they hear during interviews in class. Hearing about other's experiences can often bring valuable perspectives to one's own work. There may be students who had difficulty in their interviews and would like to talk about that with the class as well.
2. Following up this section with a fact sheet of local historical information is a good way to round out the exercise. Ask your local historical society or library if they can provide one. Guest lecturers or storytellers are also good resources.
3. Creating a time line with the class's newfound information may help the students visualize how the community has changed over the years. Draw a horizontal line on a large piece of paper with vertical branches to represent different periods of times or years. Label each branch with a fact or event from the time period. Be sure to label the whole diagram with a larger block of time (for example: the 1900's).

Follow-up Activity:

Supplement the interviews with library research using the same statistical resources about the community such as population change over time, demographics, employment and industry, cultural trends and environmental trends. Ask your school or town librarian how best to search for resources that document both the statistical data of the community in the present day and that available when the senior citizens were growing up. Provide a list of these sources to aid the students. The students will gain experience with both interactive and library research.

Concept:
Changes in population and technology affect communities over time. Observations of older residents can provide insight into a community's past, present and future.

Objectives:
Students will be able to:
• Draw comparisons between the present-day community and that of an earlier time depicted by the older residents of the area.
• Foster new relationships with senior citizens and city officials in their communities.
• Identify changes that have occurred over the past decades and their effect on the community.
• Develop a questionnaire and conduct interviews with community residents.
• Create a time line depicting their community's history.

Subjects:
Social studies

Skills:
Research, writing, public speaking, interviewing

Method:
Students interview senior citizens in their community to broaden their perspective in how their community has changed over the decades with respect to population, economics and the environment.

Materials
Sample questions (photocopy for students)
Local resources about the history of the community (optional)

Generations Apart

1. How long and where have you lived in this area?

2. Can you think of any anecdotes that depict the community setting when you first came here/when you were growing up?

3. How has the community improved/changed since you've lived here?

4. What changes do you think have not been beneficial to the residents?

5. What was/were the main occupation/s or cash crop/s?

6. What businesses have disappeared or changed into something new?

7. Were there any farms near by? Was the area residential or urban?

8. Do you think the landscape has changed over time? What are some of the most obvious changes?

9. Was there much crime?

10. What was it like for families bringing up children?

11. What were the schools like? What were class sizes like?

12. Did a large percentage of kids graduate from high school in your community?

13. Were there any periods of population increase or decrease that you noticed? How did that affect the area/community? For example, were there ever overly crowded classrooms or a lot of traffic congestion?

14. Were people sparsely settled?

15. Were people very poor/wealthy?

16. What was happening in the news?

Suggested Resources for Further Research

We suggest the following resources to help students learn more about the issues covered in *Earth Matters*. The list is not meant to be comprehensive, but as a starting point for their research.

Population Dynamics

Books:

All Our People: Population Policy with a Human Face. Klaus M. Leisinger, Karin Schmitt, and Robert S. McNamara. Washington, DC: Island Press, 1994.

Beyond the Limits. Donella H. Meadows, Dennis L. Meadows and Jorgen Randers. White River Junction, VT: Chelsea Green Publishing Co., 1992.

Beyond the Numbers: A Reader on Population, Consumption, and the Environment. Ed. Laurie A. Mazur. Washington, DC: Island Press, 1994.

Ending the Explosion: Population Policies and Ethics for a Human Future. William G. Hollingsworth. Santa Ana, CA: Seven Locks Press, 1996.

Overpopulation: Earth at Risk. Rebecca Stefoff. Broomal, PA: Chelsea House, 1993.

Preparing for the Twenty-First Century. Paul Kennedy. New York: Vintage, 1994.

The Population Explosion. Paul R. Ehrlich and Anne H. Ehrlich. New York: Simon and Schuster, 1990.

The State of the World Population. Serial. Nafis Sadik. New York: United Nations Population Fund. (Available from the UN Population Fund, information at rear).

The Third Revolution: Environment, Population and a Sustainable World. Paul Harrison. New York: Penguin, 1992.

Periodicals:

American Demographics. Monthly. Cowles Business Media, Inc. (Available from CBM: P.O. Box 68, Ithaca, NY 1485-0068, 607/273-6343, www.marketingtools.com).

Population Today. Monthly. Population Reference Bureau. (Available from the Population Reference Bureau, information at rear).

Populi. Bi-Monthly. United Nations Population Fund. (Available from the UN Population Fund, information at rear).

Teacher's PET Term Paper. Quarterly. Zero Population Growth. (Available from Zero Population Growth, information at rear).

World Eagle. Monthly. World Eagle Publishers. (Available from World Eagle, information at rear).

ZPG Reporter. Bi-Monthly. Zero Population Growth (Available from Zero Population Growth, information at rear).

Handbooks and Wall Charts:

Challenging the Planet: Connections Between Population and Environment. Report. Population Action International, 1993. (Available from Population Action International, information at rear).

The Children's Environmental Index. Handbook. Biannual. Zero Population Growth. (Available from Zero Population Growth, information at rear).

Global Migration. Wall Chart. Population Action International, 1995. (Available from Population Action International, information at rear).

Life in the World's 100 Largest Metro Areas. Wall chart. Population Action International, 1990. (Available from Population Action International, information at rear).

Measures of Progress. Poster kit (Includes "Life Expectancy at Birth," "Population Growth Rate," and "GNP per Capita"). World Bank, 1995. (Available from World Eagle, information at rear).

Population Handbook. Handbook. Population Reference Bureau, 1997. (Available from the Population Reference Bureau, information at rear).

United States Population Data Sheet. Wall chart. Serial. Population Reference Bureau. (Available from the Population Reference Bureau, information at rear).

World Population Data Sheet. Wall chart. Serial. Population Reference Bureau. (Available from the Population Reference Bureau, information at rear).

World Population: Facts in Focus. Student Workbook to accompany World Population Data Sheet. Population Reference Bureau, 1996. (Available from the Population Reference Bureau, information at rear).

The World's Youth. Wall Chart. Serial. Population Reference Bureau. (Available from the Population Reference Bureau, information at rear).

Audiovisual:

Decade of Decision, 14 min. Video. Prod. Meg Maguire and Dennis Reeder, Population Action International, 1997. (Available from Bullfrog Films, information at rear).

Future in the Cradle: The International Conference on Population and Development, 22 min. Video. Prod. Robert Caughlan and Dennis Church. 1995. (Available from the Population Stabilization Project: 1115 Merrill St, Menlo Park, 94025; 650/327-0771).

The People Bomb, 90 min. Video. Prod. CNN, 1992. (Available from Social Studies School Service, 10200 Jefferson Boulevard, P.O. Box 802, Culver City, CA 90232-0802; 800/421-4246).

When the Bough Breaks: Our Children, Our Environment, 52 min. Video. Prod. Lawrence Moore and Robbie Stamp for A Central/Observer Production/ Television Trust for the Environment, 1997. (Available from Bullfrog Films, information at rear).

Who's Counting: Population and Habitat in the New Millennium, 24 min. Video. National Audubon Society, 1997. (Available from National Audubon Society, 3109 28th St., Boulder, CO 80301; 303/442-2600; www.earthnet.net/~popnet).

World Population, 6 min. Video. Zero Population Growth, 1990. (Available from Zero Population Growth, information at rear).

Software:

Population Concepts, PC or Mac Diskette, CD. EME. (Available from Cambridge Development Lab, information at rear).

Internet:

Museum of Man: www.popexpo.net/english.html

National Center for Health Statistics: www.cdc.gov/nchswww

Population Action International: www.populationaction.org

Population Reference Bureau:
Main Page: www.prb.org
Popnet: www.popnet.org

Statistics Canada www.statcan.ca/

Suggested Resources for Further Research

U.S. Census Bureau: www.census.gov

United Nations
   Population Fund: www.unpfa.org
   Population Information Network:
   www.undp.org/popin

World Bank, Development Education
   Program: www.worldbank.org/depweb

Zero Population Growth:
   Main Page: www.zpg.org
   Population Education:
   www.zpg.org/education
   ZPG Seattle: www.cn.org/zpg

Climate Change

Books:

The Changing Atmosphere: A Global Challenge. John Firor. New Haven, CT: Yale University Press, 1992.

Earth Under Siege: Air Pollution and Global Change. Richard P. Turco. New York: Oxford University Press. 1996.

The Forgiving Air: Understanding Environmental Change. Richard C. J. Somerville. Berkeley, CA: University of California Press, 1996.

Global Warming: The Complete Briefing. John Houghton. 2nd ed. New York: Cambridge University Press, 1997.

Global Warming: Can Civilization Survive? Paul Brown. London: Blandford, 1996.

The Heat is On: The High Stakes Battle Over the Earth's Threatened Climate. Ross Gelbspan. New York: Addison-Wesley, 1997.

Vital Signs: The Trends that are Shaping our Future. Serial. Ed. Lester R. Brown. New York: W.W. Norton & Co.

Periodical:

Climate Alert, Bi-Monthly. The Climate Institute. (Available from The Climate Institute: 120 Maryland Avenue, NE, Washington, DC, 20002; 202/547-0104; www.climate.org).

Handbooks and Wall Charts:

Stabilizing the Atmosphere: Population, Consumption and Greenhouse Gases. Population Action International, 1994 (Update available Fall 1999). (Available from Population Action International, information at rear).

Audiovisual:

Cooperating for Clean Air, 37 min. Video. Horizon Communications, 1993. (Available from Bullfrog Films, information at rear).

Greenhouse Crisis — The American Response, 11 min. Video. Union of Concerned Scientists, 1990. (Available from The Video Project, information at rear).

Once and Future Planet, 23 min. Video. Prod. John Stern, King Broadcasting Co., 1990. (Available from Bullfrog Films, information at rear).

Ozone — Cancer of the Sky, 40 min. Video. Prod. Natural History Unit, Television New Zealand, 1994 (Available from The Video Project, information at rear).

Software:

Balance of the Planet. PC or Mac Diskette. Broderbund. (Available from Cambridge Development Lab, information at rear).

Focus on the Environment: Hothouse Planet. PC or Mac Diskette, CD. EME. (Available from Cambridge Development Lab, information at rear).

Internet:

Global Change: www.globalchange.org

Intergovernmental Panel on Climate Change: www.ipcc.ch

Liberty Tree: www.libertytree.org/trenches/climate/climate.html

Pace University: www.law.pace.edu/env/energy/globalwarming.html

Resources for the Future: www.weathervane.rff.org

U.S. Environmental Protection Agency: www.epa.gov/globalwarming/home.htm

Air Pollution

Books:

Air Pollution: Its Origin and Control. Kenneth Wark, Cecil F. Warner, and Wayne T. Davis. 3rd ed. New York: Addison-Wesley, 1997.

Air Pollution, Acid Rain, and the Future of the Forests: Worldwatch Paper #58. Sandra Postel. Washington, DC: Worldwatch Institute, 1984. (Available from Worldwatch: 1776 Massachusetts Avenue, NW, Washington, DC 20036; 202/452-1999; www.worldwatch.org).

Earth Under Siege: Air Pollution and Global Change. Richard P. Turco. New York: Oxford University Press. 1996.

The Forgiving Air: Understanding Environmental Change. Richard C. J. Somerville. Berkeley, CA: University of California Press, 1996.

Audiovisual:

Cooperating For Clean Air, 37 min. Video. Horizon Communications, 1993. (Available from Bullfrog Films, information at rear).

Ozone — Cancer of the Sky, 40 min. Video. Prod. Natural History Unit., Television New Zealand, 1994 (Available from The Video Project, information at rear).

Software:

Focus on the Environment: Air Pollution. PC or Mac Diskette, CD. EME. (Available from Cambridge Development Lab, information at rear).

Focus on the Environment: Our Ozone Crisis. PC or Mac Diskette, CD. EME. (Available from Cambridge Development Lab, information at rear).

Internet:

Air Pollution Control Resources: members.aol.com/cleenair

Econet, Acid Rain Links: www.igc.org/acidrain

Environment Canada: www.ns.doe.ca/pollution/air.html

Environmental Working Group: www.ewg.org/pub/home/air/air/html

Trent University (Ontario), Monitoring Acid Rain Youth Program: www.trentu.ca/maryp

U.S. Environmental Protection Agency:
   Acid Rain: www.epa.gov/docs/acidrain/ardhome.html
   Clean Air Act Guide: www.epa.gov/oar/oaqps/peg_laa/pegcaain.html
   Office of Air and Radiation: www.epa.gov/oar
   Office of Mobile Sources: www.epa.gov/omswww

Suggested Resources for Further Research

Water Resources

Books:

Cadillac Desert: The American West and its Disappearing Water. Marc Reisner. Revised ed. New York: Penguin, 1993.

Lost Oasis: Facing Water Scarcity. Sandra Postel. New York: W.W. Norton & Co., 1992.

Overtapped Oasis: Reform or Revolution for Western Water. Marc Reisner and Sarah F. Bates. Washington, DC: Island Press, 1991.

Population and Water Resources: A Delicate Balance. Malin Falkenmark and Carl Widstrand. Washington, DC: Population Reference Bureau, 1992.

Sea Change: A Message of the Oceans. Sylvia A. Earle. New York: Fawcett, 1996.

Water: A Natural History. Alice Outwater. NY: Basic Books, 1997.

Periodicals:

U.S. Water News. Monthly. U.S. Water News, Inc./The Freshwater Foundation. (Available from U.S. Water News: 230 Main Street, Halstead, KS 67056; 316/835-2222; www.uswaternews.com).

Audiovisual:

Downwind/Downstream: Threats to the Mountains and Waters of the American West, 58 min. Video or film. Dir. Christopher McLeod. Prod. Robert Lewis and Christopher McLeod in assn. with Environmental Research Group, 1988. (Available from Bullfrog Films, information at rear).

Perspectives in Science: Water, 60 min. Video. National Film Board of Canada, 1991. (Available from Bullfrog Films, information at rear).

Turning the Toxic Tide, 46 min. Video. Prod. Bill Weaver and Shivon Robinsong, Across Borders Video, 1997. (Available from Bullfrog Films, information at rear).

The Underlying Threat, 48 min. Video. Dir. Kevin Matthews. National Film Board of Canada, 1989. (Available from Bullfrog Films, information at rear).

The Wasting of a Wetland, 23 min. Prod. Daniel Elias, 1994. (Available from Bullfrog Films, information at rear).

Software:

Focus on the Environment: Water Pollution. PC or Mac Diskette, CD. EME. (Available from Cambridge Development Lab, information at rear).

Handbooks and Wall Charts:

Sustaining Water: Population and the Future of Renewable Water Supplies: A Second Update. Population Action International, 1997. (Available from Population Action International, information at rear).

Internet:

Cadillac Desert: www.crpi.org/cadillacdesert

Environment Canada: www.ec.gc.ca/water

National Wildlife Federation: www.nwf.org/nwf/water

U.S. Environmental Protection Agency, Office of Water: www.epa.gov/ow

U.S. Geological Survey: www.usgs.org

Water Education Foundation: www.water-ed.org

Water Wiser: www.waterwiser.org

World Bank, Development Education Program: www.worldbank.org/depweb/water/water.htm

Deforestation

Books:

Defining Sustainable Forestry. Ed. Gregory H. Aplet, Nels Johnson, Jefferey T. Olson, et. al. Washington, DC: Island Press, 1993.

The Dying of Trees: The Pandemic in America's Forests. Charles E. Little: New York: Penguin, 1997.

The Last Stand: The War between Wall Street and Main Street over California's Ancient Redwoods. David Harris. San Francisco: Sierra Club Books, 1997.

Saving the Tropical Forests. Judith Gradwohl, Russell Greenberg, and Michael H. Robinson. Washington, DC: Island Press, 1989.

Trees of Life: Saving Tropical Forests and their Biological Wealth. Kenton Miller and Laura Tangley for World Resources Institute. Boston: Beacon Press, 1991.

Periodicals:

Journal of Forestry, Monthly. Society of American Foresters. (Available from SAF: 5400 Grosvenor Lane, Bethesda, MD 20814-2161; 301/897-8720; www.safnet.org).

Audiovisual Aids:

Our Threatened Heritage, 19 min. Video. National Wildlife Federation, 1988. (Available from The Video Project, information at rear).

Our Vanishing Forest, 58 min. Video. Prod. Arlen Slobodow for Public Interest Network, 1992. (Available from Bullfrog Films, information at rear).

Replanting the Tree of Life, 20 min. Video. Dir. David Leach. Asterisk Productions, 1987. (Available from Bullfrog Films, information at rear).

Saviors of the Forest, 90 min. Video. Prod. Bill Day and Terry Schwartz, 1994. (Available from The Video Project, information at rear).

The Temperate Rain Forest, 16 min. Video. Dir. Don White. National Film Board of Canada, 1985. (Available from Bullfrog Films, information at rear).

Wilderness: the Last Stand, 57 min. Video. Dir. Miranda Smith, Nathaniel Kahn, and David Zieff. Prod. Miranda Smith Productions, 1995. (Available from The Video Project, information at rear).

Software:

Ecology Treks. PC or Mac Diskette. Sanctuary Woods. (Available from Cambridge Development Lab, information at rear).

SimIsle: Missions in the Rainforest. PC or Mac CD. Maxis. (Available from Cambridge Development Lab, information at rear).

Internet:

American Forests: www.amfor.org

Canadian Forest Service: www.nrcan.gc.ca/cfs

Food and Agriculture Organization of the U.N.: www.fao.org

Rainforest Alliance: www.rainforest-alliance.org

U.S. Forest Service: www.fs.fed.us

World Resources Institute: www.wri.org/biodiv/foresthm.html

Suggested Resources for Further Research

Food and Hunger

Books:

Altars of Unhewn Stone: Science and the Earth. Wes Jackson. New York: North Point Press, 1987.

Diet for a New America: How Your Food Choices Affect Your Health, Happiness, and the Future of Life on Earth. John B. Robbins. 2nd ed. Tiburon, CA: H.J. Kramer, 1998.

Diet for a Small Planet. Frances Moore Lappe. 20th Anniversary ed. New York: Ballantine, 1992.

Full House: Reassessing the Earth's Population Carrying Capacity: The Worldwatch Environmental Alert. Lester R. Brown and Hall Kane. New York: W.W. Norton & Co. 1994.

Hunger: 1998. Serial. Bread for the World Institute. (Available from Bread for the World: 1100 Wayne Ave., Suite 1000, Silver Spring, MD 20910; 301/608-2400; www.bread.org).

Mirage: The False Promise of Desert Agriculture. Russell Clemings. San Francisco: Sierra Club Books. 1996.

Tough Choices: Facing the Challenge of Food Scarcity. Lester R. Brown and Linda Starke. New York: W.W. Norton & Co., 1996.

The Unsettling of America: Culture and Agriculture. Wendell Berry. 3rd Ed. San Francisco: Sierra Club Books, 1996.

Handbooks and Wall Charts:

Conserving Land: Population and the Future of Renewable Water Supplies. Kit. Population Action International, 1995. (Available from Population Action International, information at rear).

Audiovisual Aids:

Diet for a New America, 30 or 60 min. Video. Prod. Ed Schuman and Judy Pruzinsky, KCET-TV, 1991. (Available from The Video Project, information at rear).

Famine and Chronic and Persistent Hunger: A Life and Death Distinction, 11 min. The Hunger Project, 1990. (Available from The Hunger Project: 15 E. 26th St., Suite 1401, New York, NY 10010; 212/251-9100; www.thp.org).

My Father's Garden, 57 min. Video. Prod. Miranda Smith, 1995. (Available from Bullfrog Films, information at rear).

Turn Here, Sweet Corn, 58 min. Video. Prod. Helen De Michiel, 1990. (Available from Bullfrog Films, information at rear).

Internet:

Bread for the World: www.bread.org

Care: www.care.org

Earthsave: www.earthsave.org

Food and Agriculture Organization of the U.N.: www.fao.org

The Hunger Project: www.thp.org

Interaction: www.interaction.org

Waste Disposal

Books:

The Garbage Primer: A Handbook for Citizens. Christine Mueller and Mamatha Gowda. Washington, DC: League of Women Voters, 1993.

Rush to Burn: Solving American's Garbage Crisis? Newsday. Washington, DC: Island Press, 1991.

Toxic Nation: the Fight to Save Our Communities from Chemical Contamination. Fred Setterberg and Lonny Shavelson. New York; John Wiley & Sons, 1993.

War on Waste: Can American Win its Battle With Garbage? Louis Blumberg and Robert Gottlieb. Washington, DC: Island Press, 1991.

Audiovisual:

Hot Potato, 11 min. Video. Prod. Dr. Kay T. Dodge, Center for Environmental Studies and Grand Rapids Public Schools, 1990. (Available from Bullfrog Films, information at rear).

Perspectives in Science: Toxic Waste, 60 min. Video. National Film Board of Canada, 1991. (Available from Bullfrog Films, information at rear).

Solid Solutions: Rural America Confronts the Waste Crisis, 30 min. Video. Prod. Daniel Schaffer and Rosemary Walker, University of Tennessee.1994. (Available from The Video Project, information at rear).

Waste, 29 min. Video. Prod. Lynn Corcoran, 1985. (Available from Bullfrog Films, information at rear).

We All Live Downstream, 30 min. Video. Prod. A.C. Warden and Karen Hirsch, 1990. (Available from The Video Project, information at rear).

Internet:

Cornell Waste Management Institute: www.cfe.cornell.edu.wmi

Environmental Defense Fund: www.edf.org

Greenpeace: xs.greenpeace.org/ctox.html

Keep America Beautiful: www.kab.org

Obvious Implementations: www.obviously.com/recycle

U.S. Environmental Protection Agency: Consumer Solid Waste Handbook: www.epa.gov.epaoswer/non-hw/reduce/catbook/index/htm

Office of Solid Waste: www.epa.gov/osw

Biodiversity

Books:

The Company We Keep: America's Endangered Species. Douglas H. Chadwick and Joel Sartore. Washington, DC: National Geographic Society, 1996.

The Diversity of Life. Edward O. Wilson. New York: W.W. Norton & Co., 1993.

Extinction: the Causes and Consequences of the Disappearance of Species. Paul H. Ehrlich and Anne R. Ehrlich. New York; Random House, 1981.

The Forgotten Pollinators. Stephen L. Buchmann and Gary Paul Nabhan. Washington, DC: Island Press, 1997.

Nature's Services: Societal Dependence on Natural Ecosystems. Ed. Gretchen C. Daily. Washington, DC: Island Press, 1997.

Silent Spring. Rachel Carson. New York: Houghton Mifflin Co., 1962.

Song for the Blue Ocean: Encounters along the World's Coasts and Beneath the Seas. Carl Safina. New York: Henry Holt & Co., 1998.

Song of the Dodo: Island Biogeography in an Age of Extinctions. David Quammen. New York: Touchstone, 1997.

Tracking the Vanishing Frogs: an Ecological Mystery. Kathryn Phillips. New York: Penguin, 1995.

Wildlife Extinction. Charles L. Chadiex. Washington, DC: Stone Wall Press, 1991.

Audiovisual:

Before It's Too Late, 48 min. Video. Prod. Storyteller Productions, 1993. (Available from The Video Project, information at rear).

Suggested Resources for Further Research

Biodiversity: The Variety of Life, 42 min. (video). Prod. Dal Neitzel, Greater Ecosystem Alliance, 1992. (Available from Bullfrog Films, information at rear).

Software:

Encyclopedia of U.S. Endangered Species. CD. Clearvue. (Available from Cambridge Development Lab, information at rear).

On the Brink. PC or Mac CD. Bytes of Learning. (Available from Cambridge Development Lab, information at rear).

SimLife. PC or Mac Diskette. Maxis. (Available from Cambridge Development Lab, information at rear).

Internet:

American Association of Zoological Parks and Aquariums, Species Survival Plan: www.aza.org/programs.ssp

Defenders of Wildlife: www.defenders.org/eslc.html

Econet: www.igc.org/igc/issues/habitats/#endanger

Greenpeace Canada: www.web.apc.org/~species/index.html

National Wildlife Federation: www.nwf.org/nwf/endangered

U.S. Fish and Wildlife Service: www.fws.org

University of Michigan Environmental Education Link: www.nceet.snre.umich.edu/endspp/endangered.html

World Wildlife Fund: www.wwf.org

Energy Issues

Books:

Cool Energy: Renewable Solutions to Environmental Problems. Michael Brower. Revised ed. Cambridge, MA: MIT Press, 1992.

The Energy Crisis: Unresolved Issues and Enduring Legacies. Baltimore: Johns Hopkins University Press, 1996.

Food, Energy, and Society. Ed. David Pimentel and Marcia Pimentel. Revised ed. Niwot, CO: University Press of Colorado, 1996.

If You Poison Us: Uranium and Native Americans. Peter H. Eichstaedt and Murray Haynes. Santa Fe, NM: Red Crane Books, 1994.

Oil Spills. Joanna Burger. New Brunswick, NJ: Rutgers University Press, 1997.

Audiovisual Aids:

Fueling the Future. 4 parts, 58 min each. Prod. Diane Markrow for KBDI, 1991. 58 min. each. (Available from The Video Project, information at rear).

Internet:

Center for Renewable Energy and Sustainable Technology: solstice.crest.org/index.shtml

Department of Energy: www.doe.org

Environmental Defense Fund: www.edf.org/issues/energy.html

National Renewable Energy Laboratory: www.nrel.gov

Rocky Mountain Institute: www.rmi.org

Rich and Poor

Books:

A New Look at Poverty in America. William P. O'Hare. Washington, DC: Population Reference Bureau, 1997. (Available from the Population Reference Bureau, information at rear).

Economics and Rapid Change: The Influence of Rapid Population Growth. Population Action International, 1997. (Available from Population Action International, information at rear).

Environmental Justice: Issues, Policies and Solutions. Ed. Bunyan Bryant. Washington, DC: Island Press, 1995.

Material World: A Global Family Portrait. Peter Menzel, Charles C. Mann, and Paul Kennedy. New York: Random House, 1995.

Population: A Lively Introduction. Joseph A. McFalls, Jr. Washington, DC: Population Reference Bureau, 1991. (Available from the Population Reference Bureau, information at rear).

Periodicals:

WHY: Challenging Poverty and Hunger, Quarterly. World Hunger Year. (Available from WHY: 505 Eighth Avenue, 21st Floor, New York, NY 10018-6582; 212/629-8850; www.iglou.com/why).

Audiovisual:

Circle of Plenty, 28 min. Video. Prod. Bette Jean Bullert and John de Graaf,

1987. (Available from Bullfrog Films, information at rear).

Food for Thought, 28 min. Video. Produced by Robert Dean and Roger Bingham for KCET, 1990. (Available from Bullfrog Films, information at rear).

Wall Chart:

The International Human Suffering Index. Wall chart. Population Action International, 1992. (Available from Population Action International, information at rear).

Internet:

Care: www.care.org

Earth Systems: 54 ways you can help the homeless: www.earthsystems.org/ways

UNICEF: www.unicef.org

World Hunger Year: www.iglou.com/why

World Vision:
Canada: www.worldvision.ca
USA: www.worldvision.org

Population and Economics

Books:

Beyond Growth: The Economics of Sustainable Development. Herman Daly. Boston: Beacon Press, 1997.

Blueprint for a Green Economy. David Pearce, Anil Markandya, and Edward B. Barbier. London: Earthscan, 1989.

Building a Win-Win World: Life Beyond Global Economic Warfare. Hazel Henderson. San Francisco; Berrett-Koehler, 1997.

The Case Against the Global Economy: And for a Turn Toward the Local. Ed. Jerry Mander and Edward Goldsmith. San Francisco: Sierra Club Books, 1997.

The Conserver Society: Alternatives for Sustainability. Ted Trainer. London: Zed, 1995.

The Ecology of Commerce. Paul Hawken. New York: HarperCollins, 1994.

Eco-Pioneers: Practical Visionaries Solving Today's Environmental Problems. Steve Lerner and Jonathan Lash. Cambridge, MA: MIT Press, 1997.

Home Economics: Fourteen Essays. Wendell Berry. New York: North Point Press, 1987.

Natural Capital and Human Economic Survival. Thomas Prugh, Robert

Suggested Resources for Further Research

Costanza, and John H. Cumberland, et. al. Solomons, MD: International Society for Ecological Economics, 1995.

Our Ecological Footprint: Reducing Human Impact on Earth. Mathis Wackernagel and William Rees. Philadelphia: New Society, 1995.

Our Common Future. World Commission on Environment and Development. New York: Oxford University Press, 1987.

Small is Beautiful: Economics as if People Mattered. E.F. Schumacher. New York: HarperCollins, 1989.

Valuing the Earth: Economics, Ecology, Ethics. Ed. Herman E. Daly and Kenneth N. Townsend. Cambridge, MA: MIT Press, 1993.

Audiovisual Aids:

Greening Business, 45 min. Video. Dir. David Springbett. Prod. CBC's "The Nature of Things," 1994. (Available from Bullfrog Films, information at rear).

Who's Counting: Marilyn Waring on Sex, Lies, and Global Economics. 52 min. Video. Dir. Terre Nash. Prod. Kent Martin and the National Film Board of Canada, 1995. (Available from Bullfrog Films, information at rear).

Worth Quoting: With Hazel Henderson, 9 parts, 30 min. each. Video. Prod. Florida Community College of Jacksonville, 1994. (Available from Bullfrog Films, information at rear).

Internet:

Economics Working Group: www.igc.org/econwg

EPA Office of Economy and Environment: www.epa.gov/oppe/eaed/eedhmpg.htm

Island Press: www.islandpress.com/eco-nomics/index.html

Redefining Progress: www.rprogress.org

World Bank:
   Development Education Program: www.worldbank.org/depweb/sector/econ.htm

   New Ideas in Pollution Regulation: www.worldbank.org/nipr

The World's Women

Books:

An Epidemic of Adolescent Pregnancy: Some Historical and Policy Considerations. Maris A. Vinovskis. New York: Oxford University Press, 1988.

Balancing Act: Motherhood, Marriage, and Employment Among American Women. Daphne Spain and Suzanne M. Branch. New York: Russell Sage Foundation, 1996.

Dangerous Passage: the Social Control of Sexuality in Women's Adolescence. Constance A. Nathanson. Philadelphia: Temple University Press, 1993.

Dubious Conceptions: The Politics of Teenage Pregnancy. Kristin Luker. Cambridge, MA: Harvard University Press, 1997.

May You Be the Mother of 100 Sons: A Journey Among the Women of India. Elisabeth Bumiller. Reprint ed. New York: Fawcett, 1991.

The Stork and the Plow: The Equity Answer to the Human Dilemma. Paul R. Ehrlich, Anne H. Ehrlich, and Gretchen C. Daily. New Haven, CT: Yale University Press, 1997.

Taking Women into Account: Lessons Learned From NGO Project Experiences. Ed. Rehka Mehra. International Center for Research on Women, 1996. (Available from ICRW: 1717 Massachusetts Avenue, NW, Suite 302, Washington, DC 20036; 202/797-0007; www.icrw.org).

The World's Women: Trends and Statistics. United Nations. New York: Author, 1995.

Women's Rights and Population Policy. Ruth Dixon-Mueller. Westport, CT: Praeger, 1993.

Handbooks and Wall Charts:

Educating Girls: Gender Gaps and Gains. Wall Chart. Population Action International, 1998. (Available from Population Action International, information at rear).

Reproductive Risk: A Worldwide Assessment of Women's Sexual and Maternal Health. Wall chart. Population Action International, 1995. (Available from Population Action International, information at rear).

Women of our World. Wall chart. Population Reference Bureau, 1998. (Available from the Population Reference Bureau, information at rear).

What Legacy Do They Share. Poster. Population Reference Bureau, 1995. (Available from the Population Reference Bureau, information at rear).

Audiovisual:

How Much is Enough?, 26 min. Video. Prod. Central Independent Television, 1993. (Available from Bullfrog Films, information at rear).

The World of Women; As Seen By 13 Influential Women from Around the World, 30 min. Audio cassette and transcript. Population Reference Bureau, 1996. (Available from the Population Reference Bureau, information at rear).

Internet:

Center for Development and Population Activities: www.cedpa.org

International Center for Research on Women: www.icrw.org

United Nations:
   Development Fund for Women: www.unifem.undp.org
   Women's programs: www.un.org/ecosocdev/topicse/wom-engee.htm

Finding Solutions

Books:

A Sand County Almanac. Aldo Leopold. New York: Oxford University Press, 1949.

Deep Ecology for the Twenty-First Century. Ed. George Sessions. New York: Shambhala, 1994.

Desert Solitaire. Edward Abbey. Reissue ed. New York. Ballantine, 1991.

Discordant Harmonies: A New Ecology for the Twenty-first Century. Daniel B. Botkin. New York: Oxford University Press, 1992

How Much is Enough? The Consumer Society and the Future of the Earth. Alan T. Durning. New York: W.W. Norton & Co., 1992.

Ishmael. Daniel Quinn. Reissue ed. New York: Bantam, 1995.

The Rights of Nature: A History of Environmental Ethics. Roderick F.

Suggested Resources for Further Research

Nash. Madison, WI: University of Wisconsin Press, 1990.

Sacred Trusts: Essays on Stewardship and Responsibility. Ed. Michael Katakis. San Francisco: Mercury House, 1993.

Valuing the Earth: Economics, Ecology, Ethics. Ed. Herman E. Daly and Kenneth N. Townsend. Cambridge, MA: MIT Press, 1993.

Audiovisual:

Affluenza, 56 min. Video. Prod. John de Graaf and Vivia Boe, with KCTS/Seattle and Oregon Public Broadcasting, 1997. (Available from Bullfrog Films, information at rear).

Escape from Affluenza, 56 min. Video. Prod. John de Graaf and Vivia Boe, with KCTS/Seattle and Oregon Public Broadcasting, 1998. (Available from Bullfrog Films, information at rear).

Software:

Ecology Package. Six programs available separately or bundled. PC or Mac Diskettes. Intellectual. (Available from Cambridge Development Lab, information at rear).

Internet:

Affluenza: www.pbs.org/affluenza
Edward Abbey page: www.utsidan.se/abbey
National Wildlife "Aldo Leopold: A Man for All Seasons": www.nwf.org/natl-wild/1998/aldo.html
President's Council on Sustainable Development: www2whitehouse.gov/pcsd/index.html
United Nations, Sustainable Development: www.un.org/esa/sustdev
University of Georgia, Ethics and the Environment: www.phil.uga.edu/eande
University of Gothenburg (Sweden): www.phil.gu.se/environment.html
University of North Texas, Center for Environmental Philosophy: www.cep.unt.edu
The Wilderness Society: www.tws.org/ethic

Books:

State of the World. Serial. Ed. Lester Brown, et al.New York: W.W. Norton & Co.
Vital Signs: The Trends that are Shaping our Future. Serial. Ed. Lester R. Brown. New York: W.W. Norton & Co.
World Resources. World Resources Institute. Bi-annual. New York: Oxford University Press.
World Development Report: Serial. World Bank. New York: Oxford University Press.

Periodicals:

E: The Environmental Magazine. Bi-monthly. Earth Action Network, Inc. (PO Box 2047, Marion, OH 43306; 815/734-1242; www.emagazine.com).

Internet:

Econet: www.igc.org/igc/econet/index.html
Environmental Web Directory: www.webdirectory.com
Envirolink: www.envirolink.org
Environmental Protection Agency: www.epa.gov
Environment Canada: www.ec.gc.ca
Island Press, Eco Compass: www.islandpress.com
U.N. Environment Program: www.unep.org
U.S. Environmental Protection Agency: www.epa.gov
World Bank, Development Education Program: www.worldbank.org/depweb
Zero Population Growth: www.zpg.org

Ordering Information

Bullfrog Films
P.O. Box 149
Oley, PA, 19547
800/543-3764
www.bullfrogfilms.com

Cambridge Development Laboratory, Inc.
86 West St.
Waltham, MA 02154
800/637-0047
www.cdl-cambridge.com

Population Action International
1120 19th Street, N.W.
Suite 550
Washington, DC 20036
202/659-1833
www.populationaction.org

Population Reference Bureau
1875 Connecticut Avenue, NW
Suite 520
Washington, DC, 20009-5728
202/473-1155
www.prb.org

United Nations Population Fund
220 East 42nd Street
New York, NY 10017
212/297-5026
www.unfpa.org

The Video Project
200 Estates Dr.
Ben Lomond, CA 95005
800/4-PLANET
www.videoproject.org

World Eagle
111 King St.
Littleton, MA 01460-1527
800/854-8273
www.tiac.net/users/nca/neweagle/home.htm

Zero Population Growth
1400 Sixteenth Street, NW,
Suite 320
Washington, DC 20036
202/332-2200
www.zpg.org

ZPG Population Education Materials

Earth Matters: Studies for our Global Future (for grades 9-12)

A new, second edition of this highly acclaimed curriculum. This spiral-bound book of 12 student readings and 34 innovative activities covers such topics as deforestation, climate change, hunger, poverty and the status of women. *Earth Matters* also examines the underlying clashes between economic growth and economic health. Activities include simulations, debates, lab experiments, critical thinking exercises, problem-solving challenges and a rainforest board game. #EMTT $19.95

People and the Planet: Studies for Our Global Future (for grades 6-9)

An interdisciplinary, environmental education and global studies guide in one, *People and the Planet* covers concepts and objectives central to science, social studies, math and family life education. Through 30 hands-on (and minds-on!) activities and four readings, students explore the interconnections of human population growth, natural resource use, solid waste management, biodiversity, social justice and community well-being. #PPLN $22.95

Counting on People: Lessons on Population and the Environment (for grades K-6)

Population and environmental lessons are presented in fun, interesting ways so even the very young can understand them. Essential for the elementary classroom, this unforgettable book is filled with 30 hands-on modules, delightful poems and songs, and charming illustrations. #ELMN $19.95

Multiplying People, Dividing Resources: A Math Activities Kit (for grades 5-10)

Math has never been so fun and eye-opening as with this kit of activities which make critical connections between people, resources and the environment. Now students can use real world population and environmental data to practice working with large numbers, percentages, ratios and growth curves in analyzing the world around them. Contains 19 activities and a World Population Data Sheet. #MATH $9.95

"World Population" Video (for all grade levels)

This international award-winning video presents the best-ever graphic simulation of human population growth! In this six-minute video, as time passes, dots light up on a world map to represent millions of people added to the population for 1 A.D. to the present and projected to 2020. Includes a 12-page booklet of activity and discussion questions. A must have item! #WPPV $19.95

Teachers' PET Term Paper

Lively quarterly newsletter for teachers involved in K-12 population education. Features classroom activities, resource reviews, training schedules and timely articles. #TCHR Free one-year subscription.

Popular Planet Press

ZPG's children's newsletter for students ages 8-12 includes articles, games, and ways to "Get M.A.D. (Make a Difference)." #PPP Free one-year subscription; Classroom sets of 30, one-year subscription (3 issues) $5.00

ZPG Population Education Training Workshops for Teachers

Spice up your lesson plans! Expand your teaching repertoire. ZPG offers population education training workshops through inservice programs, conferences, teacher education programs and museum programs throughout the country. With an ever broadening network of teacher trainers, ZPG now reaches both present and future teachers. Our university outreach to education methods classes has met with great success. Since 1975, tens of thousands of educators have participated in these dynamic workshops, and as a result millions of young people have benefited from population studies.

Population education helps students appreciate the interdependence of people, animals, natural resources, food, industry and land. They learn not only about the social, political and environmental impacts of population growth and change, but more importantly, how their own personal decisions will affect the quality of life in tomorrow's world.

ZPG workshops include:

• Current information on global and U.S. population trends and their impacts.
• Our award winning video, "World Population."
• Games, quizzes, a global simulation, cooperative learning exercises and problem-solving challenges.
• Complimentary teaching materials to support your population education efforts: current population statistics, scripts for classroom activities, resource lists and reference guides.
• A new perspective on population education and alternative strategies to engage your students.

• Follow-up assistance through a quarterly newsletter, phone contacts and correspondence.

Workshop length and content are tailored to the professional needs of the participants. Some are as short as an hour, others as long as a full day. Some are geared toward a specified audience, e.g., high school social studies educators, middle school life science teachers or elementary school teachers; others are open to teachers of all subjects in grades K-12. Outdoor educators and museum docents are welcome too!

For further information, or to arrange a ZPG population education workshop, contact:

ZPG Population Education Program
1400 16th Street, N.W., Suite 320
Washington, DC 20036
1-800-POP-1956

ZPG Population Education Materials

Yes, I wish to enhance my teaching and include population studies in my classroom. Please send me the materials I've indicated below. If for any reason I am dissatisfied, I may return the materials to you for full credit or exchange.

Quantity		Price Each	Total
	People and the Planet (PPLN)	$22.95	
	Counting on People (ELMN)	$19.95	
	Earth Matters (EMTT)	$19.95	
	Multiplying People, Dividing Resources (MATH)	$9.95	
	World Population Video (WPPV)	$19.95	
	Popular Planet Press (PPPP) Single copy (1 year)	FREE	
	Popular Planet Press (PPPP) Set of 30 (1 year)	$5.00	
	Teacher's PET Term Paper (TCHR) (1 year)	FREE	
	*Membership in ZPG (MEMB)	$25.00*	

Shipping & Handling Charges

Purchase amount	Domestic	Foreign
$7.99 or less	$2.00	$5.00
$8.00-$29.99	$5.00	$9.00
$30.00-$49.99	$7.00	$13.00
$50.00-$99.99	$9.00	$15.00
$100.00 and up	10% of cost	30% of cost

Rush Orders: For two-day shipping. add $10 to your shipping and handling charge. Normal orders shipped within 2 weeks.

	Total
Subtotal	
*Less 20% member discount	
DC residents add 6% sales tax	
Shipping & Handling	
TOTAL	

*ZPG members are entitled to a 20% discount on all ZPG publications and a subscription to the bimonthly *ZPG Reporter*. Quantity discounts are also available. Please enquire.

Payment Method:
☐ Check ☐ Visa ☐ MasterCard ☐ Purchase Order
Account#: _____
Expiration Date: _____
Signature: _____
Purchase Order #: _____
Ship To:
Name: _____
Address: _____
City: _____
State: _____ Zip: _____
Bill To: (If different from "Ship To")
Name: _____
Address: _____
City: _____
State: _____ Zip: _____

Unconditional Guarantee

All of ZPG's population education resources are unconditionally guaranteed. If after using any of the materials in your classroom, you are not satisfied, return your purchase in original (resalable) condition within 30 days for full credit, refund or exchange.

Mail to: Zero Population Growth, 1400 16th Street, N.W., Suite 320, Washington, DC 20036

Call 1-800-767-1956   Fax: 202-332-2302